Reading the Weather, Reading the World

Lucy Calkins, Emily Butler Smith, and Mike Ochs

Photography by Peter Cunningham

Illustrations by Jennifer DeSutter

HEINEMANN ◆ PORTSMOUTH, NH

To Seymour Simon, who has led a generation of readers to fall in love with science.—Lucy, Emily, and Mike

Heinemann
361 Hanover Street
Portsmouth, NH 03801–3912
www.heinemann.com

Offices and agents throughout the world

Cataloging-in-Publication data is on file with the Library of Congress.

ISBN-13: 978-0-325-07716-1

Series editorial team: Anna Gratz Cockerille, Karen Kawaguchi, Tracy Wells, Felicia O'Brien, Debra Doorack, Jean Lawler, Marielle Palombo, and Sue Paro
Production: Elizabeth Valway, David Stirling, and Abigail Heim
Cover and interior designs: Jenny Jensen Greenleaf
Photography: Peter Cunningham
Illustrations: Jennifer DeSutter
Composition: Publishers' Design and Production Services, Inc.
Manufacturing: Steve Bernier

Printed in the United States of America on acid-free paper
19 18 17 16 15   EBM   1 2 3 4 5

Acknowledgments

THE THREE OF US have the feeling that people get when they have climbed a major mountain together. We're looking back on the journey with a great deal of shared camaraderie and mutual appreciation. Our appreciation goes not only to each other, but also to the Teachers College Reading and Writing Project (TCRWP) staff, who have researched content literacy for decades now—leading staff development, think tanks, and institutes on content literacy, writing books on the topic, and pioneering new trails of thought. We're especially grateful to Kathleen Tolan, who leads our February Content Literacy Institute and spearheads the Project's work each year rethinking our content literacy curriculum calendars. Mary Ehrenworth has for a long while been a provocative and generous thinker on this topic, leading study groups for the rest of us and helping us keep abreast of new developments across the nation. Two of our colleagues—Audra Robb and Janet Steinberg—have been especially involved behind the scenes with PARCC and SBAC, and their insights have also informed our work.

We've benefited, too, from partners across the nation. One of us works closely with the Colonial Williamsburg Foundation (CWF), bringing a team of TCRWP teacher-leaders to Williamsburg each summer to study and develop methods of teaching and learning history. We're grateful especially to Tab Broyles from Colonial Williamsburg and to Mrs. Abby M. O'Neill for sponsoring that partnership through her significant gift to CWF.

As we began the process of drafting and rewriting this book, we had help from many corners. Our writing companion, Ali Marron, read drafts, added in sections that we couldn't write, helped us address omissions, lifted our spirits, and provided invaluable good cheer and help. Kelly Boland Hohne, Janet Steinberg, and Audra Robb kept us ever-cognizant of the instructional terrain we needed to cover. Jen DeSutter provided glorious art, helping to put complex concepts into accessible little drawings. Ryan Scala and Amy Tondreau pitched in when we really needed fresh perspectives and ideas.

We couldn't be more grateful to Katie Clements and Felicia O'Brien who shared the challenge of editing this book. Felicia inched painstakingly through the manuscript, attending to every detail, and then Katie gave the text a final check, adding her gracious, responsive, and agile prose to the book.

The book then was passed from our hands to those at Heinemann, and how glad we are that Elizabeth Valway, Senior Production Editor; David Stirling, Production Manager; and Amanda Bondi were there to do the heroic work of synthesizing all the photographs, charts, drafts, and student work into a coherent and accessible guide for your teaching. Those three and their fearless leader, Abby Heim, have spared no effort in making the book live up to its potential, and we couldn't be more grateful.

Natalie Norris helped us to pilot the book in far corners of the country. We are especially grateful to a few teams of piloting teachers. We thank Denise Bord and Rachon Miller, literacy specialists in New Berlin, Wisconsin, who rallied entire teams of fourth-grade students and their enthusiastic teachers, who shared photos and student work as the unit progressed. May Ogden taught the unit to her class in North St. Paul, Minnesota, and gave us critical feedback. Teachers from Ridgebury School in Ridgefield, Connecticut, including Kat Kasperis, also dove into the unit, providing us with critical feedback, examples of student work, and photographs of kids at work as well. There were many teachers who helped us, too, not with the entire unit but with particular lessons, by being willing to give things a try and then another. Gillian Osswald helped us assemble the student work, sifting through stacks of students' writing about their reading and helping us match the work to the text. We're unbelievably grateful to all of you.

Now, the book passes on to the marketing and sales team at Heinemann—to Lisa Bingen, Chuck Filo, and Anita Gildea—and we thank them in advance. Then, it is yours and your kids, and the real excitement will begin!
—Lucy, Emily, and Mike

Contents

BEND III Tackling a Second Research Project with More Agency and Power

An Orientation to the Unit

AS THIS BOOK GOES TO PRESS, the headline story in the *New York Times* reports that California's Governor Jerry Brown has just announced an unprecedented 25% cut in water consumption in response to the severe drought that is now in its fourth year in that state. The Colorado River Basin, which supplies water to forty million people in seven states, is losing water at dramatic rates as well. The U.S. drought monitor recently showed that 70% of the land in the western United States is abnormally dry.

So what does this have to do with this unit? For the second half of this unit, the class will study extreme weather and other natural disasters; the whole-class topic for that portion of the unit is drought. Of course, you could teach this unit by substituting a different topic into that second half. Our choice of a research focus came in part because we know it is important to support students as they read scientific technological texts; we also recognize that few topics are as important to the lives of all global citizens as the topic of extreme weather.

But the information about the drought that is sweeping across the world today has a much larger relevance to this unit, and it is this. This unit—and those that come before and after it, as well—has been designed to help educate a generation of young people to have the skills necessary to engage in the research teams and skunk works projects that will be necessary if the upcoming generation is going to solve the many problems that are fast descending on us. Ebola attacks, flooding in our cities, global terrorism, the growing gap between the rich and the poor, the diminishing middle class, the corporate takeover of schools and politics: these and other challenges require that the students we educate are ready to be inventive, thoughtful researchers, collaborators, and listeners.

In his book, *The Global Achievement Gap*, Tony Wagner points out that throughout the twentieth century, the basic skills of reading, computation,

and rudimentary writing were the focus of our attention in schools and at home. "For most students, a 'rigorous' curriculum meant having to memorize more vocabulary words and do more math problems at night." He goes on to suggest that in the twenty-first century, mastery of basic skills will no longer be enough. He writes, "We are confronted by exponential increases of readily available information, new technologies that are constantly changing, and more complex societal challenges such as global warming. Thus, work, learning, and citizenship in the twenty-first century demand that we all know how to think—to reason, analyze, weigh evidence, problem solve—and to communicate effectively. These are no longer skills that only the elites in a society must master; they are essential survival skills for all of us." His words could be a mission statement for this unit.

This book begins by inviting students to read far and wide, picking up any nonfiction text that speaks to them. The design of the unit is that students start by reading easy texts and doing important work with those texts, and then they choose more challenging texts and you help them do similar work with those more challenging texts. The texts students read in Bend I are self-selected texts. Within that context of high-interest engagement, you will teach the skills that are becoming the new essentials for researchers. No, you won't teach your students to copy facts onto index cards—how I remember copying from tissue-thin pages of the *Encyclopedia Britannica*! But you will teach readers to read in such a way that they can summarize a text, leaning on the text structure to help them determine importance. You'll teach them that when they want to read texts that are dense and inaccessible, one way to access those texts is to literally read "up" on the topic. If they start by reading an accessible text, working hard to form a basic understanding of the topic, that first text can provide a context for reading denser and more difficult tests, slotting the new information into the reader's existing knowledge. Before long, your kids will be chomping at the bit to dig into a substantial research project, and so you launch them in studies of hurricanes and tornadoes, earthquakes and tsunamis.

Effective teaching brings kids backstage to see how important big work is done. In your modeling with a whole-class research topic and your minilessons, you'll show your children that the work of heady, thoughtful research projects is well within their grasp. You'll show them that despite the Wizard of Oz's apparent power, he actually is an ordinary person doing something obtainable. Just as you teach young writers that writing does not require a quill pen and magical talent, kids need to learn that reading as a researcher is within their grasp. Research is poking and prying with a purpose in mind. Your kids know all about poking and prying; they've been doing little else since they were two and found an earthworm lying sprawled across the sidewalk. The toddler prodding the worm with a stick is engaged in a process that is not unlike the work that kids will be doing in this unit.

In the research teams that form at the start of Bend II, your children will poke and pry into topics related to extreme weather and natural disasters. Your teaching will support the skill of synthesis, channeling them to think about how new information can add to or change information they have already learned. You'll also teach kids not only to summarize what they have learned but also to write as a way to think about what they are reading and learning. As nonfiction presents complexity in so many ways, you'll exhort readers to continue tackling the hard parts of nonfiction, whether those hard parts are scientific explanations, graphs, or other potentially confusing data. After days of researching a topic of extreme weather or natural disaster, students will hold a mini-celebration to teach one another what they have learned.

Bend III will take a new turn, with students taking on a different—yet related—topic of extreme weather or natural disaster. In this way, students will practice the skills of close reading as well as comparing and contrasting. Kids will have the opportunity to compare and contrast not only the content of what they are learning but also aspects of authorial intent, such the tone and craft between texts. So, too, in Bend III, will readers practice the skill of evaluating sources to determine their credibility. The unit ends with a celebration and a nod toward activism. In other words, readers will learn not only to *read* differently after this unit but also to *live* differently.

In the upcoming weeks, as you guide students through the sophisticated work of research, know that in fact, you will be guiding them with a much bigger mission. In their book *Breakthrough*, Michael Fullan, Patricia Hill, and Carmen Crévola say, "The new mission . . . is about learning to learn, about becoming independent thinkers and learners. It is about problem solving, teamwork, knowledge of the world, adaptability." This unit has the power to change your students' lives, not because they will learn about earthquakes and Doppler radar, but because they will *learn to learn*—perhaps the single most important academic skill we can offer our students as we set them out into the world.

SUPPORTING SKILL PROGRESSIONS

In the previous unit, you supported the major shifts from third to fourth grade in reading narratives. Those shifts have corollaries in reading expository texts, and this unit will help your students meet those expectations. Before embarking on this unit, you will want to read the Informational Reading Learning Progression for fourth grade, and review the progression for third grade as well. Your conferring and small-group work will often need to shore up foundational skills that are on the third-grade progression, even while your unit advances into the new work of fourth grade. This is one of two nonfiction units we've developed for fourth grade—you'll see that some of the new challenges are tackled within this unit and others are left for *Reading History: The American Revolution*.

In third grade, your students learned the importance of previewing nonfiction texts, asking, "What kind of text does this seem to be? How does it seem to be structured?," and then using that sense of text structure to orient their reading. If the text is a traditional expository text, your third-graders were taught to read the text looking for the main idea and supporting points of the text or sections of text. They referred to that way of structuring as boxes and bullets. If the nonfiction text is, instead, a narrative nonfiction text (as most biographies are, for example, as well as many stories of achievement or defeat), your students were taught to bring a story-structure template to those texts, looking for the main subject's traits, motivations, problems, and responses and eventual resolution to the problems. That story frame, your students found, worked even when the main subject was not a person en route to becoming famous, but a cactus struggling to survive, or an immigrant group hoping to make its way through Ellis Island.

Although students were taught that basic work in third grade, it is work that requires a lot of continued instruction. You can't assume that your students are all reading texts with an awareness of the text structure. Furthermore, as texts become longer and more complex, it will be more challenging for your students to discern a text structure undergirding the texts, and simply maintaining a focus on text structure will take more work. The unit goes further, however, and helps students know that sometimes, expository texts are quite clearly organized into more specific text structures, and when that is the case, the reader who discerns this can use his or her knowledge of text structures to figure out what is important in the text (and what isn't as important). For example, if a student reading an article about California's drought reads a paragraph that describes one effect of that state's long drought, then the reader can think, "This looks like a cause-and-effect text" and can be alert for a list of effects, as well as some discussion of the cause(s). Then again, if the reader notes that the text contains cue words such as *similarly*, and *however, these differ because,* then the reader will do well to think, "This appears to be a compare-and-contrast text." That awareness can lead the reader to set up a mental or physical note-taking system of double columns, preparing to list ways the two things are similar and ways they are different.

Discerning a text's structure is not so much a goal for readers as one possible *means* to the goal. The goal is for readers to be able to sort through all the information in an informational text so as to determine the main idea(s) and the important points that go with that main idea (or those main ideas.) The reader who can distill the main ideas and important points of a nonfiction text is able to summarize. Learning to summarize requires that students can not only informally outline a text but also be selective, as summaries are brief. While a *retelling* of a text can conceivably ramble on and on and on, a summary needs to involve no more than half a dozen sentences. The Common Core State Standards (CCSS) Reading: Informational Text (RI) strand expects that by fourth grade, students will be able to describe the overall structure of text(s) (RI 4.5) and summarize the main idea of a text and explain how it is supported by key details (RI 4.2). This work is important not only because it is highlighted in the Common Core and other global standards but also because most authors of nonfiction texts write in the hope that readers will be able to do this intellectual work. Surely we hope this of our readers! The strand that supports this important work is the "Main Idea(s) and Supporting Details/Summary."

Before moving on from this strand, let me emphasize again that students need to know they cannot include minor details in a summary. They also need to be accurate when they write about what the text says. In addition, they need to learn to keep their own opinions out of a text-summary. This work is not easy but it is central to understanding what a text is saying—and is not saying.

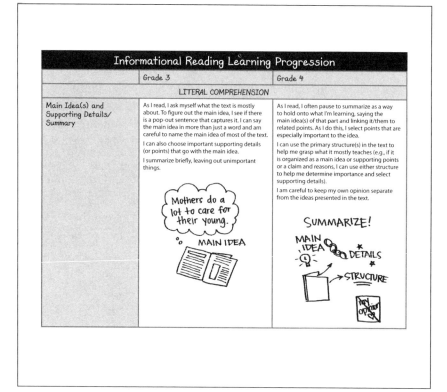

We've learned both from our own research and from a close collaboration with a team of researchers at Cognitively Based Assessment of, for, and as Learning (CBAL), a think tank at Educational Testing Service (ETS), that students who are skilled at orienting themselves prior to reading expository texts are far more likely to read those texts well. In this unit and throughout the K–5 curricular sequence, students are taught to look over a nonfiction text and note the text features and the key transitional words that can cue them into the text structure, allowing them to approach the text ready to learn in an organized way. Text orientation also allows fourth-graders to access related background knowledge. Even before a reader begins to read a particular text about tornadoes, the reader can think, "What do I know about this topic? What do I know about how this sort of text is apt to go?" and the reader will then prepare himself to read about tornadoes—the causes, warning signs, and events leading up to it, the actual tornado and its effects, and the efforts to clean up and learn from the tornado. Think how better prepared such a reader will be for discerning what is and is not important as he reads!

When reading scientific texts, it is especially important that students learn to do a kind of envisioning that they may not have had much experience with prior to now. Think, for a moment, about the illustrations you are likely to find in texts that talk the formation of hurricanes—showing the rise of warm, moist air and the descent of cool, dry air, as well as the increasing winds that make the clouds circulate. Are you imagining those illustrations might be flow-charts? Diagrams with arrows going this way and that way? Because if so, you are onto something important about the skills that you'll need to teach readers during this unit. Some reading researchers describe the envisioning work that nonfiction readers need to do as "building a mental model," and surely that is what your students will need to do when they read about scientific phenomena. Imagine a reader reading about the air flow prior to a hurricane. Chances are good that the reader has translated the words on the page into a mental sketch. She reads on, learning perhaps about how temperature plays a role in this, and so the reader adds that information into her existing mental model.

Students' stronger knowledge of structure will also support them in "Monitoring for Sense." As they consider how parts of the text fit together, it will be helpful for them to think of common ways that parts of texts tend to fit together (cause/effect, compare/contrast, claim/support, and so forth). And this work on structure will also help students in the strand called "Analyzing Parts of a Text in Relation to the Whole," as they figure out how the pieces of the text fit and how one part of a text fits with the rest. Why did that author include that diagram? Is it meant to contrast with the information in the adjacent paragraph? Is it meant to further explain information given in the start of the article? And how does this last paragraph fit with the others? Is this one part of the text explaining one of the effects? Does it answer a question that the author raised earlier? As students begin to read across paragraphs, sections, and pages, they will need to be able to start reading texts in a connect-the-dots sort of way, recognizing connections even between parts of the text that are not next to each other. This work represents a major shift for students.

Another strand addressed in this unit is "Analyzing Author's Craft." If your students have grown up in writing workshop, they will be accustomed to studying the craft of text. That is, they will be used to studying other writers' texts with the aim of improving their own writing. Studying the craft of texts as

readers may be less familiar, and this unit makes space for this practice so that students will hone their understandings of the relationship between readers and writers and will have experience reading with an attention to craft. Not only will you support their ability to recognize the craft of the text, but you'll also teach your students to discuss the goals writers may have been aiming for and the craft moves they seem to have, therefore, made.

Even fourth-graders who have been part of vibrant writing workshops will probably not come to you with a lot of experience using academic language to talk about authorial techniques used in nonfiction texts, yet this seems to be important on high-stakes. The TCRWP has devised a method for supporting this work, which we refer to as our "goals and technique cards." Essentially, this is a way to scaffold kids so they can learn how to talk about texts, saying things such as, "The author uses (you choose a technique) in order to accomplish (you choose a goal). The use of these cards makes it easy for students to learn to meet the standards for "Analyzing Author's Craft."

Another major focus for fourth grade is addressed in the strand "Cross Text(s) Synthesis." Students are coming to a point in their educational lives where they need to engage in more research. This means they will need to read across texts on a topic and be able to integrate what they have learned in order to speak and/or write knowledgeably about that topic. Again, this is critical and challenging work. The third-grade units addressed this work as well, but this year, the expectations for how fourth-graders integrate knowledge on a topic from different texts are ramped up.

As students read across texts and analyze texts more deeply and reach for more difficult texts, it is more important than ever that they be growing ideas as well. A big shift from third grade is that this year students are expected to entertain their own ideas more and more. This means that they will have an idea, read a little more, develop the idea further, take the risk to think in new ways about the idea, and perhaps write about it. They are expected to wonder and to question, "Is this always the case? Could this be connected to—?" Growing ideas is important in every year, but as students are becoming more interpretive, their work in this area should rise to new heights.

This year, you'll want to push students to reach for slightly more challenging texts as they read across texts on a topic, and they'll need to rely on their work in the "Word Work," "Fluency," and other foundational skills as they do so. Then too, as in every year, you'll want to continue to support students in the "Building Vocabulary" part of the "Word Work" strand, helping them see how to learn new terms from texts and study some of the more abstract terms (e.g., *forecasting*) across multiple texts, learning more about these kind of terms, what other terms with which they are connected, and coming to new understandings of the term. To support that continued vocabulary building, you'll see that students in this unit have multiple opportunities to learn not only the specialized vocabulary of topics related to the science of extreme weather forecasting and of natural disasters but also academic vocabulary terms, such as *observe, investigate, examine,* and *analyze.*

And as students read across texts, this will also mean that they need to ramp up their work in "Comparing and Contrasting," as well. One of the major ways that students' compare-and-contrast work will differ this year is that in third grade they were expected to compare and contrast mainly the *information* from different texts—that is, the content. That was not easy, as students were required to learn to think in a new sort of boxes-and-bullets

Informational Reading Learning Progression		
	Grade 3	Grade 4
INTERPRETIVE READING		
Cross Text(s) Synthesis	When I read two texts (or parts of a text) that teach about the same subtopic, I can find the information on a subtopic from both texts (or parts of one text) and put that information together.	As I read two or more texts (or parts of a long text) on a topic, I can collect and merge information and ideas from both texts (or parts of a long text) in a way that makes a new organization for the combined information. If there are ways to categorize the information on the subtopic, I sort information from both texts into a category.

way as they filed information into a "These are mostly alike because they. . . . But they are also partly different because they, . . . template.

That work is still important this year and can be done in much more conceptual and analytical ways as students get older and more proficient. But meanwhile, students are also expected to begin learning how to compare and contrast not only the *content* of texts but also the *texts* themselves. A student may read two books that both describe the sequence of a tsunami—one plays up the human horror, but the other stays very technical and almost objective. Is the actual information the same, and just the effect different? Or do these two sources have something different to say about tsunamis? This work relates to their work in "Analyzing Author's Craft" and also "Analyzing Perspective." This unit will begin tackling author's craft and the following nonfiction unit will take up that work and provide work on analyzing perspective.

Informational Reading Learning Progression		
	Grade 3	Grade 4
ANALYTIC READING		
Analyzing Author's Craft	I know that authors of informational texts make craft decisions with readers in mind. I especially notice when the author has done something that stands out—a repeating line, an illustration, and I think, "Why did the author do this?"	I know that authors of informational texts make craft decisions with readers in mind. I can elaborate on why the author used these techniques. One way I do this is to ask, "How would the text be different without this?" I can note the craft techniques that have been used and can say, "The author has used (this technique) to accomplish (this goal)." For example, "The author has made a comparison to help readers grasp an idea."

OVERVIEW

This unit is designed so that students start by reading easy texts and doing important work with those texts and then they choose more challenging texts. You will help them do similar work with those more challenging texts. Eventually they will dig into research projects that revolve around a class topic of extreme weather and natural disasters. At the end of the unit, students will research a second subtopic in order to provide opportunities for students to compare and contrast what they have learned and to explore more conceptual topics. In many ways, the structure of Bends II and III echoes that of their third-grade units studying animals.

Bend I: Learning from Text

In the first bend, you'll engage your kids in an "archaeological dig" through their backpacks in order to uncover the nonfiction in their lives. "Would you dig through your backpacks and pockets to assemble an evidence-based answer to the question, 'What sort of nonfiction texts fills my life?'" Soon you'll channel students to select nonfiction texts that they want to read, encouraging them to start with texts that look easy for them to read, and you will take some time to reteach them the importance of reading those texts in such a way that they can teach someone else what they have learned. As part of this, you'll return to the work on text structure from third grade. This time, however, you'll be talking less about boxes and bullets as a catch-all text structure for many expository texts, and will instead advance the notion that some texts are organized in a problem-solution structure, some in a chronological structure, and some in a pro-con contrasting structure.

While students will be reading on topics and in books of their choice, we suggest that you make use of the text *Everything Weather* as a tool for whole-class minilessons and for your read-aloud. You'll carry this text into the second bend of the unit, when you move the students into research teams focused on topics related to extreme weather and natural disasters.

After the first three sessions, the first bend takes a minor shift. Your instructional focus will be on the various ways nonfiction texts become more complex. You'll point out that the work you've taught so far is all well and good when the texts are fairly simple—when they are written to make it easy to see an underlying text structure and to figure out the main idea(s) and supporting points. But in the real world, many nonfiction texts are complicated.

You might say to students, "Sometimes I wish that nonfiction texts had their own versions of those signs that say, 'Warning!' I'm sure many of you have had that experience of seeing a cute photo on the cover of a nonfiction book, and even seeing large font in the book, and thinking, 'This will be easy,' and then you start reading and you can hardly read it."

In Bend I, there is a sequence of lessons that help readers tackle increasingly difficult nonfiction texts, equipping readers with some of the strategies they need. As part of this, you'll point out that increasingly they'll work really hard to pronounce a tricky word, only to find that even after they can say the word, they have no clue what it means.

You will also act surprised if your students don't self-initiate word banks, reminding them that the lessons they have been taught in previous years should make a lifelong difference. For homework one night, then, you suggest children create their own word banks. You'll say to your children, "If you are reading about castles, your word bank might contain words like *moat*, *armory*, *ambush*, *defenses*, and *siege*. Once you have recorded words that are key to your topic, make sure that you use those words when talking (and when thinking) about your subject. That's the only way you will get to really 'own' the words." Of course, this is fourth grade and so you can ramp up expectations from the previous year. You might do so by suggesting that kids can actually practice words by using subject-specific words to talk about everyday life topics. For an example, you could show kids that if you wanted to use castle terminology to talk about homework, you could say, "I try to build a *moat* around Friday and Saturday nights and all-day Sunday, so they are times that are free of work. But sometimes I get *ambushed* by assignments I hadn't expected. I'm working to build an *armory* of excuses so that I can keep my *defenses* up."

This first bend ends with a "boot camp" session teaching children to summarize nonfiction texts well. In some ways, a good summary serves as the bedrock to strong nonfiction reading. You'll gather students on the rug, introduce them to the idea of summary, and say, "On the surface, summary at first seems pretty obvious and easy to do, right? I mean, all you have to do is say back what's in the text, right? But it turns out that summarizing is a bit more complicated. To summarize well, you need to know what to include in your summary, how to summarize the author's points in your own words, and how the details support the author's main idea. That's a lot! Today I want to teach you that when readers summarize nonfiction writing, they organize their summaries to include what is most important to the writer's topic—the writer's main idea and the key supporting details—all the while being careful to put this into their own words." Then, instead of demonstrating how you do the work, you will coach them through the process of summarizing a familiar shared text. Once kids get started summarizing the shared text, you'll say things like, "Leah, to start our summary, let's tell the main idea and also be specific about who the author is. One way this could sound is, 'In this passage, the author's point is—' or 'The main idea of this passage is that—.'" Then you could say to the whole class, "Try out how the first sentence could go in your own words," as you give them all thirty seconds to try out their first sentence.

Soon you'll say, "Friends, I think we've got a main idea down in our own words. Now we need to find the supporting details for the main idea. To do this, it can help to think about how the text is structured. When you know how a text is structured, you can choose details for your summary that fit with that structure. Let's look at the text and our main idea: the sun and Earth work together to create the weather. Hmm, what text structure does this passage take?" You'll then give students a minute to decide before calling them back.

Working in this way, you and the class can co-construct a summary that sounds a bit like this:

In this passage, Kathy Furgang explains that the sun and Earth work together to create the weather. One detail that supports this is that the sun heats the land on Earth, which warms the air. In addition, Kathy Furgang points out that wind moves warm air around. A final detail is that Earth's rotation causes air to move and change directions, which then causes change in temperatures.

Now students will be more able to work on summarizing the texts that they are each reading individually.

Bend II: Launching a Whole-Class Research Project

At the start of the second bend, you'll launch the class in a research project on extreme weather and natural disasters, which will span the rest of the unit. You'll ask your students, "Will you think for a moment about the world events that have made the *biggest* difference in the lives of people over the last few years?" Students may suggest war or terrorism attacks, and surely they have

made a difference. But you'll counter by suggesting that nothing has mattered more than extreme weather, and to defend your claim, you'll show a series of brief, potent video clips. Students will watch highways collapse, cars peeking out from ten feet of snow, and villages swept away. After showing the clips, you'll say, "Do you see what I mean about peoples' lives being literally turned upside down? Do you see why I'm thinking that extreme weather might be the most important topic we could study right now?"

Then you'll go on to organize the class into research teams to study hurricanes, tornadoes, tsunamis, droughts, earthquakes, floods, and other kinds of extreme weather and related natural disasters. And because the crisis around access to water is *such* a huge concern, you'll propose that the whole class studies drought.

It will be important for you to talk up the importance of kids working in research teams. You might say, "I know that when you think of teams, you probably think of football teams, soccer teams, or chess teams. The teams I'm suggesting will work in similar ways. You won't be working to move a ball down the field, but instead you'll be working hard to develop some expertise on a topic. And like a football team, I'm expecting different group members will have different jobs, different roles."

You could continue, saying, "Imagine something with me: You are all grown up and you are heading to your first day of work at your new job. Depending on where you work, you might be told that your challenge is to work with a team to solve the crisis of the Ebola epidemic, or to make sure there are no power outages during the big storm that will hit your city in just a few days, or to decide how to build and staff a school in a remote mountain region. In order to solve the problem you are given, you won't pick a book off the bookshelf and start reading pages 1, 2, and 3 about the topic. No—you'll need to follow a spider web of Internet links, to talk to experts, to read lots of books, to imagine all sorts of solutions and possibilities, and ultimately to decide on a way to fix the problem. Before you can do any of this, though, you'll need to make sure that each team member knows what, when, and how he or she will work to help get the job done." And with that rallying cry, the research portion of this unit will be launched.

Although students will have learned during third grade about ways to go about conducting research, you nevertheless reteach that content, saying to them, "Will you watch as I rehearse for what I'll do as a researcher and reader, making a plan for how I'll learn more about droughts? I'm going to try to make something researchers call an action plan. You can whisper to your partner about whatever you notice me doing, and after a bit I'll stop and we'll collect some notes." Then you show students how you get started. Again, you'll point out that you will preview texts to learn about the subtopics that thread through them—and you'll bring out subtopics that students will no doubt find thread through their topics as well. Students will end up finding that whether they are studying hurricanes or tsunamis or earthquakes, there are some similar subtopics that will merit attention: the causes and effects of the event, the human story aspect, and so forth.

Each group will then do their own work of setting up their research. Imagine a group of four or six kids is studying each of these topics: hurricanes, tornadoes, earthquakes, tsunamis, and floods. Meanwhile, remember, the whole class is studying drought. Within each group, individuals or pairs of readers can then take on the job of researching a subtopic within their topic. For example, a reader or two from the hurricane group can spend a day or two studying ways of measuring hurricanes and then cycle over to the personal stories of hurricanes, while another reader comes in on the original topic.

Our expectation is that you will not have a huge number of resources on any one of these subtopics, and you presumably don't want students to spend weeks cruising through the Internet, so we suggest that the research cycles that follow are fast paced, with children not necessarily having time to complete one aspect of research before moving to another aspect. The net effect, however, will be a powerful immersion in these high-interest and important topics and present lots of opportunities to teach skills that are transferable to other research topics.

As your research teams begin to study their topics, you'll teach them key reading skills. For a start, you'll point out that readers can locate and synthesize information from a variety of texts. You will teach readers that after they have read an initial text on a subtopic, they can read several more texts on the same subtopic, and they will come to those later texts differently because of their earlier readings. They can read, thinking, "Does this add onto what I already learned? Does it conflict with what I learned?" Of course, you'll need to help students revise their notes so that the new information is slotted where it belongs in their notes. All of this will offer support to the "Synthesis" strand of the learning progression and prepare students for the post-assessment.

If some children struggle with this, you'll want to point out that the work they are doing now with extreme weather is not significantly different from the work they did in third grade. "Am I right that you learned you could take one subtopic—like elephant babies—and read a section about elephant babies in two different books, and then take what you learned from one book," and I spread out one hand, "and what you learned from the other book," and I spread out my other hand, "and bring that information together?" and I clasped my hands together.

You might remind them, "The researcher keeps notes and information from the first text in mind and reads the second text, asking, 'Does this add onto what I've already learned? Change what I learned?' The new text gets filed into mental files (or notes) from the first text."

Reading and researching a topic, of course, isn't just about taking notes on the topic. You'll also teach kids to grow ideas off their notes, to think deeply about the topic, and again, you will want to refer to the Informational Reading Learning Progression to support that work. So often, when asked to grow their own ideas, children relate to personal preferences or emotional responses only, not really grounding their ideas in specific information that they've learned. Your hope is their ideas will sound more like, "I always thought that weather forecasters had easy jobs, standing in front of maps on TV shows, but now I understand that they need to go right into the eye of the hurricane, the center of the extreme weather event, and that takes courage. It's not the image I used to have of weather forecasters!" You'll coach researchers to push their thinking, providing thought prompts that help them do intellectual work with all they've learned. As a mini-celebration, at the end of this bend, you'll pair research teams together and channel them to teach one another all they have learned and to teach each other well.

You won't be surprised that your instruction returns to a theme that was important earlier in this unit—embracing the challenges of difficult texts. It is predictable that students will encounter dense descriptions of processes and procedures, studded with difficult vocabulary and new text features, including graphs, diagrams, and charts. In easier texts, these features act as visuals to help readers understand the text. But as texts become more difficult, the text features begin to hold essential information that readers need to decipher in order to fully comprehend what is being set forth. You'll teach students to expect hard parts in their texts and to read these sections with extra alertness, rather than skimming past them. You'll start by saying, "Readers, last night

I was struggling to set up my DVD player so I could watch the new DVD I just got of *Modern Family*. I found a manual for the DVD player and turned to a page that had a lot of complicated instructions and a diagram, too, and I started trying to figure out the names and the purposes for each of the wires and the buttons. Pretty soon my brain felt like mush!" You'll gesture to show that the manual had fried your brain.

As you continue role playing the part of a frustrated reader, you can eventually tell students that you came to the realization that "my problem with the DVD player wasn't a DVD problem—it was a reading problem. More specifically, it was a *nonfiction* reading problem." This will set up a teaching point for the day: "Today I want to teach you that when researchers encounter complex, technical parts of their text, they tackle them head on. They read (and sometimes reread) everything on the page closely, pausing after a chunk to think about what it's teaching. Then, they talk or write to develop their ideas."

Bend II will culminate with time for research teams to teach each other what they've learned about their topic. When you become an expert on a topic, you don't keep your knowledge to yourself. Instead you share your knowledge by teaching others. For your teaching point, you could say, "Today I want to teach you that experts live in the world differently. They don't keep their expert knowledge to themselves. Instead, they share this knowledge by teaching the people in their communities."

Bend III: Tackling a Second Research Project with More Agency and Power

In the third and final bend, research teams will swap topics and begin studying another extreme weather or natural disaster event. Each team will trade topics with a team that studied a related topic. You might tell your researchers, "Today each research team will get a chance to deepen that work. You'll begin a crash course in a second form of extreme weather or related natural disaster. I'm going to suggest you study topics that are somewhat related to each other, because the connections will be especially explosive. Tsunami and earthquake research teams will switch topics. Hurricane and tornado teams, you will swap topics. And the drought researchers will study floods, while the flood researchers study droughts."

Initially, you will channel researchers to compare and contrast their topics. You'll start by saying, "Today I want to teach you that researchers often shift from studying one example of something to studying a second example of that

same thing. It is powerful to learn about the second example through the lens of thinking, 'How is this similar to what I already know? How is this different?'" You'll demonstrate how you plan to study a second topic, comparing it to the first. Then you'll channel students to talk with their research teams about whether they imagine following a similar action plan, and about other things they imagine they'll want to do. Then research teams will set off to read and take notes, observing to themselves, "These are similar because—" and "There are different because—."

Next, you'll teach students to do the work that experts in any field do—broaden their study from a specific subtopic to a broader issue or topic. You'll show children how they can extend the reading-across-a-topic work that they've done often in the previous two bends of the unit. "Today I want to teach you that to develop expertise on a topic, nonfiction readers go from learning about specific related topics (such as tornadoes or floods) to learning about their bigger field of knowledge (extreme weather). As a researcher's focus gets bigger, the researcher thinks more about patterns and relationships. Expert knowledge is the knowledge that a person *makes* on his or her own, by putting together specific knowledge on one topic and another topic and another topic. Experts come up with their own discoveries and ideas and hunches as they think between related topics they know well. Experts grow their own ideas and synthesize what they are learning across topics." Eventually, researchers will continue growing bigger ideas from these broader topics. You might give them an example of how this might go, asking, "Do you see how an expert's focus keeps getting bigger and bigger as his field of interest grows?"

By now, your students will be noticing patterns and relationships across texts, pushing themselves to grow deep ideas through their synthesis work. In the following session, you will show students how to take this work further, demonstrating how reading across several texts can spark deep questions that lead to in-depth inquiries.

The next day's work will help kids see their role in the larger act of reading and researching. On some level, the act of reading and researching has three parts: the author's role and agenda, the text's role as a vehicle for an author's agenda, and the reader's role and agenda. Part of this thinking extends from Louise Rosenblatt's work with the reader-response theory. What this means for the session is that while a research club might read a common text written by an author with one agenda, each reader comes to that text with his or her own research question and set of prior experiences and will take something different from the text. You'll help kids do this work by asking them to read again through the lens of structure. You'll also help kids understand the process by way of analogy. You'll explain that two people might watch the same baseball game in a different way. One might watch the game for what it is—strikes, balls, runs, and outs—while another might watch it for how to coach and manage a team. You'll say, "Readers, these two people watching the same baseball game see it so differently because they come to the game with different agendas. In the same way, readers can read texts differently, based on their particular agendas. Today I want to teach you that readers can come to texts with their own agendas. At times readers' agendas may match how the text is organized and intended to be read, but sometimes readers' agendas run counter to how texts are organized. In those times, readers organize the information they learn in the way that best fits with their own agenda."

You'll also be teaching researchers to double-check the credibility and reliability of their sources. You'll explain to readers that not all sources are created equal—some are less trustworthy than others. You'll begin by naming your teaching point, "Today I want to teach you that researchers become experts by evaluating sources in order to consider the credibility and trustworthiness of them," and you'll demonstrate with the mentor text *Everything Weather*. After that, you'll channel partnerships and research teams to check on the credibility of their sources, whether they be books, articles, or online Web content.

As your students move between different texts on their new topic, they'll be reading these texts differently, not just because they approach this topic with knowledge about a parallel topic but also because they approach this topic with more knowledge of the genre of nonfiction. In the following session, you will note this expertise and point out that one of the side effects of expertise is that they'll bring a new sort of awareness to their reading. You'll explain to them that as they continue to pick up books, this time about a second topic related to extreme weather events, they're apt to find themselves thinking: "Yep, I've read a book like this before," and then be able to describe how they expect the book to go. You'll say to kids, "In a nonfiction study like ours, it is important to study the topic we are learning about, but it is just as important to study the texts themselves, to think about how they were made and why they were made that way. Today I want to teach you that nonfiction readers think about the decisions nonfiction writers make—the ways those authors seem to want us to think or feel about a topic. This is especially important when reading several texts about the same, or similar, topics."

Next, you'll introduce to your readers the goal and technique cards, which address the various craft moves nonfiction authors make as they write information texts. You will teach students that when we see an author trying to accomplish something, we can ask *how* they do this—which techniques that author uses. You might remind them that as writers themselves, they have a wealth of techniques for achieving goals. For instance, when they want to build tension in a narrative story, they may slow down the action and add both inner and descriptive thinking. You might say, "Today, I want to teach you that readers study texts in order to find out what techniques, or craft moves, an author uses to achieve his or her goals." Then you'll model the thinking process that goes behind this work before turning over the reins to the students to explore how authors use craft techniques to achieve their aim.

Finally, the unit culminates with a celebration that lets kids wed their skills as researchers and as persuasive writers together. For two days, you'll support and coach kids to create a celebration project, a pamphlet, a video, a poster, or a speech—any text that advocates for some sort of change in the world. You might say to students, "When we become experts on a topic, it is common to find yourself wanting to share your thoughts and opinions about your topic with the world. In your studies of weather and natural disasters, many of you have uncovered places where your voices would matter, ways in which you wish things were different or where there should be change, and as a writer, it's important to remember that you have the resources to fight for that change to happen!" At the beginning of the unit, you'll ask kids to read differently. By the end of this unit, you'll see the ways in which reading differently causes your readers to *live* differently.

ASSESSMENT

Your instruction will always be informed by assessments, and those assessments will be continual. You'll use running records and other observations of your students, examinations of reading logs and writing about reading and their talk about reading, and performance assessments to track student progress and to align your teaching to what your best knowledge is of what they can do, can almost do, and can't yet do.

At the start of the year, you presumably took running records that informed you about the levels of text complexity your students can handle. Hopefully, you gave a second informal running record to any student who showed signs of being able to progress up a notch during that unit. Many students can move after they've increased their reading volume in the first weeks of the year. For students who recently began reading fiction books at a new level of text complexity, use those levels as a starting place for students' work with nonfiction. Because assessing students is a time-consuming process, it is reasonable to start students at the same level of text complexity in nonfiction as they can handle in fiction. Just keep an eye on those students as the unit begins, because often students' reading levels for nonfiction are below their levels for fiction. Be alert especially for signs of disengagement. Watch students' reading logs for possible declines in volume of reading. If you see these signs, move students down a level or so in nonfiction at the start of this unit, and then provide enough support to help them move quickly back up.

You may have taught a unit you developed on your own between our first unit and this unit. If you didn't—if this is your second reading unit of the year—then your students who enter the unit reading at benchmark will be reading level Q or R. As you match students with nonfiction books, continue to aim for approximately 96% accuracy when students are reading without book introductions or other forms of support, although you may need to allow for a bit of struggle with domain-specific vocabulary. (This may mean slightly lower accuracy expectations for nonfiction than for fiction, because nonfiction by definition will introduce new domain-specific vocabulary, which will make accuracy a bit more challenging.) Of course, it is likely that you'll have students whose levels are not yet at benchmark. Remember that during your year together, you'll be aiming to support your fourth-graders to move at least to level S texts.

If your school has access to a system that supports you in conducting running records of nonfiction texts (such as the Fountas & Pinnell Benchmark Assessment System), you might choose to use that system to support you in administering nonfiction running records to students. Even if you don't have such a system, you can use any text that has been leveled, ask students to read a snippet of it (about 100 words), and conduct a running record. The TCRWP website does not provide leveled nonfiction texts for conducting running records.

Regardless of which approach you choose, this unit supports dramatic growth. Small-group work can reinforce this. The strands of text complexity in nonfiction (see *Reading Pathways, Grades 3–5: Performance Assessments and Learning Progressions*, Chapter 5) will be enormously helpful to you as you plan your small groups. That chapter details major ways in which nonfiction texts become complex in relation to main idea, vocabulary, structure, and knowledge demands.

Know that, in general, students can read more challenging levels of nonfiction when they are reading about topics about which they have expertise. If a student is passionate about snakes, for example, he'll be able to tackle more difficult texts on that topic. Providing students with several sequenced texts on any topic will also help, so the reader first dives into the easiest text on a topic and then reads progressively more complex texts as she gains background knowledge.

Of course, literal comprehension is necessary but not sufficient, and you will also want to assess your students' higher-level comprehension, looking specifically at all the skills comprised by interpretive, analytic reading. This unit begins with a performance assessment, available in the online resources, which is designed to highlight and support these comprehension skills. The performance assessment assesses four main skills that are critically important across this unit and on the high-stakes assessments your fourth-graders will be taking. In particular, this unit focuses on these skill areas:

- Main Idea(s) and Supporting Details/Summary
- Analyzing Parts of a Text in Relation to the Whole
- Analyzing Craft
- Cross Text(s) Synthesis

More details pertaining to the assessment can be found in the Start with Assessment letter found in this unit, and in the online resources.

The biggest decision you will want to make right away pertains to the scoring of the performance assessment. In Chapter 2 of *Reading Pathways, Grades 3–5: Performance Assessments and Learning Progressions*, you will read about ways in which you can hold a norming meeting with other teachers so that all the teachers across your grade level can collaboratively score students' performance assessments, assessing that work in roughly equivalent ways. The learning progression, combined with a big effort to calibrate your assessments, can enable you and your colleagues to come to a shared view on what constitutes good, better, best work in particular reading skills.

But what we think is most important is that you try to turn as much of the assessment as possible over to the kids. What you are truly assessing is invisible—what goes in a student's mind during reading—and no one is a better judge of that than the child. You'll find a letter detailing how this work might go in the classroom in Session 3 of the unit. To support your students with this work, you'll draw on the Informational Reading Learning Progression and on student-facing rubrics created from the progression.

A word of caution: If your students have not grown up with Units of Study in Teaching Reading and therefore have never before seen the Informational Reading Learning Progression, you'll find their initial work on the performance assessment and their initial efforts to score themselves to be very rough approximations. You would probably be more comfortable if you score their pre-assessment and then ask them to work in partners on Day 3, not to self-score but to understand how you scored them and to try revising their work. That would take a fair amount of your time, however, and if it postpones the unit or the unveiling of the learning progressions, it is probably not worth the trade-off.

Once students have studied the Informational Reading Learning Progression and gleaned an understanding of the indicators that might suggest they are doing higher level work, this fills them with a sense of direction and resolve, and it puts a tincture over the whole unit. As students self-assess their work on analyzing craft, for example, you have almost painted the future teaching on that topic with a dye that makes that teaching stand out in your students' minds more across the unit. They know it is a skill that will be assessed, so they sit up and look alert! At the point in the unit when you teach about analyzing author's craft, they're apt to think, "Oh, this is about author's craft. That was on the pre-assessment." By prioritizing this work on the assessment, you've demonstrated that you place a high value on this learning, and students will likely respond accordingly.

Giving students a sense of the end goals for the unit gives them a sense of agency and purpose, as well as a feeling that they can do what it takes to grow. Carol Dweck's research has shown that students who see hard work as valuable have a growth mindset and an empowered sense of themselves as learners. Mistakes are valuable because they lead to new learning, and a new challenge is something to be welcomed with excitement. And here, students will feel empowered because they'll know what it means to push themselves to be stronger. If you want to do better, then you can absolutely refer to text structure as it relates to main ideas, for example. This is not hidden from the students. The goals are transparent, clear as day, and thus accessible.

GETTING READY

Gathering Texts

In Bend I, you will channel students to read high-interest nonfiction texts at their independent reading level. We suggest you make use of your classroom library, the school library, and the local library to assemble a great number of high-interest books. Whenever possible, group books into topic sets so that students can first read an easier text on a topic and then use that knowledge to access other books on the same topic that are increasingly complex.

In Bends II and III, students will work in research teams to read about extreme weather and natural disasters, so you'll need to assemble books on these topics for their use. These collections might include articles, books, and videos, as well as interviews, observations, and surveys. You will encourage students to be their own text collectors, but you will also want to support students in growing their collections. You might set up a time for students to visit the school or community library or invite students into the room to research and print articles outside of reading workshop.

Partnering Students

Across the unit, you'll want to partner students in different ways. For Bend I, you will find it advantageous to pair students in same-level partnerships. Partners reading around similar levels of text complexity will encounter overlapping complexities in the texts they read, and you'll recruit them to tackle those complexities together, trying out strategies you teach and even creating their own. You may choose to layer in additional support for partnerships by first channeling them into duplicate copies of high-interest nonfiction texts.

In Bends II and III, students take on team-based research projects on topics related to extreme weather and natural disasters. You'll probably invite students to write you quick letters about the topics they would like to study. Teachers who piloted the unit found it helpful to give students some choice while also reminding them that they will switch topics at the end of Bend II. Assembling the research teams takes a bit of behind-the-scenes engineering, but it will be worth it. You might channel students whom you know will work well together to study the same topic, and you'll also consider the texts that you have for a particular topic alongside your students reading levels so that you help match readers to books they will be able to read independently.

Conducting Read-Alouds alongside the Unit

The read-aloud text we recommend for the unit is National Geographic Kids' *Everything Weather* by Kathy Furgang. There's much to love about this book. Your students will be in awe of the text, from the sections about bizarre weather events to the compelling photographs, diagrams, and humor. You will likely admire the book's snippets of text that are perfect for quick strategy and skill instruction. While you probably won't read this book from cover to cover, it is sure to become a favorite as you share excerpts in read-aloud and in lessons. During Bends II and III, you'll continue to use sections of *Everything Weather*, as well as some additional texts such as *DK Eyewitness: Hurricane and Tornado* by Jack Challoner and *Hurricanes* by Seymour Simon. You will also want to make your own selections of texts to read aloud to your class during the latter parts of the unit. Choose texts that you find engaging, and encourage your students to share texts they think would be helpful for the class, too. You will want to carve out a separate chunk of time each day, outside of reading workshop, for reading aloud sections of these texts.

✥ ONLINE DIGITAL RESOURCES

A variety of resources to accompany this and the other Grade 4 Units of Study for Teaching Reading are available in the Online Resources, including charts and examples of student work shown throughout *Reading the Weather, Reading the World*, as well as links to other electronic resources. Offering daily support for your teaching, these materials will help you provide a structured learning environment that fosters independence and self-direction.

To access and download all the digital resources for the Grade 4 Units of Study for Teaching Reading:

1. Go to **www.heinemann.com** and click the link in the upper right to log in. (If you do not have an account yet, you will need to create one.)
2. **Enter the following registration code** in the box to register your product: RUOS_Gr4
3. Under **My Online Resources**, click the link for the ***Grade 4 Reading Units of Study***.
4. The digital resources are available in the upper right; click a file name to download. (For any compressed ("ZIP") files, double-click the downloaded file to extract individual files to your hard drive.)

(You may keep copies of these resources on up to six of your own computers or devices. By downloading the files you acknowledge that they are for your individual or classroom use and that neither the resources nor the product code will be distributed or shared.)

Dear Teachers,

Before you turn the page and begin the journey of this unit of study, we want to remind you that it is enormously helpful to establish some baseline data on what your kids can (and can't yet) do as readers of nonfiction texts. The world today is rapidly escalating expectations for nonfiction reading and chances are good that your children will need to get into high gear soon in order to meet the exciting (and potentially overwhelming) expectations for nonfiction readers. These global standards may, for instance, require fourth-graders to read across a collection of nonfiction texts that teach about the same topic, categorizing information from both texts in a way that makes a new organization that synthesizes the combined information. Add to that the fact that on standardized assessments, kids are being asked to take on incredibly ambitious work, work that we, as educators, are often unsure that we could do. It is easy, then, for students to feel demoralized and overwhelmed by the tasks ahead.

To counter these feelings, and to help fourth-graders make progress along these lines, you and your colleagues need the tools to communicate your literacy goals and pathways to children and to support them as they progress along those trajectories. Your children need access to low-stakes assessments that allow them to think about the progress they are (and are not yet) making toward that important work. To support these goals, you'll want to give a performance assessment before you begin this unit. This work will give you and your students a crystal-clear path forward.

You'll see that the assessment asks children to read more than one text and to do some high-level comprehension work. Much of what they're being asked to do is work they won't yet have been taught to do yet, so don't be dismayed if it seems hard for them. The hope is that by the time of the post-assessment, this work will seem more within reach. But if it still seems ambitious, you can find some consolation in the fact that research suggests that checklists and rubrics are especially helpful if they are challenging for kids, establishing a horizon for them. We're quite sure this work will be challenging for your youngsters.

The texts will be too hard to read for kids who are working well below benchmark. You could, of course, develop your own easier assessment, inserting these questions into easier texts. Alternatively, you could read these passages aloud, while letting children follow along. Certainly you will learn nothing about children's abilities to do higher-level thinking if they can't read the text at all! Your running records will tell you the level of text complexity a child can handle, and this assessment is meant to measure higher-level comprehension skills. So while reading the passages aloud isn't a perfect solution, it's better than the other options.

In a world where people rarely agree on anything, there is unanimous agreement that the biggest problem with most classroom-based assessments is that too often, nothing is made of the data. Please, please, don't neglect to score this for or with your kids within a few short days as they need the feedback, and they need the rubrics and learning progressions to be in their hands.

Best of luck to you with the performance assessment—and the unit!

Thanks,

Lucy, Emily, and Mike

Reading and Learning
with Intensity

IN THIS SESSION, you'll teach students that nonfiction readers make a commitment to learning from texts by making connections between what they already know and care about and the text.

GETTING READY

✔ Organize students into matched-level partnerships. These might be continuations of the partnerships from the first unit in the year, or they could be new partnerships. Assign one student to be Partner 1 and one to be Partner 2.

✔ Be ready to give each student a new, nonfiction book baggie, with an expository book or article you have specially selected. The selected texts should be within reach, contain a Table of Contents, have headings or topic sentences that make it easy to glean the author's points—the main ideas and supporting details. Ideally, partners will have the same text (see Active Engagement).

✔ Be sure students have a pocket folder with blank reading logs, a pen, Post-it® notes, and a reading notebook.

✔ Ask students to bring their backpacks with them to the meeting area (see Connection).

✔ Keep chart paper and markers at hand (see Connection).

✔ Bring a magazine to the minilesson (see Teaching).

✔ Choose a demonstration text to read aloud throughout the bend. We have chosen *Everything Weather* by Kathy Furgang as a demonstration text. If it is very important to you, you can choose another text, but the topic of weather is heavily embedded throughout the unit, and is one we strongly recommend (see Teaching).

✔ Prepare a chart titled "To Read Nonfiction Well . . ." This will become an anchor chart for Bend I (see Teaching).

T ODAY WILL BE A BIG DAY. Bring out the trumpets, the red carpet, the fanfare. Today your students will be setting aside their fiction and will begin to read high-interest expository books and articles. A primary goal for this first portion of the unit is for kids to devour huge amounts of text, reading with volume and engagement that equals that which they've demonstrated while reading fiction.

You'll remind students of nonfiction reading skills and strategies they know from third grade that you expect they will bring to their fourth-grade work. "Last year, you learned that readers take the time to orient themselves to a text," you might say, and then you will teach that when orienting to a text, readers draw on prior knowledge—even when the topics are a bit tangential. When reading a book on droughts, knowledge of evaporation and of irrigation can help. "You know that readers read to glean the main ideas," you'll remind students, and you'll extend reading for the author's points by suggesting that your students do not engage in a stop-and-go sort of reading in which they aim to record every passing fact, definition, date, and statistic. You can trust that many students' natural inclination is to read for random factoids, not reading in large chunks and gleaning the main ideas of text, and it will be this latter sort of reading that you support. This is important because when youngsters approach nonfiction texts as if reading is a sort of Trivial Pursuit game in which the goal is to capture every passing fact, those youngsters can't easily glean the most important ideas. In this lesson, and indeed in this unit, you support the sort of nonfiction reading that you engage in when you read the newspaper, a magazine, a high-interest nonfiction book, a website on a topic you care about. In so doing, you not only support readers' skills, but you support them in becoming lifelong readers of nonfiction, purusing nonfiction as an extension of all their other interests in life.

To loosen kids' grip on the sort of nonfiction that involves inching through texts and copying down facts, you'll ask children to refrain from note-taking at all for now. This will change soon. A few days from now you'll channel students to record summary-like notes, but even then, you won't encourage them to read with pen in hand, pausing to write every few lines, but will instead suggest that when they reach the end of a chunk of text, they can use note-taking as a way to take stock of what they've learned. To make it likely that students read with fluency, engagement, and high levels of understanding, you'll channel them to read very accessible and engaging texts, and to read in ways that make it likely they connect to the topic. Later, on what is likely to be the fourth day of the unit, you will support students as they begin to read harder, more complicated nonfiction texts. But that part of the bend is yet to come. For today, your goal will be to rev students up and build excitement and energy for the new unit. The more fanfare you build, the more volume you'll get!

"To make it likely that students read with fluency, engagement, and high levels of understanding, you'll channel them to read very accessible and engaging texts, and to read in ways that make it likely they connect to the topic."

Be sure to prepare your library so that your classroom becomes a place to study ancient Egypt and termites and star basketball players. Consider creating book bins around some high-interest topics. For today, you'll channel students to read accessible and structured expository texts in partnerships.

Today, you'll also help students choose books that will be enticing for them to read for the next few days. It would be ideal if you can do a bit of investigation beforehand, finding out what your students are passionate about (especially those who tend to be resistant readers) and see if you can't find some books on those topics. You'll want to champion this unit by emphasizing that students will have the chance to develop more expertise on chosen topics, and to immerse themselves in new studies. For many fourth-graders, a nonfiction unit of reading is an exciting opportunity.

Like so many of our first sessions, this one calls on students to take charge of their reading lives. You'll begin by teaching them that taking charge of one's reading life is a matter of mindset—of choosing one way of reading over another (much the same way they choose to read a text like it is gold, rather than like a curmudgeon). You'll show them how seeking connections to a text and its subject matter is one way nonfiction readers engage.

Reading and Learning with Intensity

CONNECTION

Ask students to bring their backpacks to the meeting area. Then channel them to do an archeological dig through their belongings to determine the kinds of nonfiction reading they do.

Before students gathered, I said, "Readers, I'm going to ask you to do something surprising. Would you bring your backpacks with you to the meeting area?" Once they had assembled, the floor space brimming with backpacks, I continued. "Readers, today we launch a new unit, this time focusing on nonfiction reading. I thought before we get started we might take a minute to think, 'What sorts of nonfiction texts already fill my life?'"

"Would you and your partner do a sort of archeological dig, only this time, instead of digging through layers of earth to find shards of old pottery that could be assembled to learn about an ancient civilization, would you dig through your backpacks and pockets to assemble an evidence-based answer to the question: 'What sort of nonfiction texts fill my life?'"

Kids set to work and I rotated among them. To one, I said, "Wait, wait, you're passing right past your math workbook. Might there be nonfiction writing in it? How would you categorize that kind of nonfiction writing? Word problems and directions?" To another I said, "You know what—other kids are searching through backpacks—try something different. How about searching through your clothes? Hey—labels! I never thought of that!" To yet another, I said, "Wait. Really—you want to use just one word to name all the different kinds of nonfiction writing in this book?" Opening to the index as an example of a different sort of nonfiction text, I said, "Look again. What are the different kinds of nonfiction writing that go into even this one book?"

With the class, compile a list of the kinds of nonfiction texts students found, emphasizing the point that nonfiction is all around them.

After a few minutes, I reconvened the class. "In just three minutes you have found *so* many kinds of nonfiction texts that fill your life! Let's record these. Call out some of the kinds of nonfiction you found." I jotted students' suggestions on a sheet of chart paper as they called them out.

This activity takes the prize for being out-of-the-box! It's a bit messy and a bit tangential to the real point of the day, but remember that this first connection needs to launch not just the day's minilesson but also the unit.

The challenge in this minilesson and in many minilessons is to do this work quickly. This task could consume the entire class period, if you let it—and it is not worth that amount of time! Use your voice, your gestures—everything you've got—to create an urgency right from the start, and stay within the time frames we suggest.

After a few of the expected categories, I gestured toward Sophia to share, knowing what she'd say. "Clothing labels." I also knew Jack wanted to put candy ingredients on the list, so I called on him, too. Before long we had a long list that made a clear point: "As you can see, boys and girls, you are nonfiction readers *all day, every day*!"

Point out that if their families had been asked to list kinds of nonfiction reading that fill their lives, the lists would be similar and longer. Use this to drumroll the importance of the unit.

"Readers, look at all of the nonfiction reading you do each day! It is everywhere. I want to make a really important point, though. If this wasn't you sitting in this meeting area, doing an archeological dig of the nonfiction texts that fill your life, but if instead your families were doing that same work, they'd probably be holding whatever they use to carry their work—briefcases, pocketbooks, laptops, trays of incoming and outgoing work—and if I had asked *them* to study the nonfiction reading that fills their days, your families would have listed all these and even more kinds of nonfiction. As you get older, nonfiction takes up more and more of your reading life. There are standards, or guidelines, for the kinds of work that kids should do in school, goals kids should reach in all subject areas. In elementary school, these standards suggest a kid's reading life—across the whole day—should be divided pretty equally between reading fiction and nonfiction, but by high school, the standards suggest that a kid's reading life should be two-thirds nonfiction, one-third fiction! That makes this unit an important one."

❖ **Name the teaching point.**

"Today I want to teach you that as you get older, you don't just read *more* nonfiction, you also read nonfiction *differently*. Grown-up nonfiction readers make a commitment to learning from a text, by making connections between what they already know and care about, and the text."

TEACHING

Point out that readers have a choice to read nonfiction texts in a waiting-for-the-dentist way, or with reading-to-become-smarter engagement.

"When you listed the kinds of nonfiction texts that fill your world, one thing you didn't note is that there are at least two utterly different *ways to read* nonfiction. You can read a nonfiction text—any text—in what I call a 'Waiting for the Dentist' way. Or you can read the same text in a 'Reading to Become Smarter' way.

"Right now, let's all show what 'Waiting for the Dentist' reading looks like." I leaned back in my chair, crossed one leg over the other, and began nonchalantly flipping through a magazine I had brought over for this purpose. I gestured for the students to join me, acting out a lazy kind of reading, flipping past imaginary pages, bored looks on our faces. "Exactly! We've all seen people in waiting rooms, picking up a magazine to kill time. They flip open the magazine, scan for tidbits that look mildly interesting, thinking, 'Ah! Here's an interesting picture!' or 'That's a funny ad.' Then their time is up, and they drop the magazine.

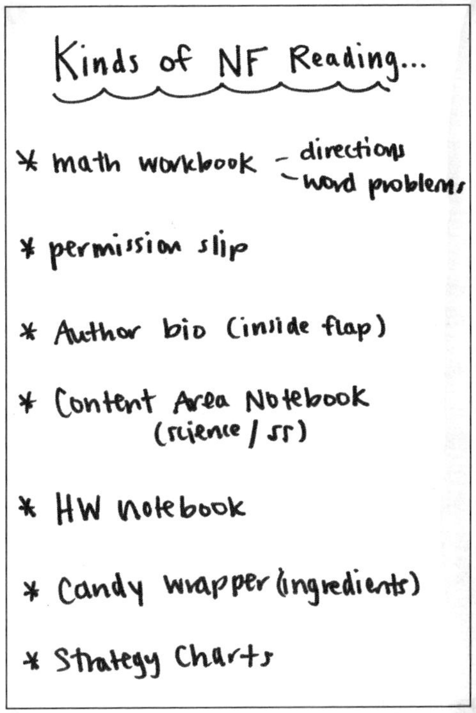

FIG. 1–1 One teacher's chart of the various kinds of nonfiction found in students' backpacks

"Here is my question. How many of you have done that kind of nonfiction reading?" Some hands went up sheepishly. In contrast, I shot my hand up proudly. "I read that way *a lot*. I read junk mail that way, and parts of books and newspapers. But here's the thing: as I do that sort of reading, I'm looking for texts that I want to *really read*. And when I want to learn from a text, it is almost as if I flip a mental switch and now I read, *committed* to learning from the text. Then I make my reading work look very different."

Explain that to commit to learning from a text, a reader has to care about the topic. Sometimes, readers get themselves to care by connecting the new topic to something they already care about.

"I know you've heard people talk about the need to 'make a commitment' to a team or a project. Perhaps a coach has said to you, 'Are you willing to make a commitment to gymnastics?' My point is that for you to learn from a text, the first step is to make a commitment to doing so. You need to care about the topic. Sometimes, of course, you already *do* care about the topic. Other times, readers need to have ways to get themselves to care about a topic. And one way to do that is to build connections between what you already know and care about and that new topic."

Help kids connect to the topic of the whole-class read aloud by activating prior knowledge and considering what they care about.

Holding up *Everything Weather*, I said, "So before we dig into our new read-aloud book, let's try to make connections to it. Look over the book with me and let's think, 'What do we *already* know and care about that connects in *some* way to this topic?'" I looked at the book silently, giving the class a minute to think as well.

"If you don't know a lot about the science of how weather works, you can still connect to the topic, right? Think about what you *do* know about weather—and for a minute, try to make the topic matter to you. Make it feel like a big deal."

I gave the children a moment to do this.

"Are some of you thinking about ways in which the weather has affected your plans—made you cancel a ballgame, a vacation, a school day (!)—or ways the weather has made just an average Saturday into a great day? I am.

"Is anyone thinking about the extreme weather that's been happening—who remembers seeing ten feet of snow in Buffalo last November? Imagine those people opening the door to go out of their house and all they see is a wall of snow. Are any of you remembering the tornadoes that swept through some parts of the country? How about the droughts? The weather ends up having a pretty big effect on people's lives, doesn't it? Right now, turn and talk to your partner about why you think that a book on weather is going to be super important and interesting—and talk that way even if you are kind of pretending. You can pretend your way into being connected to a topic. Turn and talk!"

Debrief, naming what you have done that you hope students learn to do any time they read.

After letting children talk for a moment, I said, in a hushed aside, "Did you notice what we did just now? We could have picked up this book *Everything Weather* in a sort of ho hum way, but by thinking about things we care about that are related to this book, this topic, I think we're all more ready to read this with interest, with commitment. The point

When students were in third grade, they learned a variety of techniques for revving up their mind for reading nonfiction, including noticing all the parts of the text, and thinking about how the book may go. This takes it to the next level, since you are asking students to not only think about the book itself, but their own prior knowledge and personal connections to the topic at hand.

We want to instill in our learners the positive learning mindset of "I can learn, and I want to learn." Albert Bandura's research into self-efficacy has been a major influence on this session.

isn't that weather is an interesting topic (though I think it is) but instead, the point is that to rally yourself to read *any* nonfiction book well, it helps to take a minute to make a connection to the topic." I unveiled a new chart, which would become the anchor chart for the bend, to be added to in the coming days and weeks.

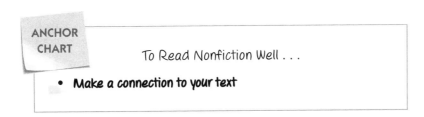

ANCHOR CHART

To Read Nonfiction Well . . .

- **Make a connection to your text**

ACTIVE ENGAGEMENT

Set partners up to practice what you just taught. Give each reader a new book and ask them to make a connection to the topic of their text.

"I'm going to distribute new Nonfiction Baggies to each of you." I held up one of the baggies, one measly book sitting inside it. "You might be thinking to yourself, 'That's not much of a book baggie!' And you'd be right to think that. In fact, after today's lesson you are going to have a chance to browse baskets of books and fill your baggies to the brim. For right now, though, I've given each of you an article or a book—a text I chose especially for you and your partner. You'll see that you both have identical texts in your baggies." I began to hand the baggies out as I continued talking.

"You may be interested in the topic already—or you may not." Leah looked curiously at her book on the digestive system. "But here is your job: get yourself to care about this topic. And try to do that by using the strategy we just tried. Think, 'What do I know and care about that connects to this topic in some way?' Get started on the work of becoming committed to this text. You can talk together as you do this. Partner 2, go first."

I listened in as Anthony pointed to a photograph in his book about wolves. "I know a little bit about wolves because I have a dog and they look pretty similar. I know they are related."

"Yeah, dogs and wolves come from the same ancestors," Colin said. "I watched a show about it. Only dogs became pets, though. Not wolves!"

Reconvene the class, asking a student to share how he became connected to a topic that at first glance seemed distant and not quite interesting to him.

I called readers back to attention. "Let's hear from some of you who at first glance thought, 'Hmm, . . . I'm not so sure I *do* know or care about this topic,' but who found a way to connect." I scanned the room for volunteers, then called on Jason to share.

Jason said, "Well, my book is about orchestras and I thought you had given me someone else's baggie probably because I have *no* interest in orchestras. I don't like that boring kind of music. But then I saw it has a chapter on the conductor and I was thinking that conductors and coaches might be sort of similar, and I am really interested in soccer coaching. So I'm not really interested in the whole book but maybe just in that part."

I nodded. "And the good thing, Jason, is that your interest is going to give you a new way to think about what you read, too. That might be true for others."

LINK

Prepare students to go off to read, trying out today's strategy before picking new books to add to their nonfiction book baggies.

"Readers, today start by independently reading the text you and your partner have in your baggies. As you read today, take time to be a committed reader by trying to connect to the topic you are reading about, no matter what it is!"

"I'm expecting that you'll fill up your baggies over the next few days. You can start choosing books when you finish the text I chose for you. For now, please select texts that look easy for you—texts you can read along at a good pace, reading a ton of them! As we move further in the unit, I'm going to show you how you can deliberately reach for harder nonfiction—but that part of the unit will only work if you start off with texts that are easy for you."

"And, I'm also going to ask you to *not* write about your reading. Again, we'll get into that later. Too often, I see kids inching through nonfiction books, copying down half the information—and getting almost no reading done! Today should feel completely different than that. Off you go!"

The progression of student work in this unit goes from more to less supported. Today you set students up to read nonfiction texts that are supported with subtitles that help the reader navigate the text. You can find suggested texts in the online resources. Students will work through those texts in partnerships, receiving extra support. As they do this, you'll have a chance to support them in choosing texts to read over the upcoming bend. Be sure you steer them toward especially accessible texts, texts they can read with minimal difficulty.

Launching the Unit by Getting Accessible Books into Kids' Hands

TODAY you will probably divide your time between helping students choose books and articles for their baggies, giving text introductions to help readers get started, and, overall, helping to get the new work of this unit off the ground.

Initially, your students will only have one expository nonfiction text to read, so obviously this won't keep them doing nose-in-the-book reading for long. What it does mean, however, is that to start, all readers have something to read, and you have time to help them make wise decisions about their upcoming reading agenda. Use independent reading time today to help rally kids to choose small collections of texts that are apt to be accessible and interesting enough that they will read them with commitment.

Presumably you will already have leveled the nonfiction texts in your classroom library. You may have done this using Fountas and Pinnell's leveling system for nonfiction texts, which is as good a system as any, or you may have relied on published Lexile levels. Know that in either case, most teachers find it harder to bucket nonfiction books by level, and certainly harder to match readers to books with precision because a nonfiction book will be harder or easier for individual readers based to some extent on that individual's prior knowledge of the topic. So a nonfiction book might be accessible to a reader who is steeped in that topic, and not to a similar reader whose knowledge of the topic is thin. This means that matching readers to nonfiction books will be more complex work that will need more constant vigilance than matching them to fiction books.

This does not mean, however, that you might as well give up on any effort to be sure readers are reading texts they can handle. We've often witnessed that during nonfiction units, a significant mismatch between kids and books will lead to students hardly reading anything. Remember, kids' reading levels plummet every summer—you don't want them plummeting whenever you teach a nonfiction unit as well!

You'll probably put nonfiction books into bins or baskets that combine several text levels, and channel kids to the containers with books that most closely match their interests, if possible. We also recommend you teach kids that by reading the easiest book on a topic first (even choosing to read a very, very easy book on a topic to start), the reader can provide himself or herself with the prior knowledge necessary to tackle slightly more challenging books on that same topic. The easier books allow readers to build some background knowledge so they're better able to handle the more challenging texts.

As you assist readers in locating texts they want to read, use this as a chance to tell them a bit about their topics, and to help rally their commitment to the topics. If you see a book on hurricanes, point out that the number of hurricanes in this country is skyrocketing, and ask if they've ever experienced a hurricane or seen one on a news show. Wonder, together, what the difference is between tornadoes and hurricanes.

(continues)

MID-WORKSHOP TEACHING   Taking the Time to Share

"Readers, a reading researcher named Alan Purves once said something interesting about reading. He said, 'It takes two to read a book.' He went on to explain that the books he remembers most are those he has shared with someone else.

"I thought, therefore, that as we start this unit, it makes sense for you to think about a way that you could share your book with your partner. Right now, look over what you have read and think about how you'd like to share the book. Will you read a part of it together? Talk about the topic? Come up with some connections from your own life? Think about questions you'd like to ask the author?

"Take a quick moment to decide, then do some sharing."

Provide readers with limited background knowledge of their topic with text and topic introductions.

Keep an eye on readers who may have limited background knowledge and schema on their text's topic. While you have pre-selected some books on behalf of all your partnerships today, you may still see a reader or two who may need additional support connecting to her topic. In these instances, in addition to channeling readers to easier books on the topic, you might also provide a brief text or topic introduction. For example, if a pair is reading about medieval times, you could quickly activate your readers' prior knowledge of kings, queens, and knights, and then teach them briefly about their roles.

Help readers dig into nonfiction by linking new work to ongoing work.

Meanwhile you'll also want to help get the new unit off the ground. Always at the start of a unit, it is important to move quickly among the kids, helping to recruit them into the work of the new unit. You'll use table compliments, quick small groups, and voiceovers to rally kids to keep up the same habits they began during the first unit of the year. You'll teach more on previewing a text in the coming days, but if you catch a child looking at the back cover blurb of her book, name what the child is doing and compliment it. "I love that you are remembering that some of the habits of narrative reading are true for all reading. It's smart to read the back blurb of a book so you can get a better idea about what you'll be learning." To another table you might say, "Are you all noticing that once Fatima decided on a book to read independently, she logged it in her reading log, just as we have been doing all year? Will each of you take a moment—once you've chosen the book you'd like to read today—to jot that book into your reading log?"

Taking Stock and Making Resolutions

Channel students to self-assess how their first day of nonfiction reading went, noticing what their strengths were, as well as areas for improvement.

"Readers, before you go any further with your nonfiction reading, I would like for everyone here to take a moment to reflect. Earlier this year, we talked about the fact that people don't get better at something just by doing that same thing over and over and over again. You read nonfiction today, and you can read it every day for the next few weeks, and yet not necessarily grow as a nonfiction reader. Instead, getting better begins with you being honest with yourself. What works about the way you read nonfiction—and what doesn't work? What could you do to improve? Would you jot some notes about how your reading went today—what was good about it? What was less good about it?" I gave students just a minute to jot their reflections, then had partnerships cluster together, so they were sharing in foursomes while I listened in.

After a few minutes of sharing, I brought the group back together and summarized, using this as a time to rally them to tackle the unit with dedication. "I heard many of you saying that you love reading nonfiction because you learn new information and can become experts on all sorts of different topics. This is so true, we are all going to become experts and have so much exciting learning ahead of us! I also heard you saying that you sometimes fall into some bad habits, like skipping headings or just looking at interesting pictures and not really digging into nonfiction texts. We'll be sure to guard against this kind of reading in this unit—you can't become an expert by not paying really close attention and giving reading your all."

BUILDING YOUR NONFICTION READING LIFE

Readers,

Earlier today, you searched your backpacks for an answer to the question, "What sorts of nonfiction already fills my life?" Tonight I hope you continue to think about this and also try to make your nonfiction reading life richer. Think about the things you love—a sport, an author, a music group, an animal, a cause, a place, a game. There are nonfiction texts connected with that topic. Your job tonight is to try to find some of those texts.

This may mean searching online for websites on the topic, it may mean going to the school or local library to research books, or it may mean asking people (including me and your family) for help.

A final option is to bring home the books you are reading in school and continue reading them. The most important thing for now is that you are reading nonfiction at home as well as at school. Continue to read without doing any writing about your reading, and be sure to use your reading log to record the amount of reading you are doing.

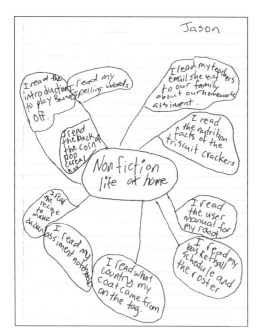

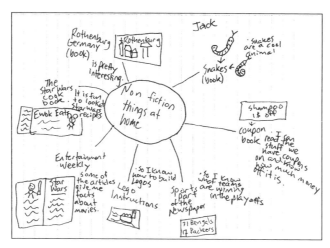

FIG. 1–2   Nonfiction that fills Jason's and Jack's lives

Session 2

To Learn from Nonfiction, Readers Get Their Mental Arms around the Text

YOUR CHILDREN will enter today's workshop with baggies brimming with books that they've chosen because they are accessible and high interest. The session launches a line of work designed to help students get their mental arms around these accessible books, reading in such a way that they glean the author's points—the main ideas and supporting details. Today you remind kids that when reading nonfiction, it is important to take time to preview the text and based on that, to generate expectations for how the text in its entirety will go. Tomorrow, you talk about pausing to extract the main idea and supporting details.

If you are thinking, "Didn't kids learn that in third grade?" you are right, this was an important part of their third-grade nonfiction instruction. But as nonfiction texts carry more and more information, determining what's critically important and culling that from the minutia must continue to be front and center in any effort to help kids read nonfiction.

The work that you'll be teaching today and over the upcoming days is as important as anything you could teach your students. As Tony Wagner, the author of *Creating Innovators*, reminds us, in this twenty-first century, it has become essential to help students to deal with the overwhelming influx of information that is at their disposal. After all, it used to be that the teacher's job was to deliver content—the capitals of the states, the elements of the Periodic Table—to students who needed that content. Teachers brought knowledge—like the clay tablets from the mountains—into classrooms full of kids who had no other access to that knowledge. But now, as Wagner points out, knowledge is like air—it is everywhere. Any student can, with one click of a button, access the entire Library of Congress. What this means is that whereas your job as a teacher was once to deliver knowledge, now your job is to help students deal with the overwhelming barrage of knowledge that is out there. Another way of saying this is that your job is to help students determine importance.

Teaching kids to read in ways that allow them to determine importance is, of course, no small charge. Try handing a learner a highlighter and asking the youngster to underline what is important. You'll quickly find that either nothing is highlighted—or everything is. This session doesn't take kids the distance—it simply reminds them that as readers of

IN THIS SESSION, you'll remind students that nonfiction readers preview texts by surveying the parts of the text as well as activating prior knowledge to anticipate how the text might go.

GETTING READY

✔ Ask students to bring a book from their baggie to the meeting area to discuss with a partner (see Connection).

✔ Be ready to pass out white boards and dry erase markers, one for every four to five students (see Teaching and Active Engagement).

✔ Keep chart paper and markers at hand (see Teaching and Active Engagement).

✔ Keep *Everything Weather* by Kathy Furgang or whatever text you have chosen as your demonstration text at hand (see Teaching and Active Engagement).

✔ Display the anchor chart "To Read Nonfiction Well . . ." with a new bullet added that says "Preview" (see Teaching and Active Engagement).

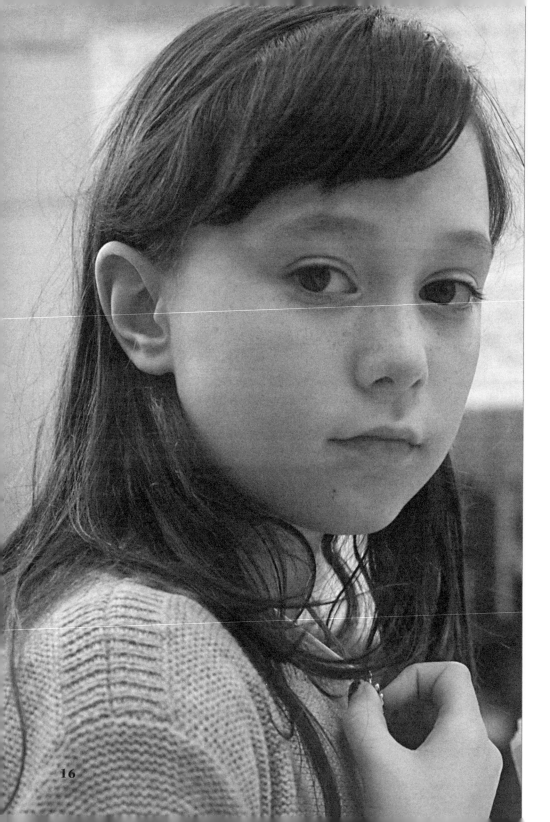

nonfiction texts, they need to be culling the essentials from all they read, and one way to do this is to read, aware that nonfiction texts have parts. Readers of expository nonfiction chunk as they read, and think about what they have learned, part by part.

"Your job is to help students deal with the overwhelming barrage of knowledge that is out there. . . to help students determine importance."

Of course, in previous years your students have already learned to think of parts of texts in relation to the various ways that texts are structured, and tomorrow's teaching will remind them of all that prior instruction. Soon after that, readers will be encouraged to choose challenge texts and you'll help them read these more difficult texts in the same way you help them read accessible texts today. For now, this unit follows the advice, "Add flour slowly, stirring all the while." The hope is that for now, your teaching and your students' thinking will focus on the topics that are front and central in texts—on mushrooms and pirate ships, miniature horses and roller coasters—and your instruction will accentuate the importance of that focus.

To Learn from Nonfiction, Readers Get Their Mental Arms around the Text

CONNECTION

Ask students to bring a new book they anticipate reading today to the meeting area. Channel them to look over the books, connecting with the topic and generating questions.

"When you come to the meeting area, please bring a new book or article that you'll start reading today. I'm hoping that you choose a text from your baggie that will be easy for you to read quickly."

Once the children had gathered, I continued on. "Fourth-graders, listen up. Researchers say that to learn *anything*, you need to connect the new information you are learning with what you already know. You did that yesterday, when you took the text I had put in your book baggie and found a way to connect personally with the topic of that text.

"You've each got a new book with you, so will you take a minute to study the cover of your book, flip through its pages, maybe skim what's written on the back cover? And, as you do, think about how the topic connects to other things you know and care about."

I let the children do this and at one point voiced over, "Remember yesterday that Jason didn't start off being that interested in reading about the symphony, but then he realized that conducting a symphony is a bit like coaching soccer, so that part of the book became more interesting to him. The other thing that happened yesterday is that as you connected with your topic, you found yourself asking questions such as 'Will the tiger have any of the habits that our cat has?' Leo's reading a book about a man riding a high-wire bicycle across the Niagara River, and he wonders why people do those high-risk activities. How many people die?

"Do this work with your partner. Leaf through your books together. Think about how the topic connects with what you already know. What does that make you expect to learn? What does it make you wonder? Take just a minute to do this for each of your books."

Debrief, naming the replicable parts of what you have just asked students to do, and setting up today's teaching point as a second thing readers do before they read.

After just a minute or so, I intervened. "I think you are seeing that making connections can help you turn that switch so you go from 'Waiting at the Dentist Reading' to 'Reading to Learn.'

One of the challenges of the connection is that it should engage students, but also stay brief, so as to protect the streamlined quality of the minilesson. In this connection, you channel students to take a minute to talk to each other. Be aware that some teachers struggle to punctuate minilessons with tiny bits of turn-and-talk because whenever they set kids up to talk, that talking becomes a Very Big Deal and lasts a long time. You'll want to practice turn-and-talks so that you can say to kids "What did you eat for breakfast: turn and talk" and the room can erupt into talk, and then ninety seconds later you can call, "Come back to me," and the kids can instantly be with you. This particular talk interval will be longer than ninety seconds, but for the entire minilesson to be ten minutes (okay, twelve!) it can't be much longer. If you aren't able to do these interludes briskly, then skip them. You can instead ask students to take a minute to think quietly, alone, about the questions you could instead set them up to discuss.

"But there are other critical things to do before you start reading, and one of those is to preview the text in a way that helps you anticipate what you'll learn. I know you learned last year (and for years before that!) about the importance of previewing a text, of revving up your mind to get ready to read. Yesterday, I noticed many of you jumped straight into reading. I understand your eagerness to dive in, but I want to remind you of something."

❖ Name the teaching point.

"Today I want to remind you that nonfiction readers preview texts. They survey the parts of the text, paying attention to headings and topic sentences, and they use what they already know about the topic to think, 'This part seems to be about . . . and this other part seems to be about . . .'"

TEACHING AND ACTIVE ENGAGEMENT

Rally students to take seriously the suggestion that they orient themselves to a nonfiction text before reading it by highlighting relevant reading research.

"Readers, I'm not sure if you realize it but there are grown-up researchers who devote their whole lives to studying not just topics like rain forests and hurricanes—but readers. One of those organizations that studies readers also write the tests that kids take to get into college. Some researchers at that organization—called ETS—told us that when they study kids as nonfiction readers, what they find is that any kid who begins reading a nonfiction text by looking over the whole text and thinking, 'How might this whole text go?' ends up being a *way* better reader than a kid who just gets a text, opens it up, and starts plowing through it. So the work that you have been and will be doing today turns out to be *really* important.

"These researchers are clear that if you want to get stronger as nonfiction readers, then instead of just diving right into nonfiction texts, you need to take control of your own reading and boss yourself around a bit. You need to say, 'Hold on. Don't start reading yet. Look over the text.' Then you need to study the cover of a text, the Table of Contents, and the headings, photographs, diagrams, and other text features as well. And as you do that, you try to figure out how the whole of the text seems to be organized. I know this work is not new to you; you spent a lot of time as third-graders orienting yourselves to nonfiction texts before diving in."

Preview a nonfiction text, using knowledge of the topic to imagine how the text is apt to go. Recruit kids to function as researchers, chronicling what you do.

I distributed a few white boards into the group so that everyone was sitting within whisper-distance of someone with a white board, then said, "Will you be whisper-researchers, working together quietly to record ways you see me getting ready to read?" I gestured toward our "To Read Nonfiction Well . . ." anchor chart where I had added the word "Preview," signaling that I hoped students would help me fill the bullet in. "There's stuff I do, that nonfiction readers do, even before settling down to read an opening paragraph. That's what I want you to research."

This suggestion we're giving to readers about the power of previewing a text isn't one we educators should take lightly, either. Substantial research has shown that teaching children to preview a text well is one of the most powerful reading interventions known today.

ANCHOR CHART

To Read Nonfiction Well . . .

- Make a connection to your text
- **Preview**

Preview the whole text and predict how it might go.

I picked up *Everything Weather*, put it on the document camera, and started flipping through it, modeling the predictable mistake my students were likely to make. "Oh wow—look at this cool fact! 'Doppler radar is so sensitive.'" I stopped myself. "No, wait, I want to read this book in a more grown-up way. I better get myself ready to read in a way that gets me thinking about how the whole text is apt to go."

"Let me start over again." I flipped back to the front cover. "Hmm, . . . *Everything Weather*. Before I even preview any further, I'm already thinking of some of the subtopics this book might contain. I haven't read a book on weather for a while—maybe ever, but the weather affects my life so I pay attention to it, and I know about it from watching the news on television. I also know how nonfiction books tend to go. They are usually organized into subtopics. Since this book is called *Everything Weather*, I expect it might first explain about basic kinds of weather—like rain and snow—but then maybe it will also teach me about storms—like hurricanes and tornadoes. Let me skim the Table of Contents and see what it shows me."

I flipped to the Table of Contents, and read through the chapter titles. "Let's see, 'What's the Weather?'; 'Weather Extremes'; 'Weather Predictions'; 'Fun with Weather.' Looks like this book covers a lot of different angles. And this is interesting: I was right that the book begins with types of weather and then teaches about extreme weather, but then there are two more big sections I didn't expect—one on weather predictions and another on fun with weather. I wonder what those will teach?"

Invite students to name the replicable work you have done previewing the book thus far.

I turned to the students and said, "Are you thinking about what I've done so far to preview this book? Talk about what I am doing in a way that will work even if you are reading on a totally different topic. For example, if you wanted to get started reading about gorillas, what does my work suggest you could do?"

I gave students a moment to talk and to record onto their white boards, and then I continued.

Demonstrate the process of previewing a page. Notice aloud what the headings might reveal about the upcoming text content.

"I'm going to turn to the chapter 'What's the Weather?' to see what it will teach me." I reached for the book still on the document camera, and I opened to the first page of that chapter and thought aloud.

To accentuate what you hope students do not do, it can help to do that thing, and then self-correct. It also helps demonstrate the positive learning mindset of approximation, that it is okay to make mistakes and brush the dust off one's pants and to try again—a learning attitude that research has shown to produce achievement in student learning.

Notice that as I shift into a demonstration, I make very clear the process I am using to do this thinking. That is, I don't just say, "The four main sections in this book are about . . ." I actually spell out what I'm thinking about the weather book in a way that will transfer to any book. "I'm thinking of some of the subtopics the book will contain, I'm thinking about how nonfiction books tend to go . . ."

"Hmm . . . the section title says, '*Weather . . . or Not*?' and then there are all these headings '*Everybody talks about it, but what is weather? Weather is the condition of the air or atmosphere. Temperatures rise and fall. Air warms and cools. Winds can be fast or slow,*' and I see some text boxes with photographs, examples of weather. I mean, I know about weather from everyday experience, but, oh, this is cool—there is a text box that says 'What Isn't Weather?' I hadn't considered that there is some stuff that seems like it would be weather but isn't, such as seasons.

"It looks like this section is going to teach me some of the basics about weather. This section is almost like an introduction to the topic 'weather.' After all, the title of this book is *Everything Weather*."

Again ask kids to record the replicable strategies they saw you using, then share their observations, leading you to synthesize findings onto your anchor chart.

Then I turned to the kids and said, "I could go on, but will you compare notes and think again about what else I do to preview a book? As you do this, remember to try to name what I do in ways that would work even if you were reading a book on something totally different."

Again I gave the children a moment to record notes detailing ways that nonfiction readers get ready to read. After a minute, I said, "So readers, hold your white boards up so I can see what you've noticed." They did, and I scanned the white boards. "Each of you has used some different words to name this work, but you are essentially saying the same thing," I said. "Let me see if I can capture what you are all saying on our chart." Then I added to our anchor chart:

ANCHOR CHART

To Read Nonfiction Well . . .

- Make a connection to your text
- **Preview the whole text and predict how it might go**
  - **Use prior knowledge of the topic**
  - **Scan the text features**

Preview the whole text and predict how it might go.

LINK

Repeat the teaching point, stressing that by previewing, readers generate a sense of the whole text. Point out that as they read, readers pause to think about whether they learned what they had anticipated or they were surprised.

"The important thing for you to realize is that now that you are in fourth grade, you don't just read *more* nonfiction, you also read nonfiction differently. Right now, use your thumb and your forefinger to make a peephole that is the size of a camera lens." I made one of these. "Try reading your book, looking through that peephole." The kids dramatically bent over their books and started reading that way.

I stopped the kids. "The way you are reading now, looking through a tiny peephole, is the way that unskilled readers read nonfiction. They are looking only at the very words that are in front of them. They don't have a sense for the whole text, for how the parts go together and what those parts say, altogether. By looking over the whole text before you read (or at least the chunk you are about to read), you alter your reading so you are not just seeing through a little peephole. You are putting one part of the text together with another part. That's a big deal.

"The best way to get your mental arms around the whole text is to take the time to preview in a way that gives you the larger plan for the whole book or even just the whole chapter. Today you'll continue to read easy, quick nonfiction, and to read without taking notes. Just read to learn. The two things I am going to ask you to do are these. First, make sure that you preview the whole text before you dive in. And second, after you read a chunk of your topic, pause to think, "Did this teach me what I expected to learn, or am I a little surprised by what I'm learning?"

TODAY, AS IN THE PREVIOUS SESSION, you'll need to interact efficiently with lots of kids, making your presence felt across the whole room, and do this in ways that rally most of the class into the work of the unit.

Research and support previewing.

There will be a small window in which you can research whether and how kids preview their books, so be ready to notice that work right away. It will help if you carry with you the Informational Reading Learning Progression tabbed "Orienting." That is, if the book is titled *Whales*, you can expect your less experienced previewers might do little more than say to themselves, "Hmm, . . . I bet this book will be about whales." Those readers would benefit from learning how to generate more specific expectations. If the text contains a Table of Contents, then you can teach readers to use it to say, "I think the book will first tell about how cool whales are, and then there will be a part about people who are killing them." You might leave these children with cue cards that remind them to think, "In specific, I think it'll say . . . Then it will also tell about . . ."

Some of your students will easily make connections to their prior knowledge on the topic, or perhaps any interests they have that are linked. Commend these students for carrying over what you taught them in the last session, and nudge them to take this a step further by considering the text structure of their books in their preview. Coach them so their book orientations sound more like this: "The book begins with a few chapters that go through the history of this team from long ago until now, and then it tells about the problems with the stadium and how they solved those, and then it compares the team of today with the earlier times . . ."

Check that readers are matched to books.

Be alert to signs that a child is holding a text that is impenetrable. Frankly, we've come to expect that whenever a class begins working in a nonfiction unit of study, a fair number of children will be working with texts that are too hard for them, until you intervene. One resource to guide you is the "Monitoring for Sense" strand of the

Informational Reading Learning Progression. You can also spot those children just by standing in the doorway of the classroom. Scan the room, and note children whose heads are like revolving fans. Gather the disengaged readers, let them know what you noticed, and tell them to double-check whether they can read their texts smoothly enough that they understand the content.

Reading specialist and author Richard Allington writes, "An astonishingly simple strategy that needs to be added to every classroom is the three-finger rule. Just tell kids to read the first page or two of a book (depending on the number of words on a page) and to hold up a finger for every word they cannot read. If they reach the point that

---

MID-WORKSHOP TEACHING   **After Generating Expectations, Readers Think, "Did the text unfold as expected?"**

"Readers, I need your attention for a minute. Will you recall what you expected the parts of your book would be before you started reading today?"

I gave the kids a minute to recall this. "Here is my question: were you right? Or was the text different from what you expected? Talk with your partner about whether you felt the book did—or did not—meet your expectations for it." I allowed for a minute or two of conversation before adding the teaching point.

"I'm asking you this because researchers constantly revise their ideas about the nonfiction in their hands. Researchers may come to the text expecting one thing, but then they read on and revise their thinking. Nonfiction readers constantly anticipate what a chunk of text will say, then read, check, and if necessary, revise their own thinking."

---

they are holding three fingers up, the book is probably too hard" (*What Really Matters for Struggling Readers: Designing Research-Based Programs*, 2012, 79).

You may ask whether it is reasonable for students to read nonfiction as well as fiction with 96% accuracy: How can they tackle informational books if they need to know most every vocabulary word before they are even given access to that book? This is a reasonable question. There are a fair number of experts on this topic who concur that you can almost take out the domain-specific words (the vocabulary words that the text aims to teach, for example: barometric, meteorologist, and anemometer in a text about weather), and then check that the kids are reading the rest of the text with 96% accuracy. The key thing is that readers need to have a strong enough grasp of the context that they can piece together what the text is saying enough to develop an approximate understanding of those challenging new vocabulary words.

Teach readers other ways to monitor for sense.

In addition to using the "Monitoring for Sense" section of the Informational Reading Learning Progression, you can teach kids other ways to think metacognitively, that is, to think about their own thinking as they read. In Richard Allington's book, *What Really Matters in Response to Intervention*, he lists a number of strategies to use when a book stops making sense. This list includes briefly slowing down reading, briefly pausing to think, whisper reading, rereading, skipping words, and sounding out words. You'll identify several of these strategies in Session 4, but some of your readers may benefit from them today as well.

Keeping Focused to Keep Reading Volume High

Introduce research on reading volume. Coach readers to reflect on their volume of reading and be sure they are holding texts that are good fits.

"Readers, before we end today's workshop, I want to tell you one more thing that reading researchers have found. They have a rule of thumb that says kids can read something like three-fourths of a page a minute. That means in forty minutes of actual reading time (not counting time for talking and writing about reading) kids should be reading about thirty pages. Right now, will you look at your reading log to see if you read something like thirty pages in your forty minutes of reading?" I gave students a minute to do this, and then asked, "What did you find?"

Readers called out, "I read *half* that!" and "I wasn't even close."

I nodded. "That is something else that researchers have found—when kids read nonfiction, reading often slows to a crawl. But that is not okay. You may not read three-fourths of a page a minute, but you certainly can read half a page a minute . . . and that means you are going to have to push yourself to increase your speed and your focus. But if that alone won't work, chances are really good that you are reading a book that is not the right fit for you. You need to be able to read it smoothly, rolling right along, not doing a stop-and-go thing. So please, before you leave class today, make sure you are reading a nonfiction book you can read easily."

REFLECTING ON YOUR NONFICTION READING LIFE

Readers, tonight continue digging into nonfiction texts. Find and read them *everywhere* you can! Read the sports page. Read the video manual. Read the back of the Lucky Charms cereal box.

As you do that nonfiction reading tonight, notice how you are doing it. Think about what is working for you. What isn't working for you? How can the work you do in school make a difference in your reading life outside school?

As you do that reading, here is an important challenge. After you have read, create two ways to represent your reading work in your reader's notebook. First, make a page that will divide the notebook between the fiction and nonfiction portions. Use this divider to represent your nonfiction reading life. Decide whether you will use it to show the places you read, the kinds of nonfiction you read, the topics you like best, the strategies you use when you are reading nonfiction, or anything else that matters about you and nonfiction reading. You can use pictures, words, boxes and bullets, diagrams, maps—whatever you want.

After you have made the divider page, would you also write about your nonfiction reading, making the first entry in this portion of your reader's notebook? Record insights you have about yourself as a nonfiction reader, and resolutions, too. Come to school prepared to share these and talk about them.

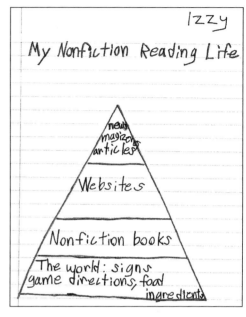

FIG. 2–1 Izzy creates a diagram of her nonfiction reading life.

◆ A DAY FOR ASSESSMENT ◆

Dear Teachers,

We hope that today for you'll return your students' performance assessments, which presumably you'll have scored yourself, to them. Today you can recruit your students to look with great earnestness at their work, considering why it received certain scores and noting ways in which it can be improved, both on the spot and across the unit.

If you haven't had time to score, we urge you to adapt our scoring recommendations so that you coach kids to score in partnerships. The most important thing is for kids to get their work back and to think about their work using the learning progressions, beginning now, at the start of the unit.

Too often, children come to you believing their abilities as readers are fixed and beyond their control. "I'm a bad reader," a child will say. "I can get the words, but I can't get those questions." Through this assessment, you help challenge the notion that success in reading is hardwired into a child's DNA. Your goal will be to rally kids to take their own learning in hand, and to have the courage to say, "I'm the kind of person who wants honest feedback so I can learn, learn, learn." You will make it crystal clear to kids that when they apply strategies, work hard, revise their first understandings, and get help, their reading will get dramatically better, right before their eyes.

In our Online Resources, we detail how this day might go. You'll need to make decisions with your colleagues, and we encourage you to draw on your students' experiences working with rubrics and learning progressions in Unit 1 as you plan. Let us share two pieces of advice. Don't postpone today—it is a big deal that kids get feedback and access to the rubrics and learning progressions now. Even if you do not feel ready: go forward. Their work with these tools, early in the unit, will shape their focus and energy moving forward. Secondly, don't let today swamp your schedule and drag on. Confine the important work into one period, and then return to the unit.

—Lucy, Emily, and Mike

Text Structures Help Accentuate What Matters

THINK ABOUT A TIME when you were reading a somewhat impenetrable book for a course you were taking. Do you remember that sinking feeling as more and more new information came your way and you realized you could never grasp it all? Think how frequently kids will experience that feeling—after all, they know less about the world and therefore more of what they read will be new for them. How easy it must be for youngsters to want to call "Uncle" when reading nonfiction.

And for good reason. When kids read narratives in the first unit of study, they only had to pay attention to more or less one essential macro-structure: a character has wants and desires, a problem, and a resolution! While narratives exhibit one macro-structure, informational texts exhibit several, often within the same text.

This session aims to give students strategies for holding onto the important information and concepts from nonfiction texts. You'll remind them again that it is important to preview a text prior to reading it, gleaning the major parts of the text and generating expectations for how those parts will go. This time, however, you'll suggest that oftentimes the text cues readers into anticipating that it will be structured in one of several common ways. When readers recognize the way a text is structured, that knowledge can help them know what is apt to be important in it.

In this minilesson, you use a video segment to teach kids that noticing cues about a text's structure can help a reader structure his or her way of learning from it. The particular videotape that you show students is structured in a problem-and-solution fashion. A reader could, on the other hand, see this structure differently—perhaps as main idea and supports—and that structure, too, could help a reader to cull out the most important things.

IN THIS SESSION, you'll teach students that nonfiction readers sometimes notice the structures in a text they are reading and use those structures to help them determine the information that is most important.

GETTING READY

✔ Cue the video clip "Phoenix Zoo: The Phoenix Zoo Saves the Arabian Oryx" from YouTube. A link to this video is provided on the online resources. If you are unable to access the video, you could substitute an excerpt from a high-interest text with a clear text structure, or you could choose to share the transcript from the video with students by projecting it and reading it dramatically (see Teaching and Active Engagement).

✔ Ask students to bring their reading notebooks and a pen to the meeting area (see Connection, Teaching, and Active Engagement).

✔ Prepare to display the chart "Common Nonfiction Text Structures," as well as individual copies of the chart for students (see Teaching, Active Engagement, and Link).

✔ Prepare to read aloud a section from *Everything Weather* that uses transition words to show text structure. We have chosen the passage "Droughts" from the "Dangerous Weather" section on page 23 of *Everything Weather* (see Teaching and Active Engagement).

✔ Prepare to display "To Read Nonfiction Well . . ," (see Link).

✔ Leave Post-it notes on tables for students to mark up their texts (see Link).

✔ Prepare to display "To Teach Well . . ." chart from Grade 3, Unit 2 *Reading to Learn* (see Share).

✔ Prepare to distribute "Researchers Take Notes that Follow the Structure of Their Texts" anchor chart from Grade 3, Unit 4 *Research Clubs* (see Homework).

Text Structures Help Accentuate What Matters

problem – solution
Compare – contrast
Cause – effect
Chronological

CONNECTION

Give students an opportunity to share with others the work they did the previous night, using the divider page in their reader's notebook to represent themselves as nonfiction readers.

"Readers, I've been hearing about the crazy, grand divider pages you made to launch the nonfiction portion of your reading notebooks and to represent yourself as a nonfiction reader. Will you show your partner what you made, read excerpts from what you wrote, and see what you can learn about each other as nonfiction readers by doing that? Turn and talk."

"I asked you to do this work last night, to get your notebooks ready for nonfiction reading. It was great to listen in just now, to hear the excitement and enthusiasm you all have for this new chapter in your fourth-grade reading lives.

"For the last few days I have asked you *not to write while you read*, to instead just take in the text. Today, though, we are turning a corner with our nonfiction reading, and your reader's notebooks will now play a bigger part. Starting today you'll be using your notebooks to take notes as you read. But it's important to think about *how* you will take these notes, and how you will determine what the most important information in the text is, what is worthy of being noted. In some cases, the text itself can actually clue you in to this."

❖ **Name the teaching point.**

"Today I want to teach you that once readers move beyond previewing expository texts to actually reading them, they often notice the way the text is organized. Expository texts have a few common structures: problem/solution, compare and contrast, cause and effect, and chronological."

TEACHING AND ACTIVE ENGAGEMENT

Play a brief video, asking students to take notes about the most important information.

"Readers, I want to show you how it can help you determine what is most important in a text if you recognize the way the text is structured. If you don't know the structure of a text, if you can't tell how it is organized, you often feel as if

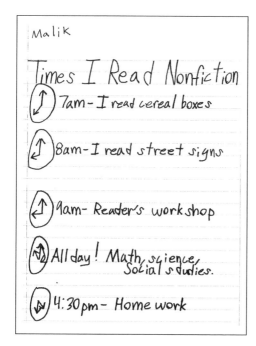

FIG. 3–1   Malik shares his homework, "Times When I Read Nonfiction."

every bit of information is equally important. When you know the structure, though, it is almost as if you are given a way to highlight some parts of the text and to skim past other parts.

"Instead of reading a text together, let's watch a video. This is a news clip; it's sort of like a newspaper article. Your aim, while you watch this video, will be the aim that most nonfiction readers have. You want to learn about this topic, you want to hold onto the most important information. As you watch it, record what you think is the most important information in the piece. Use a page in the nonfiction section of your reading notebook. You ready? It will go quickly, so pay attention!"

I played the video, about a goat-like animal called the oryx, and how the Phoenix Zoo intervened to save it from extinction. As we watched the video, I knew many students would be simply recording facts about the Arabian oryx in a list-like fashion. But I hoped that part way through this, they'd note a text structure undergirding the video.

Invite readers to share their notes with their partners.

I played the full video (only a little more than a minute long), and asked students to read each other their notes. Most of them, predictably, had not noticed that twenty seconds into the video, the news reporter says that the animals nearly went extinct from overhunting and habitat loss, and that the Phoenix Zoo took nine of the oryx to save them. These statements could have clued the students in to the structure of the text, that there was a problem, and that the Phoenix Zoo was providing a solution to that problem. If students had noticed that structure, they may have altered the way they took notes and listened.

Quickly remind students of typical nonfiction text structures. Play the video again, this time asking students to consider text structure while taking notes.

"Before we listen another time, I want to point out that you might say this text is organized in a boxes-and-bullets way—all about the oryx, with main ideas and supports. But it may be more complex than that. I'd like you to dig deeper and ask yourself, 'How are the boxes and bullets organized? How do they go together?' It helps to keep in mind some common text structures that nonfiction takes, and some words that may clue you in." I pointed to a chart listing some options:

Common Nonfiction Text Structures

Structure	Transition words
• Chronological	• first, then, next, after that, finally, before, after
• Problem/solution	• a problem is, a solution is, if . . . then . . . , so that
• Cause and effect	• because, since, reasons, then, therefore, so, in order
• Compare/contrast	• different, same, alike, similar, although, but, yet, or

It is important that you realize that this session teaches students one way to cull the main ideas and supporting points from a text. This is just one way, not the only way. In some instances, determining the structure of a text helps, but in others it is simpler to read a text and to ask oneself, "What were the main things the author wants me to take away?" The important thing is that readers have strategies to determine importance while reading.

You will notice that in this minilesson, we are saving the meat of the teaching for after students have attempted the work. This may seem somewhat odd at first—why not teach students about the specific structures before they are asked to do the work? Wouldn't knowing the text structures make their note-taking easier? Of course it would. But we think the contrast between frantic note-taking without any structure in mind and ease of organized note-taking with a guiding text structure in place will help drive our teaching point home.

We want to emphasize that watching this video and doing this work is important. The Teachers College Reading and Writing Project staff developers had a real aha when we watched this and saw the way an awareness of text structure allowed the main idea to click into place for us. If it is some trouble showing a video to your kids, consider doing it anyhow.

"This time, expect to hear a clue early on that the piece is organized in one of these ways, and then try to take notes that are organized in a way that matches the way the text is organized. The video goes quickly—you know that—so open to a fresh page in the nonfiction section of your notebook. You ready?"

I played the video again, and this time, right after the newscaster said that the animals were nearly extinct and the zoo took them in to save them, I said, "Bingo!" I paused the video and then replayed just that part and paused it again.

I turned my attention to the class. "So what are you thinking? How is this text organized? I paused right here for a reason. The reporter just said something very important." I reinterated the reporter's statements. "Does this help you figure out how this nonfiction piece is organized? What structure it is? Are there specific words that can clue you in? Turn and talk."

Students burst into conversation. "Use the chart for help," I voiced over. After a minute I reconvened the class.

"Readers, most of you are suggesting that this text is organized into a problem/solution structure. I heard you say this is the problem: the Arabian oryx was nearly extinct. And this is the solution: the Phoenix Zoo created a habitat for them. Some of you even said the problem is a number of animals on the planet are going extinct and the solution is that zoos are working to preserve endangered species. Make sure your notes reflect this structure—and get ready to watch the rest of the video." I resumed the video clip while students took notes.

Debrief in ways that make the work transferable to another text. Support that transfer by reading aloud from the model text and asking students to listen for clues to the text structure.

"The important thing is that when you are watching—or reading—an expository text, and you know how it is organized, that structure helps you know what is most important. Let's try this work again in our read-aloud, *Everything Weather*. I am going to reread the passage 'Droughts,' and when you think you might have a clue as to how this section is organized and how your notes might go, give me a thumbs up." I read in a way that emphasized transition words:

Droughts

Droughts are serious weather events. Droughts occur when an area does not get enough seasonal rainfall or snowmelt. **As a result**, *the area's water supplies shrink. Droughts* **can affect** *large geographic areas and have serious long-term* **effects** *on the land.*

I eyed the class and said, "Any guesses yet? Turn and talk, how do you think this section is structured?" I let partners talk for a moment or two, and then I called the class back.

"I hear many of you saying that this section seems to be talking about the causes of droughts and the effects of droughts. Chloe noticed the words 'effects' and 'affect,' and she thought those sounded like they fit with cause and effect. And Jasmine saw 'as a result'—she said that wasn't on our chart but that it sounded like something was happening because of something else, a cause.

If you can display this on the document camera, that will support students' work.

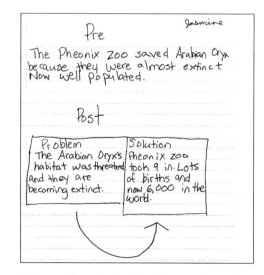

FIG. 3–2 Jasmine's notes after watching the video twice

"Now that we know the kind of mind work (and note-taking) this section is asking us to do, we're probably going to be reading to learn more about how droughts happen and what happens after they occur. I am going to reread this paragraph and then read on. As I do, please take notes to show what you're learning, in a way that reflects the text structure of the section."

Droughts

Droughts are serious weather events. Droughts occur when an area does not get enough seasonal rainfall or snowmelt. As a result, the area's water supplies shrink. Droughts can affect large geographic areas and have serious long-term effects on the land. Droughts can dry up creeks, rivers, and lakes; kill trees; and ruin crops, gardens and lawns. Drought conditions also make wildfires more likely when lightning strikes the dry ground.

"Okay, friends. Take a moment to show each other your notes and to talk: what are the causes and effects of droughts?" The room was electric with the buzz of talk.

LINK

Send readers off with a charge to think about how nonfiction texts are structured, and also with a charge to self-assign their own goals for the workshop.

"Readers, we have been accumulating strategies to add to our nonfiction reading toolkit, strategies that you can use for the rest of your life." I drew kids' attention to our anchor chart and revealed a new section to reflect the day's teaching point.

ANCHOR CHART

To Read Nonfiction Well . . .

- Make a connection to your text
- Preview the whole text and predict how it might go
  - Use prior knowledge of the topic
  - Scan the text features
- **Figure out the text's structure and use it to determine importance:**
  - **Problem/solution**
  - **Compare/contrast**
  - **Cause/effect**
  - **Chronological**

You may notice that we have for the first time in this unit advised students to take notes on what they are reading. We still do not want students to read with pen in hand, stopping to record each and every fact. Instead we will encourage them to read large portions of texts before pausing to note-take. Too often, the rush to record notes leads students to inch their way through expository texts, stopping constantly to jot facts. Transferring all the information from the source to the students' page is not an advisable form of note-taking, and students need to learn to digest larger chunks of nonfiction texts in one go.

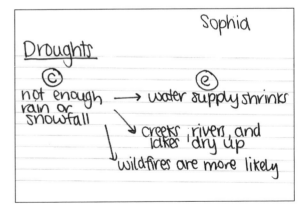

FIG. 3–3 Sophia's notes reflecting the cause-and-effect structure

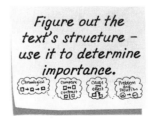

"Today, I'm going to ask you to read your nonfiction differently. I've left some Post-it notes on your tables. Before you read, look over the text you'll be reading and flag the ends of chunks of the text. You'll be marking places where you'll pause to recall what you just read.

"Then as you read, try to discern how the text is structured. I'm also giving each of you a smaller copy of the 'Common Nonfiction Text Structures' chart that can clue you in to one text structure or another—keep it near you as you read and tape it into your notebook.

"As you read, use that text structure to help you learn from the text, to help you take mental notes. Don't take actual notes until you reach the flag you've put at the end of a chunk of text. At that point, take abbreviated quick notes that mirror the structure of the text you are reading.

"If you are starting a new text, continue to read those that are easy for you. Tomorrow our workshop will turn a corner and we'll be thinking about how to do all this work when texts are getting harder, and I'll be asking you to bring one challenge text to do that, so keep an eye out for it. For today, stay with texts that are easy for you to read.

"You have *lots* to do today! Off you go."

Rally the Class to Do the New Work You've Launched

TODAY YOU RAMPED UP EXPECTATIONS for your readers, so you'll want to start the workshop by scooting about the room, making sure that readers are previewing their texts and using the Post-its you've given them to mark the ends of chunks of text. To help you with this, be sure to carry with you the "Main Idea(s) and Supporting Details/Summary" section of the Informational Reading Learning Progression. When you have a chance, help readers to begin thinking about the text structures they detect. Then you'll want to be sure that students are not inching through the texts with pen in hand, recording each passing factoid, but that they are instead reading large chunks of text, pausing only at the ends of a chunk to jot what they have learned. At that point, ideally they will be taking notes that mirror the text structure of the text. If they are not, take the opportunity to remind them of the importance of this, linking their independent work to the work of the minilesson.

There will be lots of new challenges once students begin to take notes. First and most importantly, they've been asked to take notes that reflect the text structures embedded in what they read. Those structures won't always be readily discernible (and sometimes, the texts won't be well structured!). Sometimes the text will have a structure that spans the entire text; other times, the structures will start and stop, and not necessarily at the intervals students have chosen to chunk. You won't necessarily be able to figure out how a text is structured as you move quickly among the kids, so you may not be able to give feedback on this.

As you do this, it is important to note that students don't need to be highly proficient at reading with an awareness of text structure. It is fine if they attempt to do this and the structures that they see in any one particular text aren't the same as what you see. The goal is not to be precisely accurate. Instead, the goal is to help students take in larger chunks of nonfiction text, to see how parts of the text relate to each other, and to note big ideas and organizational structures instead of fixating on teeny tiny facts. It is more important that students feel successful at doing this than you fretting too much over whether the structure they suggest is exactly correct.

(continues)

MID-WORKSHOP TEACHING   Readers Read in Ways that Prepare Them to Teach Others

"Readers, can I stop you?" I said, and waited for their attention. "When you read nonfiction, it is like you are taking a course on a topic—and one really great thing about taking a course is that you can then turn around and teach someone else what you've learned.

"Later today, I'm going to set a few of you up to teach seminars to each other on the topic you are reading about. Here's the thing: to teach someone a course on what you've read, you need to remember what you learned last year about writing informational texts. Remember how important it was for the nonfiction books you wrote to have some sort of logical order—if you were writing about what dogs eat, the book might have been organized around breakfast, lunch, and dinner, or around wet food, dry food, table scraps, but it couldn't just bounce around. The course you teach others about your topic also has to have a structure, a larger design to it. You can't just jump around and teach random facts.

"So right now, will you look over the notes you have taken so far today, and the text you have read, and make sure you are on track to be able to teach someone else about this topic? Work alone to be sure you have notes that have chunks to them, parts to them, and make sure those parts capture some big subtopics (like dog's breakfast) or big ideas.

I let children work for a bit, and at one point voiced over to say, "Remember that the books you are reading have structures to them, and you can borrow those structures. So as you read, think about what kind of organization that author has used (and I tapped the chart listing the options) and then use that text structure to help you take notes from the reading.

"Back to your reading—and your lesson planning!"

Lead a small group to support discerning the help with main idea and organizational structures.

You may find you have a small group of readers who need lots of help moving from collecting factoids to recognizing main ideas. Some kids may need more help especially reading for the main ideas their text conveys. These readers may be more apt to collect specifics than to add those up to form bigger ideas about the author's points. Today, you'll likely want to convene a small group of these readers. Ask them to start their books, thinking, "What's this mainly about?" and "What is the author's main point?" Their answer is likely to be broad. "This is about Mt. Everest." Ask them to keep reading, asking, "Specifically, what is it about?" Expect that they'll focus their answer as they read on. Then teach them that at the end of one paragraph and the start of another, it helps to ask, "Is this more information about the same main idea, or is this something new?"

You could also show them that they can use the specific bits of information they collect to come up with a main idea. For instance, if a reader is reading about giraffes and notices they have *weird, long lips, big eyes that pop out of their heads, long necks,* and *tail hairs that twitch,* you might channel that reader to ask, "What facts go together? How do they go together?" This kind of work will generally lead a reader to find the main idea.

Another day, with this same group, you might coach them to use their "Common Nonfiction Text Structures" chart as they are reading, encouraging them to preview the upcoming text at key intervals, and to pay attention to transition words to figure out the structure of that upcoming text.

When students work on previewing, coach them by saying, "Let your eyes sweep across the lines of the text, and when you come to a transition word, such as *because, but, if,* or *so,* it should be like a radar wave going 'Bing!' when it detects a signal. Your brain goes 'Bing! Ahah! This might be something important.' After you detect a transition word, ask yourself, 'Does this tell me anything about the text's structure? If so, what?'"

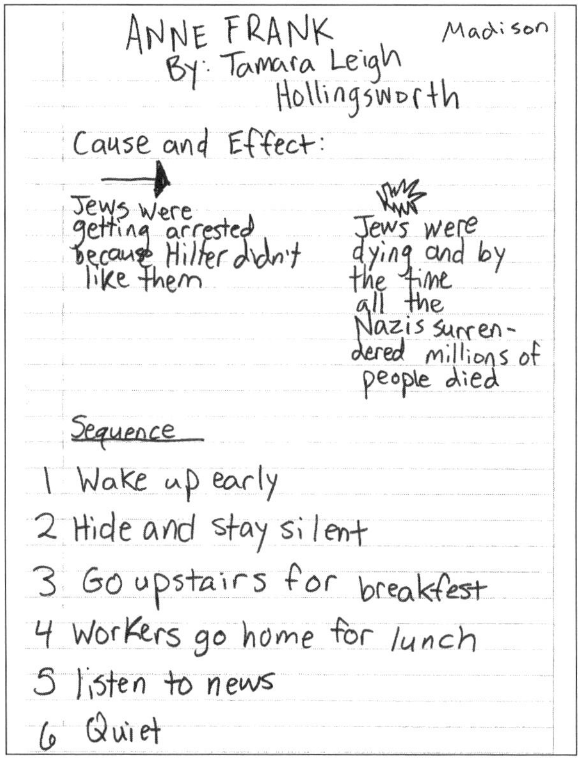

FIG. 3–4 Madison's note-taking of cause-and-effect and sequence structures

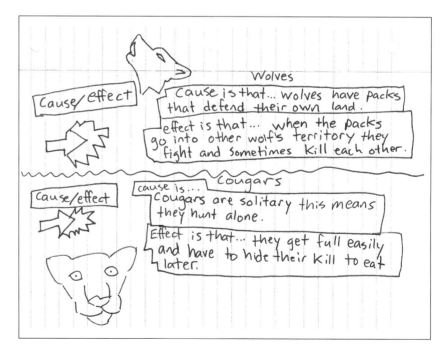

FIG. 3–5 Anthony's note-taking of a cause-and-effect structure

Teaching Others and Teaching Well

Remind students of what they learned in third grade about teaching others, and give them a minute to finalize their teaching plans.

I hung a chart I borrowed from the third-grade classrooms. "Take a minute to look over this chart about teaching others—you'll probably remember it from third grade."

"With this chart in mind, take a moment right now to make sure you are ready to teach others about your topic. You will want to review your notes, and you may also want to mark parts of your text that you'll show to your students, or that you'll read aloud."

Channel students into foursomes and set them up so that one member of the foursome teaches, while the others listen carefully to learn.

"Partners, right now team up with another partnership and decide who will begin teaching first. Those of you who are listening, it is really important that you listen in ways where you are trying to learn about the other person's topic. Try to make sense of what the 'teacher' is saying and when things are confusing to you, let your teacher know."

As students worked, I coached the listeners to listen with intensity, to show their interest by pulling in close, watching the "teacher," and showing a high level of engagement. Most groups got through two students before I stopped them.

Ask readers to prepare for tomorrow's workshop by selecting a challenging text that they want to work on reading over upcoming days.

"Readers, until now, I've asked you to read books that are on the easy side for you. You should take your baggie home with you tonight and continue reading these books. Tomorrow, we're going to start a stretch of days working on slightly harder texts. Before tomorrow's workshop, will you choose a harder text that you can read with some work? Make it a challenge text."

To teach well . . .

- Know the main ideas and supporting details
- Use an explaining voice
- Use gestures
- Use a teaching finger to point out charts, illustrations, and diagrams to help explain

NOTE-TAKING WITH STRUCTURE IN MIND

Readers, I asked you to take your nonfiction reading baggie home with you tonight so that you could continue to practice the work we did today. I've also sent you home with a chart that you might recognize from third grade. I gave you this chart to remind you of ways you might take quick, brief notes as you come to the end of a chunk of text. While you are reading, think about the text's structure and ask yourself, "How can I organize my notes to mirror the text's structure?"

Perhaps you'll be reading about an environmental disaster and what conservationists are doing to solve the problem. You could, for example, make a T-chart labeling one side "problem" and another "solution." Or you could jot a list of problems and draw arrows pointing toward possible solutions. I bet I'll see a lot of other formats for quick notes. You might jot boxes and bullets, sketches, T-charts, timelines, or Venn diagrams. You might even invent a creative new way to take notes.

Remember this: be sure your notes somehow match the structure of what you are learning, so they aren't just one long list of facts. Let the text's structure guide you. If you need a reminder of some possible text structures, glance at the "Common Nonfiction Text Structures" chart that you have taped into your notebook. You'll remember most of this chart from third grade.

Also, for the last few days the focus of your nonfiction reading has been on books that are easy reads for you. Starting tomorrow, we are going to tackle more challenging texts. Tonight, don't forget to look through the assortment of texts in your baggie and select one that you think will push you, will be a challenge for you. You will need to bring that to tomorrow's minilesson.

ANCHOR CHART

Researchers Take Notes that Follow the Structure of Their Texts

BOXES AND BULLETS

Main Idea or Subtopic

- Supporting detail
- Supporting detail
- Add more bullet points if your text includes them

SEQUENTIAL

Main Idea or Subtopic
1. First thing that happens
2. Second thing that happens
3. Add more steps if your text includes them

COMPARE AND CONTRAST

Similarities between two things
- First similarity
- Second similarity
- Add more similarities if your text includes them

Differences between two things
- First difference
- Second difference
- Add more differences if your text includes them

CAUSE AND EFFECT

An action that happens first; the reason something else happens	→	What happens as a result; the consequence of the first action

Detail about the action; add more details if your text includes them

One result of the action; add more results of the action if your text includes them

PROBLEM AND SOLUTION

A problem	→	A solution to the problem

- Detail about the problem
- Detail about the problem
- Add more details if your text includes them

- Detail about the solution
- Detail about the solution
- Add more details if your text includes them

Session 4

Embracing the Challenge of Nonfiction Reading

PRIOR TO THIS SESSION, you encouraged students to tackle easy nonfiction texts. Now you ask students to select texts that are a notch more challenging, and you begin a sequence of sessions aimed to help them tackle these texts of increasing complexity. This will become a minor theme of this unit, and the major focus of the first nonfiction unit next year. Your goal is to help students name the challenges these texts can pose in ways that help galvanize them to meet those challenges. Your hope is that this session allows them to feel empowered and strategic rather than overwhelmed.

To prepare for this work, we recommend you look over a collection of nonfiction texts that represent the increasing complexity of texts your students will read. As you read over these texts, notice the increasing challenges they pose because a major goal of your teaching is to help students become prepared to handle these texts. One thing you will find is that while easier expository texts are organized by subtopics that are clearly flagged with headings, or with white spaces that function as headings, more complex expository texts may switch from one main point to another without subheadings that signify the change. In more complex texts, the structural underpinnings of the text are often obscured by the sheer volume of information—and some of that information may not be relevant to the main point of the text.

The vocabulary demands on readers also increase as texts become more complex. The easier books include definitions for key terms, either as a synonym right beside the word or in a nearby glossary. More challenging books don't always include a synonym, but if you read right around the difficult word, you can usually glean what it means. And as books become harder still, you are expected to grasp the meaning of an entire page and use that meaning to speculate what the unfamiliar word might mean.

Then, too, as readers progress toward increasingly difficult texts, those texts can be challenging because they contain such a density of information. Sometimes the specific facts—the statistics, the dates, the names—are meant to be illustrative of bigger principles that may never even be explicitly stated. In those instances, readers are expected to

IN THIS SESSION, you'll teach students that although there are a variety of ways that nonfiction texts can pose challenges, when readers are aware of those ways they can get themselves ready to tackle the hard parts.

GETTING READY

✔ Ask students to bring the challenging texts they selected for last night's homework assignment to the minilesson.

✔ Keep chart paper and a marker at hand (see Teaching and Active Engagement, and Mid-Workshop Teaching).

✔ Provide small groups of students with short chunks of a deliberately challenging nonfiction text. Students will use these texts to discern some of the common challenges of complex nonfiction texts. Here we recommend using chunks of "A Sport," Lexile 1140L. This text can also be found in the online resources. (see Teaching and Active Engagement).

✔ Prepare to hand out white boards and dry erase markers (see Teaching and Active Engagement).

✔ Prepare to display "Common Nonfiction Text Structures" chart (see Conferring and Small-Group Work).

✔ Prepare to display "To Read Nonfiction Well . . ." anchor chart (see Share).

✔ Prepare a chart with the title "What to Do if My Book Stops Making Sense" (see Mid-Workshop Teaching).

compose bigger ideas from the wealth of factual detail, leaving most of the specific facts behind and holding onto the bigger ideas and insights.

"Your goal is to help students name the challenges these texts can pose in ways that help galvanize them to meet those challenges."

Students should come to the session today with a challenging text, which they selected for homework last night. If you have some students who are reading below benchmark and you feel that reading these challenge texts in sync with one another and with a text introduction would be beneficial, you may decide to begin your conferring today by gathering these students into a guided reading group. This added scaffold will set them up for success in implementing the work of the minilesson.

Embracing the Challenge of Nonfiction Reading

CONNECTION

Tell readers that in many endeavors, there are signals that note when things become more challenging. Point out that sometimes nonfiction books are deceptive, looking easier than they are.

"Readers, in many fields, there are ways to signal 'rough seas ahead.' At the beach, they hang up special flags to say, 'Storm approaching' or 'High winds expected.' On ski mountains, there are signs at the top of any trail saying green circle—easy terrain—or double black diamond—take your life in your hands.

"Sometimes I wish that nonfiction texts had their own versions of those flags, those signs. I'm sure many of you have had that experience of seeing a cute photo on the cover of a nonfiction book, and even seeing a large font in the book, then you start reading and you are completely surprised by the text. It's tough going!"

One of the reasons nonfiction texts are so challenging for kids is that often the books are disguised as being easier than they are. So when you ask, "Have you ever had the experience of seeing a nonfiction text that is packaged as an easy text and is, in fact, extremely difficult?" the truth is that you already know for certain that kids have encountered that. It is rampant, everywhere.

Connect this to the work students will do with their challenge texts.

"I know that last night you all chose challenge texts to spend some time tackling today. I'm hoping they are not only challenging, but that they are also super interesting to you, because you are going to have to want to read them. Right now, tell your partner some of the connections you think you'll bring to your book—and show your partner your book." I gave the students just a minute to talk before I reconvened the group.

"So today we are going to turn a corner in our nonfiction reading when we tackle these more complex texts. Even though there are a bunch of ways that nonfiction texts can be hard, when readers are aware of those ways, they can get themselves ready to tackle the hard parts.

"And today, instead of me teaching you what exactly it is that makes certain nonfiction texts hard, I thought we could figure it out together, by examining some more challenging nonfiction texts, and investigating what makes them so challenging."

❖ Name the teaching point.

"Today I want to teach you that there are a bunch of ways that nonfiction texts can be hard, and when you know some of these ways, you can get yourself ready to tackle the hard parts."

TEACHING AND ACTIVE ENGAGEMENT

Recruit kids to join in a study of what makes nonfiction texts challenging. Distribute passages that illustrate common challenges and rally small groups to analyze for sources of difficulty.

"Readers, we're going to do this work together today, but I started a little bit on my own last night. My thought is that in today's minilesson, instead of me telling you the things that make texts hard, you and I can do a bit of an investigation, and see if we can list some of the challenges that occur often in nonfiction texts. Last night, I went to my bookshelf and pulled out a few nonfiction texts, and tested them on myself. I looked mostly for texts that were really hard to read, hard to follow. It didn't take me long before I had a little stack of 'Hard to Read Nonfiction Texts.' Are you willing to join me in asking, 'What makes these hard?'" Students nodded their heads and I heard a few murmurs of "Yeah!" and "Of course!"

"I've taken snippets of a text for us to work with today. I'm going to ask you to work with your partner and another nearby partnership. I'll give each group a text excerpt as well as a white board and marker for you to jot your observations about what it is that makes the text excerpt you are working with so hard."

I quickly clustered the students into foursomes, and distributed a different section of the text and a white board to each group. I circulated as readers worked, culling some of what I heard to record on a shared chart.

I knelt down next to a group reading the section titled "Why Swim." They had circled all the statistics embedded in their passage and were staring silently at the excerpt. "So, what makes this nonfiction text hard?"

Why Swim

According to the Centers for Disease Control and Prevention, in the United States in 2009, 36% of children ages 7–17, and 15% of adults swam at least six times per year. In addition, swimming is considered the fourth most popular form of recreation in the United States. One hour of swimming can burn off up to 650 calories, more than you would burn off through other kinds of exercise, such as walking or biking. The US Census Bureau states that swimming is one of the most popular activities among children and teens (ages 7–17). But an estimated 65 million people in the United States still do not know how to swim.

"It's filled with numbers," Leah said. "Every sentence has numbers. Even that second sentence that didn't look like it has a number had 'fourth' in it."

I pushed a bit, challenging her suggestion. "So what? You guys are pros with numbers. I see you in math. Numbers don't scare you."

"We're not scared of them," Rafael laughed, "but they seem distracting. There were so many of them, that we couldn't figure out what we were supposed to learn about swimming."

We suggest that the texts you distribute are brief and are exaggerated examples of common challenges your students face in complex nonfiction texts. There are more texts available in the digital resources. We suggest the article "A Sport," which is challenging on many levels. We have taken this text and divided it into chunks for various groups to work with. Each section of text provides its own challenge, is brief, and highlights a common way that the nonfiction texts your students read are apt to be challenging.

"Think about how that could be true for nonfiction texts in general. What are you noticing here that makes challenging nonfiction hard?" I left them to jot, while I moved on to coach a new group.

Gather ideas from students about what makes complex nonfiction hard. Add students' contributions to chart.

After a few minutes of enthusiastic conversation, I drew the class back together. "What were you noticing with your texts? When it comes to nonfiction texts that are hard to read and hard to follow, what is it that makes them so hard?"

Leo started us off. "My group had the section with the heading 'Reasons Why,' which ended up being sort of weird. We thought it was gonna tell us reasons why people swim, you know, like for exercise, or to compete, or because it's part of their job. But instead the article was all about the different kinds of swim strokes. So after we read it we thought 'Reasons Why' maybe means why you would use all the different strokes."

There are many different kinds of swimming strokes. Some of the most common strokes are the front crawl, back crawl, butterfly, breaststroke, and the side stroke. Some of these strokes require a flutter kick—that is, short back and forth kicks with feet and toes outstretched. Other strokes—like the sidestroke, butterfly, and breaststroke—involve more specific kicks. Some swim strokes are made for fast, short distance swims, others are designed for long distance swimming.

"Very interesting. Did any other groups find they had headings that were somewhat misleading, that led you to believe that the section would be about one topic or idea, but then ended up being about something totally different?" Several hands were raised throughout the meeting area.

"Let's get this down." I flipped to a sheet of fresh chart paper and quickly wrote the heading, "Tackle the Hard Parts of Nonfiction Reading" and recorded the first challenge.

Tackle the Hard Parts of Nonfiction Reading

First, notice . . .
- Misplaced, misleading, or poetic headings

Other texts posed other difficulties, and soon the class had compiled their observations into this list:

Tackle the Hard Parts of Nonfiction Reading

First, notice . . .
- Misplaced, misleading, or poetic headings
- **Fact overload**
- **Confusing beginnings that don't directly introduce the topic of the text**
- **Long detours with extra information that can pull you away from the main idea**

Tackle the Hard Parts of Nonfiction Reading...

First, notice:
- *Misleading headings*
- *Fact overload*
- *Confusing beginnings*
- *Long detours & extra information*
- *Graphs and diagrams*

Then, take action:
- *Read and reread*

- *Ask, "What is this part teaching?"*

- *Talk and write to understand*

It is not uncommon for someone other than the author to add headings into a text right before publication, and those headings may be misplaced, breaking the actual structure of the text, or may, as in this example, give readers a bum steer. Sometimes the challenge isn't misplaced or misleading headings, so much as artsy ones. The presence of misleading headings absolutely makes reading nonfiction texts more difficult.

Tackle the hard parts.

LINK

Send kids off to read, encouraging them to not shy away from the challenges that nonfiction offers, but to notice and embrace those challenges.

"Readers, someone once said 'Perseverance is the hard work you do after you get tired of the hard work you just did.' Sometimes nonfiction reading can feel like that. One thing that is true about challenge is that you can choose to avoid it, or you can choose to embrace it. The readers who build their nonfiction reading muscles are readers like you: readers who persevere and embrace the challenge of nonfiction reading. I'm hoping you'll embrace the challenges so you'll be able to learn a ton from them.

"Remember, the first step is to name the challenge. Then, you have to take action or do something about it."

"Today, while you are reading, be on the lookout for the challenges we've found, and others, too, so we can all help each other as we read."

Coach Predictable Challenges Students Might Face

TODAY as your students go off to tackle their slightly more difficult texts, you'll want to support them in this work. As always, a particularly helpful way to support them when the challenges are predictable is through small-group instruction. The "Monitoring for Sense" strand of the Informational Reading Learning Progression can assist you with teaching points for these small groups.

Readers might need to shift mental gears as structures change across a text.

Some texts switch structures across paragraphs and sections of a text. Teach readers to be flexible and alert to these changes. You might gather a small group of students and give them all the same text. Begin by pointing out what specifically you want them to notice. "Let's read this passage from *Hurricanes* by Seymour Simon. Let's read for transition words to figure out the text's structure. Then, we are going to need to be

ready to switch mental gears if we notice the structure changing. I'll read the text, and you should follow along in your copy." Read aloud, emphasizing the transition words as you go:

> All hurricanes form in the same way. They **begin** life in the warm, moist atmosphere over tropical rain waters. **First**, the atmosphere gathers heat energy through contact with ocean waters that are above 80 degrees Fahrenheit to a depth of about two hundred feet. **Next**, moisture evaporating from the warm waters enters the atmosphere and begins to power the infant hurricane.

Prompt the students to talk about the text structure, and to use transition words as their guide. "Hmm, . . . What kind of text structure is this paragraph? I see these

---

MID-WORKSHOP TEACHING   Monitoring for Sense

"Readers, can I have your eyes, please?" I waited as partners placed bookmarks, Post-its, or thumbs into the bindings of their books to mark their place. "I can see by the expressions on your faces that each of you is tackling your challenge books with grit and pluck, but I want to take a moment to harken back to one other thing you need to be doing. Do you remember learning, earlier this year, that readers absolutely *must* check that reading makes sense? When your book stops making sense, you can't just read on and on . . . Instead, you need to stop and think, 'Huh?' and then *do something*. Will you tell each other some of the things you do when meaning breaks down?"

The room erupted into talk, and I listened, jotting furiously. "Readers, let me share what you said." I read off a list I'd generated while they spoke, which I later made into a class chart:

What to Do If My Book Stops Making Sense

First, stop and think "Huh?"
Then do something about it!

- read forward with mind on fire
- reread a part of text
- whisper-read aloud until it makes sense
- slow down reading for a bit, then speed back up
- pick a new just-right book

"So get back to reading your challenge book. But as you read, remember that while you are tackling the hard parts, you'll also remember this all-important tip: monitor for meaning, and when it breaks down, *do something*."

---

transition words *begin*, *first*, and *next*. Hmm, . . . What do you think? Turn and talk." After just a minute call the group back together, pointing out the chronological structure of the text.

Common Nonfiction Text Structures

Structure	Transition words
Chronological	first, then, next, after that, finally, before, after
Problem/solution	a problem is, a solution is, if . . . then . . . , so that
Cause and effect	because, since, reasons, then, therefore, so, in order
Compare/contrast	different, same, alike, similar, although, but, yet, or

"Readers, you're right. It's pretty clear that this paragraph, is organized with a chronological structure. Seymour Simon's text is begging us to do the brainwork of timelining in our minds the steps for hurricanes to begin.

"Let's read on, continuing to be flexible readers. In this next paragraph could any other structures be at play here?" Keep the group together as students each turn to their own copy of the text and read.

> *The growing hurricane forms bands of clouds and winds near the ocean surface that spiral air inward. The air is heated by warm ocean water, creating strong winds and forcing them to rise higher. This increases the power of the hurricane and leads to stormy conditions over huge areas. Hurricanes can easily last more than a week and may strike Caribbean islands days before whirling north and west into the United States.*

After students finish reading, coach them to look at key transition words to think about if other text structures might be at play. "Okay, what do you think? What other text structures might be at play here? Take a look at the key transition words for help." Guide readers to notice not only words like *growing* and *before*, but also to notice words like *by*, *creating*, and *leads to*, which indicate cause and effect.

After you have guided readers to work with a shared text, push them to open their own challenge texts and try out this work with their independent reading.

Readers might need help understanding more complicated sentence structures.

You might gather another group of readers with their challenging nonfiction books and help them navigate the complex sentences in their books. You might begin by saying, "Earlier today, we looked at ways nonfiction texts are getting hard. Well, I want to let you know that in the challenge books you're reading now, not only can reading long passages be difficult, but also reading sentences can be tricky, too. We can even find challenging sentences in *Everything Weather*." You might open to page 7 and turn the book so that the text faces the kids. As you begin teaching, play it up, leaving exaggerated pauses between each sentence. "It used to be that books went like this. Sentence one: We rely on the sun, rain and wind to survive. Sentence two: Weather can turn bad. And sentence three: Weather can seriously mess up our lives. But now authors are smushing all that information together into one sentence. Look here. Kathy Furgang wrote, 'We rely on the sun, rain and wind to survive, but when weather turns bad, it can seriously mess up our lives.' That's a lot, huh?"

Name why this is important for readers to know. "Readers, what this means is this: as texts get harder, one single sentence can hold so much information. We have to think about what each part tells in order to understand the whole sentence. Will you help me do that with this sentence?" You might model for students how you work through the first two parts of the sentence, saying, "So the first part is naming all the kinds of weather that are important—sun, rain and wind, and that connects to the second part because those must be the kinds of weather that can turn bad. Sun can turn bad, and rain can turn bad, and wind can turn bad." You might ask students to try this with the third part of a sentence, considering what that part tells and how it fits with the rest of the sentence.

Then, channel students back into their own challenge books, coaching them to try this work. You might say, "Readers, will you give this a try in your book? Find a sentence like this, one that holds a ton of information. Once you find it, will you share it with a partner next to you? Name the different parts and tell what's in each part. Then, continue reading, looking out for these long sentences that contain a ton of information!"

The Challenge of Complex Nonfiction Is the Complexity

Channel readers to share the work they did today. Ask them to tell their partner what work they did to tackle their challenge book and what strategies they used most.

I gathered the class in the meeting area and called for their attention. "Readers, I am *most interested* in hearing how you grabbed your challenge book by the horns. What work did you do to tackle the tricky parts of the book? What strategies did you most use? Turn and share with your partner." I leaned in to listen to partnerships talk.

After a bit, I asked the class to listen as a few kids talked about the challenges they encountered and how they addressed them. Madison shared that she practiced reading forward and rereading hard parts. Leo noted that he used previewing a text to help him tackle the hard parts by asking, "What is this part going to teach me?" Alyssa explained that her book began with a long story about people bringing a chimpanzee baby into their house to live like another kid and so she thought the article was about baby chimps, but then it changed around and left the chimps behind totally and just talked about animal language and human language, too.

I asked if any of the others found texts that started in a way that was deceptive, and many agreed that yes, often times they had to read a lot of the text before they were sure of its main topic. And many did include long detours. "So all in all," I said, "it seems like one of the hard parts

ANCHOR CHART

To Read Nonfiction Well . . .

- Make a connection to your text
- Preview the whole text and predict how it might go
  - Use prior knowledge of the topic
  - Scan the text features
- Figure out the text's structure and use it to determine importance:
  - Problem/solution
  - Compare/contrast
  - Cause/effect
  - Chronological
- Tackle the hard parts of nonfiction reading:
  First, notice:
  - Misplaced, misleading, or poetic headings
  - Fact overload
  - Confusing beginnings that don't directly introduce the topic of the text
  - **Long detours with extra information that can pull you away from the main idea**
    Then take action:
    - **Read and reread**
    - **Ask, "What is this part teaching?"**

about reading more complex nonfiction is that it is just that—more complex. You almost need to be thinking in pencil, ready to erase your first decisions as you read on and the text changes." I added another bullet to our anchor chart, summarizing the work of the day.

"I'm hoping that naming these challenges will help you to at least see what is causing you trouble in the challenge book you are trying to read. One word of caution: your reading work will be slower as you work on your challenge text. You should probably spend just a portion of your reading time wrestling with it, and then shift to reading a text you can read, read, read."

 # TALKING ABOUT YOUR CHALLENGE BOOK READING

Readers, tonight, as you read a nonfiction text or two, keep reading and tackling the hard parts of your challenge books. You might also take a moment this evening to talk about your books with a reading friend or family member. Researchers who study learning say that talking about reading is one of *the most powerful* things you can do to become a better reader. Some possible points of discussion could be:

- Talk about your book's subject. What are you learning? What does your family know about your topic?
- Talk about how your nonfiction book is challenging in a good way. What's tricky? How are you tackling reading challenges?

Enjoy your conversations!

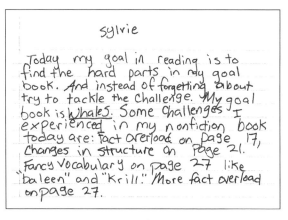
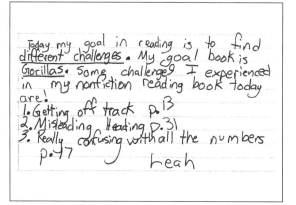

FIG. 4–1   Sylvie and Leah reflect on their conversation about their challenge books.

Session 5

The Challenges Posed by Texts that Are Structured as Hybrids

Y OUR STUDENTS HAVE EXPLORED the fact that nonfiction texts pose many challenges for readers. They've listed some of those challenges, and become more accustomed to thinking, when they encounter a challenge, "Ah, yes, I knew this would be hard in this way."

This session highlights a predictable source of text difficulty that students will encounter more and more as they tackle increasingly complex texts. Students who have been taught to consider the structure of a text and to make their notes match that structure will predictably encounter difficulties, because many complex texts are hybrids. Picture this. You are reading an article in *The New Yorker* profiling the world's best female fighter in mixed martial arts, and the author moves from telling about the fighter's daily diet and training regimen, to providing the backstory of her rise to fame (which coincidentally includes an explanation of the techniques involved in a move called *juji gatame*). The author then moves on to information about the world of the Ultimate Fighting Championship (UFC) and the polarizing impact of the fighter on that world, and from there to a recent interview with the fighter, to the UFC's current business model, and so on and so on. Sometimes these complex moves are made within just one paragraph! And yet the article is a cohesive whole.

Or perhaps you are listening to a TED talk about motivation given by Daniel Pink, and Pink moves from a personal anecdote about his (self-acknowledged less than wildly successful) time in law school, to a claim that business practices today need to change, to an explanation of a research study called the candle experiment.

To read *The New Yorker* or to listen to many TED talks, your students need to be able to move from thinking about what they know about how to read and listen to narrative nonfiction, to what they know about how to read expository texts. We are expected to make these mind moves in a seamless way, responding to cues in the text.

This session helps students read with this sort of flexibility, adjusting expectations and strategies as they progress through a sequence of text structures. Your minilesson will help readers become aware that a nonfiction text often contains many parts, and it will

IN THIS SESSION, you'll teach students that one of the challenges nonfiction readers face derives from the fact that many texts are hybrid in structure. Readers of hybrid nonfiction use authors' signals to determine which lenses to read through and how the different parts of a nonfiction text fit together.

GETTING READY

- ✔ Ask students to come to the meeting area with their challenge text (see Connection).
- ✔ Display the "Common Nonfiction Text Structures" chart (see Connection).
- ✔ Write several famous quotes on a sheet of chart paper. Students will read and then analyze for what common nonfiction text structure these quotes take (see Connection).
- ✔ Select several nonfiction texts that contain both narrative and expository parts.
- ✔ Locate and print a number of hybrid texts from the online resources; these texts will be for students to read and notate (see Teaching and Active Engagement).
- ✔ Prepare to pass out blue and green colored pencils for students to use to label their articles (see Teaching and Active Engagement).
- ✔ Display the "Coding Nonfiction Texts: Signals Authors Use" chart (see Teaching and Active Engagement).
- ✔ Prepare to display "To Read Nonfiction Well . . ." anchor chart (see Link).
- ✔ Prepare to pass out individual copies of the "Cross Text(s) Synthesis" strand of the Informational Reading Learning Progression, grades 3 and 4 (see Share).
- ✔ Links to the TED Talks on YouTube are available in the online resources (see Homework).

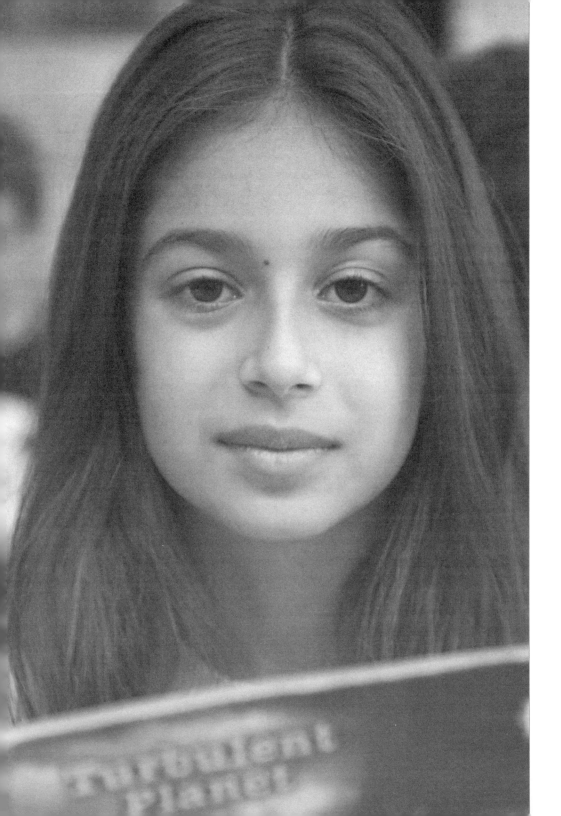

encourage readers to read, thinking about how those parts fit together.

You may be thinking, "My students are only nine now. Can they really do this work?"

> *"You will help students realize that when texts are a collection of different parts, each with a different text structure, it is important to use different lenses for the different types of nonfiction."*

It is true that *The New Yorker* is a long way off for your fourth-graders. Still, it's always important to teach with an eye on where you are going, where you are hoping to take your students. They will probably not leave your class as avid readers of *The Wall Street Journal*, but someday you want them to be. And so they will need to know that when reading nonfiction, texts are not always just one form or another; they are not always purely expository or purely narrative, purely compare and contrast or purely problem and solution. Instead, texts can be what we call "hybrids"—texts that are made of a collage of different parts.

You will help students realize that when texts are a collection of different parts, each with a different text structure, it is important to use different lenses for the different types of nonfiction. To help your students come to this realization you'll not only pantomime wearing different lenses as though they were different eyeglasses through which to look, but also you'll ask kids to inquire as to what signals authors give to help them determine when an author writes narrative or expository passages.

The Challenges Posed by Texts That Are Structured as Hybrids

CONNECTION

◆ COACHING

Set children up for today's minilesson by reminding them of the text structure work they've already done.

"Readers, a few days ago, we spent time exploring the various structures that nonfiction texts can take, and we talked about how knowing that structure can help a reader determine what information in the text is most important. Remember how much easier it was to take notes on that Arabian oryx news clip when we realized that it followed a problem/solution structure? Don't forget, you can always refer to the "Common Nonfiction Text Structures" chart if you need a reminder of the variety of structures texts can take as well as the words that cue us to these structures." I gestured toward the chart.

Common Nonfiction Text Structures

Structure	Transition words
Chronological	first, then, next, after that, finally, before, after
Problem/solution	a problem is, a solution is, if . . . then . . . , so that
Cause and effect	because, since, reasons, then, therefore, so, in order
Compare/contrast	different, same, alike, similar, although, but, yet, or

Ask partners to read famous quotes and figure out the structure each quote takes.

"I've got a little challenge for you. Will you read these quotes by famous people and see if you and your partner can see a nonfiction structure embedded in each? It's not easy to do this—the teachers in the staff room struggled with it too—so see what you can do!" I flipped to a sheet of chart paper where I had listed the quotes, and read each quote aloud.

> *"Get your facts first, and then you can distort them as much as you please."*—Mark Twain

> *"Alone we can do so little, together we can do so much."*—Helen Keller

> *"And so, my fellow Americans: ask not what your country can do for you, ask what you can do for your country."*—President John F. Kennedy

While minilessons follow a predictable structure, it's also important to provide variety for your students so that your teaching comes alive and engages students. You won't want to spend too long on this activity, but the teachers and students who piloted this unit found it to be one of their favorites.

"If you can't fly then run, if you can't run then walk, if you can't walk then crawl, but whatever you do you have to keep moving forward."—Rev. Dr. Martin Luther King, Jr.

"A bird doesn't sing because it has an answer, a bird sings because it has a song."—Maya Angelou

Then I said, "Which quotes seem to fit with which text structure? Turn and talk with your partner." I leaned in to coach as kids played the game.

Madison and Taylor jumped right into their work. "That one by Mark Twain could be chronological because it has transition words *first . . . then . . .*" Madison said.

"Yeah, and I think the Helen Keller quote could be problem and solution," said Taylor. "Like the problem is people can only do a little by themselves and the solution is they can get a lot done with others."

I gave the students just a minute to talk before I drew the class back together.

Highlight that another source of difficulty in nonfiction texts is that many contain both expository and narrative parts.

"All this talk of text structure is making me think of another way structure gets complex in hard nonfiction. Sometimes, texts are what we call 'hybrids.' I'm sure that word is familiar. Who here has heard of hybrid cars? A hybrid car has a gas engine and an electric motor, so it has two different power sources that help the car run. The same is true for a hybrid text. A hybrid text has two very distinct parts to it, a narrative part that sounds like a story, and an expository part that feels like it's teaching a ton of information."

Explain that readers read narrative and expository texts with different lenses. Emphasize that the challenge with this work is knowing which lenses to use while reading.

"Sometimes you can be reading an informational text, and you encounter a long story, embedded in the text, and you say to yourself, 'Ding, ding, ding! This is a story!' Then you think, 'I need to put on my glasses for reading for story!'" (I pantomimed sliding a pair of glasses on.) "Or, you may be reading a narrative about the true story of an amazing dog and come across a part where you say to yourself, 'Whoa! Hey now! Time for the reading for information glasses!'" (I pantomimed sliding one pair of glasses off and putting another pair on.) "I think that is common, and the challenge is that readers need to be ready to change alongside the text. After all, when the text is a story, we want to use our lenses for reading a story. When the text is expository, we need to be really reading for information."

"But here's the thing and this is the big challenge: you need to be able to recognize *when* you need to use *which* pair of glasses. It's like you need to hear that 'Ding, ding, ding!' or that 'Whoa! Hey now!' in your head as you are reading, and know which pair of glasses to put on."

Teachers, your delivery of this part is key. The "Ding, ding, ding" and the "Whoa! Hey now!" should be said in entirely different tones to emphasize the idea that they represent different lenses. When you repeat those phrases in the next part of the lesson, try to say each phrase the way you said it the first time. This will hopefully start to get those phrases going in students' own minds.

Point out that authors usually signal a change in structure. Suggest you are not sure how they do that and invite kids into an inquiry.

"Authors generally work hard to signal to you about the kind of reading you need to do. Sometimes they let you know by making a new heading or a text box. But other times, especially in texts that are more challenging, like the ones you are reading now, there are no headings to guide you, so authors need to signal in some other way. I wish I could tell you exactly what cues they use to let you know when to read through one lens or another, but I'm not entirely sure myself. So I thought today we could do an inquiry, studying some hybrid texts (or patchwork texts) to discover which signals the authors use to let readers know what kind of lenses to bring to their reading. This will not be easy work, but it is extremely important. What do you say? Are you with me?"

Name the question that will guide your inquiry.

"The question you'll be exploring is this: 'What signals do authors give to readers to let you know when a part of a text should be read through the lens of story and when a part should be read through the lens of reading for information?'"

TEACHING AND ACTIVE ENGAGEMENT

Provide a brief explanation of how the inquiry will go before getting students started.

"So let me tell you a bit about how this will work. I know you have your own challenge texts with you, but I thought we might work first with texts that I've brought that I know for sure are short hybrid texts. They contain parts that require different ways of reading. In a minute, I'll pass these texts out, one to each partnership. Will you and your partner read the text I give you aloud to each other and really study it, thinking about places where the text calls for you to read with the lens of story, and places where it is calling for you to read with the lens of reading for information?

"You can use these colored pencils to draw little sunglasses in the margin next to a part to show what lens you think you need to read it through." I uncovered a chart to guide students in their work, and I gave the colored pencils to two students to pass out.

Coding Nonfiction Texts

Blue sunglasses: narrative parts (lens of story)

Green sunglasses: expository parts (lens of reading for information)

- chronological
- problem/solution
- cause and effect
- compare/contrast

I distributed texts to partners, saying, "Then, and this is the *really* important part, you'll need to push yourselves to think even harder, really squeeze your brains to think, 'What actual *signals* do authors give to let us know when a part should be read through the lens of a story or when it should be read through the lens of reading for information?'"

You might decide to call on a student to repeat the directions for the inquiry to the class. It's a good assessment of how clear you were in your own directions and a chance for the class to remember the procedure they'll be following. Make the expectation clear that whichever student repeats directions, it is important for him or her to repeat them in the order in which they were given. Many teachers also find it helpful to have a chart listing the directions (or to project these instructions for the class with a document camera or interactive white board). They develop their chart by turning the directions into steps (e.g., Step 1: With your partner, read a text aloud to each other; Step 2: . . .). This will help students who might have difficulty remembering and following oral directions to better access the curriculum.

"Okay, everyone, start inquiring."

As partners worked, I coached in, saying things such as, "How is the text talking to you?" and "Is the text talking about a specific subject, or a subject in general?"

Convene students and highlight what you heard or have students share out their observations and construct a chart.

After about five minutes of reading and discussing the articles, I gathered the students back together. "So, how did it go? What sorts of clues did you gather? Was it clear to you when you needed to put on your glasses for reading for story (I pantomimed sliding on a pair of glasses), and when it was time to switch over, put on those reading for information glasses?" I pantomimed removing one pair of glasses and sliding on another. I displayed a new sheet of chart paper with the heading "Signals Authors Use to Let Us Know When to Read with a Certain Lens" and prepared to jot what I heard.

Jasmine started us off. "Our article started like a story. The author set up a scene that made me make a movie in my mind. 'The sun had come up over Alexandria in Egypt. Then the ground began to shake. People woke all over the city.' It didn't sound like a typical nonfiction lead. Sounded more like a story. Right away we knew we needed the blue sunglasses." I jotted Jasmine and her partner's noticing right onto our class chart, adding "Reads like a story."

"Ours was totally different!" Angel added. "We started right in with our green sunglasses, reading for information." I prompted him to read a bit out loud. "'All plants get energy from the sun. But some plants can't get all the nutrients they need from sunshine, water, and soil. Some of these plants live in places with poor soil. Others have no roots to take in nutrients. So they eat tiny animals, frogs, and insects. These are plants that eat meat.' Our author started out by kind of asking a question, and then answering it. Kind of like main idea and supporting details and setting up what she'd be teaching us." Angel's observation went into the second column.

After a few more minutes of discussion, we had a thorough list of textual signals that authors use to signify when to read for story and when to read for information.

LINK

Congratulate readers on beginning the challenging work of choosing the appropriate lenses to read through. Send them off to read, reminding them to draw on all they have learned.

"Readers, you should be proud of yourselves. It is tricky work to study texts and think about the signals authors use to let us know to read in a narrative way or an expository way. The chart we've made together is a good start. I bet if we looked at other texts, we'd see that not all authors use these signals. Authors might use other signals, and we should add those signals to our chart as we discover them.

Coding Nonfiction Texts
Signals Authors Use ...

Narrative Lens
Reads like a story...
• *Character*
• *Setting*
• *Problem/Resolution* Uh.Oh. → OK.

Treats a thing or group like a character. Hello. Hello. Hello.

Expository Lens

Weather

• *Tells all about a topic*
• *Tells a big idea and details* — Tornados cause harm.
• *Tells about groups of things* Storm / Tornado Hurricane

"As you go off to read today, I imagine you'll be keeping feelers out for those other signals authors might use when they switch from writing in a narrative format to all-about writing. If you notice those other signals, will you flag them with Post-its so we can add them to our chart? Continue, of course, drawing from our list of nonfiction reading strategies that we have been developing this week, specifically taking note of what you do to tackle the hard parts of nonfiction reading." I then drew their attention to our growing anchor chart, and I read the new section I had added on hybrid texts.

ANCHOR CHART

To Read Nonfiction Well . . .

- Make a connection to your text
- Preview the whole text and predict how it might go
  - Use prior knowledge of the topic
  - Scan the text features
- Figure out the text's structure and use it to determine importance:
  - Problem/solution
  - Compare/contrast
  - Cause/effect
  - Chronological
- Tackle the hard parts of nonfiction reading:
  First, notice
  - Misplaced, misleading, or poetic headings
  - Fact overload
  - Confusing beginnings that don't directly introduce the topic of the text
  - Long detours with extra information that can pull you away from the main idea
  Then take action:
  - Read and reread
  - Ask, "What is this part teaching?"
- **Notice if a text is hybrid and figure out which lens to read through, and when**
  - **Narrative lens**
  - **Expository lens**

Notice if the text is hybrid – use your lenses to read.

Support Students as They Tackle Challenge Books and Hybrid Texts

TODAY AS YOU TAKE UP YOUR CONFERRING MATERIALS, you might tab different sections across the learning progression in both the Narrative Reading as well as the Informational Reading sections. You'll also observe readers with a keen eye on behaviors and habits, and you'll also likely anticipate some predictable problems. Above all, you'll want to continue supporting readers with the work they are doing in their challenge books. Simple kidwatching of reading behaviors can tell you a lot about how things are going. Scrunched faces may indicate that a reader is thinking, or it may indicate struggle. If you see a reader on the same page for several minutes, you might support that reader to monitor for meaning, or rally the reader to keep up the volume. Lingering long on one page may also signal that the text is providing too great of a challenge, and you might channel a reader to try out a new challenge text or to read the text with a partner to provide some extra support.

For the last few sessions, students have been taking notes as they are reading, and you might choose to study students' reader's notebooks and notice trends. Watch for students who are taking overly copious notes. It's likely you'll want to gather these students together first. "You're reading like a copy machine!" you might say with a warm smile. "You're writing down every single fact you're reading, just like a copy machine would make a copy of every fact. Your hand must be getting tired!" Then provide a possible solution. "I'm thinking that instead of jotting *everything*, it would help to read a large chunk of the text, maybe even read for ten or twenty minutes, and then stop and *then* take notes about what's important. As you read, pay attention to the text structure—often the way a text is organized helps you to know what's *really* important to pay attention to." You might launch students into reading, and then leave them to work with a partnership. Return a good while later and coach students as they consider the text structure and take notes in ways that mirror the text's structure. Be sure the "Nonfiction Readers Take Notes that Follow the Structure of Their Texts" chart is handy while you do this work.

MID-WORKSHOP TEACHING **Thinking across Hybrid Texts: How Do These Parts Go Together?**

"Readers, I have to share some of the work Jason has been doing. His challenge text is a book called *Shark Attack!* He realized that the text started with narrative nonfiction, telling a story about a man named Rodney who survives a shark attack, and then actually it tells the story of other people who have survived attacks as well. The last bit of the chapter, however, switches to expository, and tells about ways people can prevent shark attacks, including telling about shark cages. I asked Jason the obvious question, 'How do these parts go together?' and he said . . ." and I passed the baton to Jason.

Jason cleared his throat. "They go together because even though one part is narrative and the other part is teaching all about shark cages, it's almost like problem and solution. The problem was Rodney's shark attack and the attacks other people got too, and his solution is to prevent the attacks with things like shark cages."

"Readers, see how you can sometimes synthesize across different parts of a hybrid text? It helps to step way back from the text and to think about the pieces of the text in far-vision ways. It also helps to keep common text structures in mind, asking, 'Is this part chronological? Is it problem and solution? Or perhaps it is cause and effect?'

"Right now, partners, will you ask each other the question I asked Jason: 'What are the parts of your text? How do they go together?'"

The children talked for a bit, and then I asked them to continue thinking about those questions as they turned back to their reading.

On the other hand, some readers' notes may already exhibit a degree of proficiency. These readers might be jotting main ideas as they read and suggesting key details that fit with those main ideas or taking notes in ways that mirror the structure of their text. Coach these children to imagine a wider array of taking notes than they might initially have imagined. For example, we have found that it is helpful if you teach them that readers sometimes sketch or list as a way to record information. The important thing will be to show children that any of these ways of taking notes can be done poorly, or done well. To demonstrate poor note-taking, you might open to a diagram in a book and start copying it bit by bit, replicating it precisely in your notebook (trust that your students will do this if you do not model not to). Then, explain that what will really help you hold onto information is to read a chunk of text, and then pause to sketch what you learned from the text. Emphasize the variety of ways this work could go. You can demonstrate that a student might decide to sketch the layers of the Earth's crust, or a diagram of the solar system, or a model of a coral reef.

Of course, whether researchers are listing or are sketching, it is important that they work efficiently, and yet capture enough information that their notes are useful later. Headings make a world of difference, as do captions for sketches. In fact, you will want to suggest that writing around the sketch notes can help. Labels can infuse a sketch with tons of information. Into the sketch about the coral reef, the student can label the plants and animals that live there, and the threats to the environment. This initial sketch can then turn into a series of sketches that show changes in a place over time.

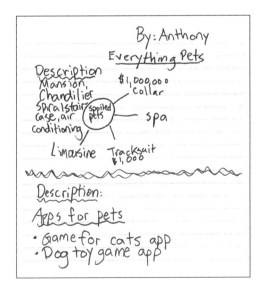

FIG. 5–1   This reader used a web and bullets to organize information.

Captions added to a diagram can help readers capture what they learned through the process of reading and sketching.

Notice the use of literary language as a sign of transference.

To support children in transferring the work they did with fiction into this unit, you'll want to see if children are applying literary language to the reading of nonfiction. For example, in your first unit of study, you encouraged your students to speak of the narrator, the setting, the character's traits, the motivation, and the obstacles when talking about their texts. Many of these terms are equally apt for use in describing narrative nonfiction, and noticing whether your children use this terminology when discussing nonfiction will reveal not only the extent to which your earlier teaching is "sticking" but also the connections that students are making between the two types of texts. Some of those terms will not, in fact, transfer perfectly into narrative nonfiction reading, but even if you need to point out to a student that the main character in a biography is referred to as the subject, not the protagonist, you'll want to celebrate that that reader made the effort to transfer knowledge from one domain to another. If some of your readers kept an index card in front of them during the preceding unit with literary terms on the cards, you'll want to take note of whether those readers dust off those old scaffolds for this new occasion.

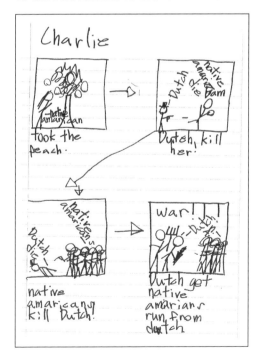

FIG. 5–2   Charlie's sketch notes

Self-Assessment with Learning Progressions

Channel readers to self-assess how they synthesize nonfiction texts.

"Readers, I've got to tell you that I love the way you are really striving to understand your nonfiction texts. And you are doing this *hard work* with such good spirits.

"As you tackle the hard parts of nonfiction reading, it can help to keep an eye on your progress, and to think, 'How am I doing?' The good news is there are tools to help you know *how* you are doing and *where* you are going, to let you know what's *next*.

"I've made copies of a strand of our learning progression that I think relates to the work you have been doing. This strand asks you to keep tabs on how you are thinking across texts and parts of a text. The fancy word for this is 'synthesizing.'" I passed out copies of the learning progression.

"Take a moment to read across the progression. Be brutally honest with yourself. Ask yourself, 'How am I doing?' then 'Where am I going?' and then 'Where can I go next?'"

After moving around the room to coach students, I paused to remind them to use the progression as a tool for goal-setting. "Readers, be sure to use this progression to push yourselves. The point of this is not to simply say, 'Yes, I'm doing that.' Instead the point is to identify goals you need to reach for in your reading. Be tough on yourself!"

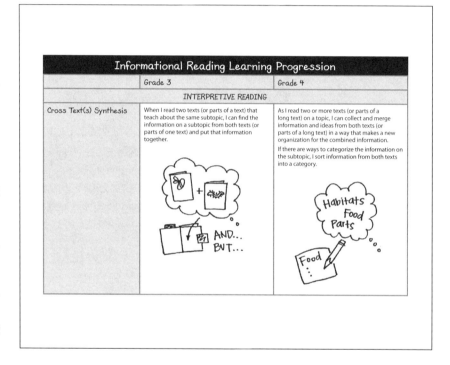

STUDYING HOW TEXTS ARE PIECED TOGETHER

Readers, for tonight, I'm going to ask you to continue to work with texts that are hybrid or patchwork. It is important for you to become more experienced at thinking about complex texts and the ways they are made like a quilt. Texts that are well written can be like patchwork quilts. They might have different pieces, each with a different text structure, but the whole text also fits together in some clear way.

It would be good for you to practice seeing how texts are made—almost turning them inside out to see the seams. I'm going to suggest for tonight, if you can get in front of a computer, that you watch a TED talk. YouTube has a channel for students called *Talks to watch with kids*: https://www.ted.com/playlists/86/talks_to_watch_with_kids (see recommendations from that listing below). Watch the talk at least twice, and as you do, think, *how is this TED talk made*? What are the parts of the talk and how do they go together?

If you have more time, of course you should continue reading whatever nonfiction texts you have been reading while at home. This time, be aware of the challenges that the text you are reading poses.

A Quick List of Recommended TED Talks for Kids

Arthur Benjamin: A performance of "Mathemagic"
http://ed.ted.com/lessons/a-performance-of-mathemagic-arthur-benjamin

Beau Lotto + Amy O'Toole: Science is for everyone, kids included
http://www.ted.com/talks/beau_lotto_amy_o_toole_science_is_for_everyone_kids
_included?language=en

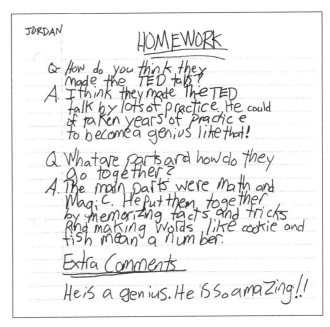

FIG. 5–3   Jordan reflects on how a TED Talk was made.

Tackling Tricky Vocabulary through Reading, Note-Taking, and Conversation

IN THIS SESSION, you'll teach students that when readers look *in* and *around* new vocabulary words, they can often figure out their meaning.

GETTING READY

✔ Prepare to display "Figuring Out the Meaning of Unknown Words" chart (see Teaching). ✋

✔ Select a passage from the demonstration text that contains tricky vocabulary. We have selected a passage from the "Here Comes the Sun" (page 13) section in *Everything Weather* (see Teaching and Active Engagement).

✔ Gather text sets representing possible research topics for the upcoming bend, and display them for students to browse (see Link).

✔ Prepare to display "To Read Nonfiction Well . . ." anchor chart (see Link). ✋

✔ Prepare to pass out individual copies of the "Word Solving, Building Vocabulary" thread of the Informational Reading Learning Progression, Grades 3 and 4 (see Conferring and Small-Group Work).

✔ Find several examples of idioms or figurative language in the demonstration text (see Mid-Workshop Teaching).

✔ Choose a passage from the demonstration text that contains numerical data or statistics. We have selected a line from page 10 in *Everything Weather* (see Share).

T HIS SESSION EXTENDS the work with challenging nonfiction texts, equipping students to handle two more of the challenges that they're apt to find. Specifically, you focus on the challenge of unfamiliar, often domain-specific, vocabulary words, and of understanding what complicated numbers and statistics in texts mean.

By fourth grade, most of your students can probably use their word-attack skills to proounce unknown words. In previous years, when solving a word, a reader was apt to have a flash of recognition and to be able to think, "Oh! *That's* what it says!" Now, however, students are much less likely to recognize the word once they have pronounced it. This makes morphology newly important, as according to a recent synthesis of studies by Tim Rasinski and others in *Educational Leadership*, 60% of the new words students encounter will be words whose meaning can be illuminated by even a fairly cursory knowledge of root words, prefixes, and suffixes.

Another dynamic will happen when your students read. The words students encounter now will often have multiple meanings, and texts may reference a secondary meaning, not the primary one. This means that students need to monitor for sense. If they read that people locked aliens up on Ellis Island, your hope is that they won't happily go along with the image of little green space men (aliens) being locked up near the Statue of Liberty!

Then, too, vocabulary will be challenging for students because of the sheer density of new words. They won't be able to master all those words immediately, and therefore they'll need to learn to think about which are important. They need to learn that the words that are important in nonfiction texts are apt to reappear, and that if the reader pays alert attention to the larger meaning of the text, usually that attentiveness to meaning will allow the reader to intuit the meaning of the unknown word.

And of course, best of all, we want students to learn words as they learn content, and to come to own those words as their own, being able to use them in interactions with each other and in their thinking about the new content.

Tackling Tricky Vocabulary through Reading, Note-Taking, and Conversation

CONNECTION

Engage the students by sharing an example of the way another student reached to develop his or her vocabulary.

"Readers, will you take a minute and tell your partner about the text you watched last night—if you were able to watch a TED talk. If someone watched and listened to an especially interesting talk, tell others about it."

The room erupted into conversation. After a bit I brought the class back together. "I'm amazed at the sheer variety of topics you learned about! It has always been interesting to me that a really great nonfiction writer has the ability to get readers interested in anything. There are best-selling writers who have written nonfiction on exclamation marks. I mean—who starts out saying, 'I'm dying to learn about exclamation marks'? But a great writer can lure us to be interested. There are famous and fascinating nonfiction texts for grown-ups on warts, and on chickens. Who would think, right?

"How many of you have ended up being interested in topics you never dreamt would interest you?" I signaled for children to show this with a thumbs up, and many did so.

Nodding, I said, "Finding the world to be more interesting than you realized is the reward from all this hard work you are doing. Today, I want to continue addressing ways that nonfiction texts get hard. I was asking some of you about how your text is hard, and a fair number of you mentioned vocabulary. Am I right that the sheer number of new words can be a bit much?"

The kids nodded, and I said, "Let me tell you a story. Bear with me for a moment, you'll see how it connects. The other day a friend of mine told me about a funny thing that happened when she was at the circus with her young son. The clowns came out—you can picture them, right? Colorful clothes, big curly wigs, face paint, the red noses—the whole costume. So the clowns started in on their routine—lots of silly things going on, everyone was laughing, and then my friend's son called out, 'Look, Mom, a urinal!'

"A *urinal*? she thought—what is he talking about? When she looked at the clowns and then looked back to her son, she realized that he said *urinal*, but really he meant *unicycle*!

Over the years, students may have become accustomed to the more "mainstream" nonfiction topics that inhabit their worlds—soccer, cooking, the Civil War, dogs. By opening their eyes to the variety, the seemingly endless wealth of nonfiction topics, you are helping them to become even more connected to the genre, and are working to create lifelong, passionate nonfiction readers, and not simply readers who read nonfiction texts because it's a "school thing."

"I'm telling you this story because I've been thinking about that little boy. He was trying to use a new word: *unicycle*. He could have just said, 'Oh, look,' and pointed, not using any fancy terminology. Instead he tried to use a new word. Even though he got it wrong, the next time he sees a unicycle he probably won't call it a urinal! He learned something—he built up his vocabulary—by taking a risk.

"This is important for you as nonfiction readers because you often come across words or terms you don't know and you want to be a risk-taker! The density of hard vocabulary in nonfiction texts is another way those texts can be challenging."

❖ **Name the teaching point.**

"Today I want to teach you that if readers look *in* and *around* new vocabulary words, you can often figure them out."

TEACHING

Provide students with an explanation of the broad mental work readers do to figure out the meaning of unknown words.

"Sometimes when you're reading you'll know right away that you don't know a word or term. Other times we might know the word, but the meaning is different in a new context. So you have to be problem solvers. I want to teach you a mantra that one of my teachers taught me that has helped me figure out the meaning of words. He used to say, 'Look in, and look around.' This might sound a bit simple, but it's not really. Let me show you." I uncovered a chart with the words and some guiding tips and questions.

Demonstrate your own reading work for the students, thinking aloud as you apply the strategy.

"Let's get started with this. We're going to read a bit from page 13 of *Everything Weather* and when we come to a word or term for which we're not certain of the meaning, we'll pause and look in and around the word to think about possible meanings." I projected a passage from the book using a document camera and read aloud.

Life Under Pressure

Feel that? Here on Earth, the air presses against us with a force of about 15 pounds per square inch.

"Hmm, . . . Life Under Pressure—well, right there—that word 'pressure.' I know the word pressure—like peer pressure or tire pressure—but I'm not 100% certain what it has to do with weather. Let me start by looking into the word. If I *look into* the word, I see the word 'press'—yes, press means to force, but forcing what? Looking into the word gives me a start, but I think I have to *look around* the word to figure out what it means in *this* text."

Here on Earth the air presses against us . . .

Figuring Out the Meaning of Unknown Words

Look in...
- **Root words**
- **Suffixes**
- **Prefixes**

Look around...
- **What do you picture?**
- **What's happening?**
- **Is it positive or negative?**
- **What type of word is it?**

"So, in this text they are talking about pressure, about force, but it's a force coming from the air . . . and the air creates a force. Hmm, . . . this is pretty cool—we're not just learning about weather, we're also learning new meanings of familiar words!"

Recap the work you've just demonstrated.

"Did you see the way we needed to read and check our understanding of the words in the text? Looking in and looking around helped us figure out a new meaning, build up our vocabulary, and learn more about what the text is teaching us."

ACTIVE ENGAGEMENT

Set students up to practice the strategy with you in the next sentence.

"Let's practice this together by reading the next sentence and thinking about the ways we can build our vocabulary and our understanding of this topic." I reread the text, focusing on the second sentence of the paragraph.

Life Under Pressure

Feel that? Here on Earth, the air presses against us with a force of about 15 pounds per square inch.
<u>*You can't really feel atmospheric pressure, but it does play a role in weather prediction.*</u>

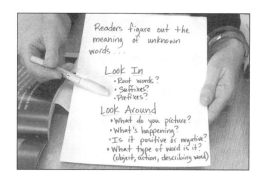

FIG. 6–1 One teacher's version of this session chart

"Look at this sentence and think about the words that are less familiar—some might be unknown altogether, others might be words you know but need to check the meaning of in this text. When you have one or two in mind give me a thumbs up.

"Now, turn to your partners and discuss the words you are less familiar with and what their meanings might be. Remember that you can look in and look around the word to help you figure out these meanings and build your vocabulary."

After giving the students a few minutes to talk in their partnerships, I called them back together. "I heard many of you talking about the word *atmospheric*—it's a tricky one to say, but more importantly we need to figure out the meaning. I heard some of you say that when you looked into the word, you saw the word 'sphere'—and then you said that the Earth is a sphere. So in terms of this paragraph it seems as though atmospheric pressure might be something like Earth pressure."

LINK

Wrap up the lesson, reminding students that figuring out the meaning of unknown words is another one of the jobs they have as informational readers.

"Readers, you began a hard text two days ago. How many of you have finished reading that text?" Kids signaled. "How many of you think you've gotten what you wanted out of the text and you probably should quit it and try another?" Again, children signaled. "How many of you are reading the hard text, it's going well, but you need more time?" More kids signaled.

"Readers, you have just two more days to read any nonfiction text that you want, on any high-interest topic, and then we're going to launch into research projects. So I'm hoping you think carefully about how best to spend your precious reading time. Some of you may want to continue with the text you have been reading or to choose another challenge text. Others of you have been hankering to read about some topic all along, and you don't want this little window of time to go by without getting to that topic. And some of you may want to preview the research topics that I'm suggesting in our next bend of the unit. I've put those bins out on the window shelf by our library, and you can browse those books and choose a book—and a topic—to start in on, if you want.

"The truth is you can be reading almost any nonfiction text and you will encounter new vocabulary words, so I don't need to steer you too much. And I also want to remind you that you just have two days to really cement all that you have learned in the first bend of this unit. So use the anchor chart as a reminder, and try to do all that work . . . while also looking in and around the new vocabulary."

It often helps to break the steps of a process down for students during an active engagement. In this case I wanted to be sure that the students had actually identified words to discuss. As students mature, they are sometimes afraid to admit that they don't know a word or term and I want to ensure that they see this as an absolutely acceptable, even desirable, practice.

Notice that the text chosen for this lesson is very short, yet presents a variety of possible challenges—words that students are probably familiar with, but have new meanings in this context, technical terms students may not know at all, and a scientific concept enhanced by numerical values that will probably confuse many fourth-grade readers.

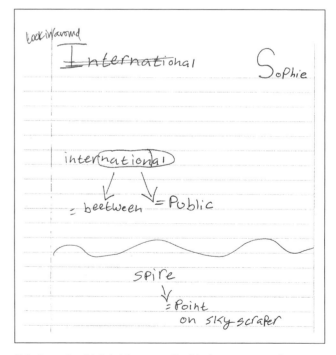

FIG. 6–2 Sophie's jottings are the kind you may see later during the independent reading portion of the workshop.

To Read Nonfiction Well . . .

- Make a connection to your text
- Preview the whole text and predict how it might go
  - Use prior knowledge of the topic
  - Scan the text features
- Figure out the text's structure and use it to determine importance:
  - Problem/solution
  - Compare/contrast
  - Cause/effect
  - Chronological
- Tackle the hard parts of nonfiction reading:
  First, notice:
  - Misplaced, misleading, or poetic headings
  - Fact overload
  - Confusing beginnings that don't directly introduce the topic of the text
  - Long detours with extra information that can pull you away from the main idea
  Then take action:
  - Read and reread
  - Ask, "What is this part teaching?"
- Notice if a text is hybrid and figure out which lens to read through, and when
  - Narrative lens
  - Expository lens
- **Figure out the meaning of unknown words:**
  - **Look in the word**
  - **Look around the word**

"I'll admire the decisions you make. Those of you who will be continuing to read the challenge text you have underway—get started." They left the meeting area. "Those of you who are thinking you want to spend these next two days on a high-interest text that you've been hankering to read, you can head off." They left. "Those of you who are thinking about previewing the text sets we'll be studying in the upcoming bend, get started." They dispersed. "Will the rest of you pull in, and let's talk about what you are planning to do today," I said.

While it's wholly true that our job is to teach children to read nonfiction well, it's also our job to teach children how to learn. One way to do this is to ask kids to self-assign their plan for the day, which allows kids to practice being independent, self-regulated learners.

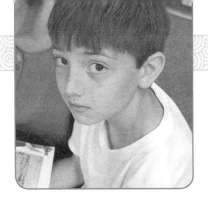

Readers Use the Learning Progression to Take Stock of Their Development

TODAY YOU MIGHT DECIDE to use this time to assess what effect your teaching is having on kid's learning. The Informational Reading Learning Progression is a useful tool for studying students' work and progress. The sections on "Word Work" and "Building Vocabulary" will be particularly useful today. Observe students from a distance, peer over shoulders, study Post-its, glance through the pages of notebooks, talk and listen—all of these interactions will provide information about the effectiveness of your teaching and the specific areas of growth and need for groups and individuals. Keep records of what you discover and jot down ideas for how to move readers forward.

Some of your students will probably need support tackling the tricky words they encounter in their nonfiction texts. Watch out for students who tend to mumble through words in their texts or skip tricky words altogether. This is a particularly troublesome habit. Not only does it interrupt meaning in the text the student is currently reading, but it also robs the reader of an opportunity to refine word-attack strategies and to build vocabulary. Consider this sentence from *Everything Weather: Freezing rain falls during the winter when rain freezes immediately as it hits a surface*. If a student mumbled through or skipped over the words *immediately* or *surface*, she would probably still be able to understand what freezing rain is and move forward in the text, but she would not have practiced word-attack skills or positioned herself to recognize either of these words more quickly the next time she encountered them, and she would not have had the opportunity to begin to build up her understanding of these words by recognizing them in a new context. That is, while a reader may have heard an adult say, "You need to clean this room immediately," she will benefit from seeing the word used in a different context so as to understand the multiple ways words can be and are used.

Help students transfer the word-solving strategies they learned in other genres and grades to their work in nonfiction.

If you decide that there are a cluster of students who need a series of small-group lessons on handling texts that contain lots of tricky words, you could start by reminding them of the strategies they learned in third grade. You might say, "I know that you have learned many strategies for climbing the hurdle of hard words and I thought it would be helpful to remind you of some of these strategies you were taught last year." This particular chart was first developed inside a fiction reading unit, so you could invite readers to consider ways in which it needs to be revised to support work in nonfiction texts.

Support readers in self-assessing their strategies for figuring out unfamiliar words.

The "Word Work: Building Vocabulary" thread of the Informational Reading Learning Progression will also be a handy tool for you as you confer and work with small groups. You might say to a group, "Readers, when you come across words that you know how to say but aren't sure what they mean, it's important to have a toolkit of strategies to help you. This learning progression can help you self-assess the strategies you are using to build vocabulary and it can give you a sense of next steps." You could then distribute the "Word Work: Building Vocabulary" thread of the Informational Reading Learning Progression, channeling students to think about where their skills are on the progression and about what they might need to do to move up the progression.

"Readers, may I have your eyes?" When students were looking my way, I continued. "Do you remember at the beginning of the year when I would say, *May I have your eyes?* and a few of you grimaced at me? Remember I had to explain, 'I don't *literally* want your eyes. That's grotesque! What I *mean* is I want your attention. I want you to look at me.'

"When we had that conversation about figurative language we talked earlier about how sometimes people use words not *literally*, but *as if* they meant something else. Nonfiction writers do this, too. Check out the stuff I pulled from Kathy Furgang's writing in *Everything Weather*: *wind howling*, *rain pounding*, *winter's icy grip*. She

could have said *Rain drops against windows*. But she didn't, did she? She wrote, *Rain pounds against windows*. She talked about the rain as if it were a fist or a hammer. She didn't mean that rain actually has fists clenched and it bangs its fists against the windows. But it does mean that rain can get so strong and loud it's *as if* it had banging fists.

"When you come to such language, it's important to ask yourself, 'Is this what the author *literally* means, or is the author comparing something *as if* it were something else?' Remember, the author is not only trying to keep us reading, but more importantly to teach us. So you must ask yourself, 'What is the author trying to teach me?'"

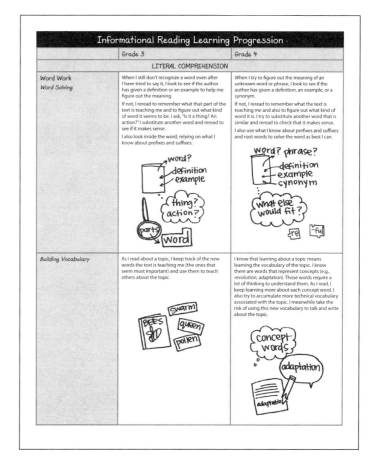

Making Sense of Statistics

Gather readers back to the meeting area. Teach readers not to skip over the numbers, but to take the time to understand and appreciate the relevance of this information.

"Readers, let's gather together for a moment," I said, even though it was unusual to convene the class in the meeting area at the end of reading time. Once children had gathered, I said, "Over the last few days we have been talking a lot about how books can be hard, and the ways we can tackle hard nonfiction texts. We've been thinking a lot today about strategies for figuring out the meaning of unknown words. But it's not just the words we need to pay attention to, we also need to pay attention to the numbers and statistics we are reading.

"I want to teach you how to understand the information provided by numbers. And the key is to visualize and make comparisons. Let's work on this together for a minute. Let me read a few sentences from *Everything Weather* to you. This came from a page in the beginning of the book (page 10).

> *Run! Tornadoes can travel up to 70 miles per hour. The average speed is 10–20 mph.*

"Let's take the first one—seventy miles per hour. Can you visualize that? About how fast is that? It can help to think about this speed in relation to what you know. When might you have traveled close to seventy miles per hour?" Several children called out cars, that a car traveling just above the speed limit on the highway would hit that speed, and that was pretty fast. Then, we tried the same process with the second sentence, visualizing and making comparisons to help us understand the statistic.

"Take a minute to look back in your books to find some places where you can think more about and learn from the numbers in your texts." I gave children a minute to do this. "Share one of the statistics you found and what you learned from studying it with a partner."

In books that are especially well written, authors often help readers to interpret statistics. For example, in The Big Thirst, *Charles Fishman points out that Americans spent 21 billion dollars on bottled water in 2009. That's such a large number that it is unimaginable to most readers. But Fishman made the number more understandable by writing, "We spend about 29 billion a year maintaining our entire water system in the United States—the drinking water treatment plants, the pump stations, the pipes in the ground, the water treatment plants. So as a nation, we spend very nearly as much on water delivered in small crushable plastic bottles as we do on sustaining the entire water system in the country" (p. 135). The work Fishman did to make his statistics comprehensible is the work that your readers will need to do when authors don't do it for them.*

DESIGNING WORD BANKS TO CAPTURE NEW WORDS

Readers, tonight when you bring your books home and read, will you remember work you did last year when you built your own word bank of words related to the animal inquiry you were doing? You don't want to be the kind of learner who waits for a teacher to tell you to build a word bank—by now, that should be second nature for you.

If you are reading about castles, your word bank might contain words like "moat," "armory," "ambush," "defenses," and "siege." Once you have recorded words that are key to your topic, make sure that you use those words when talking (and when thinking) about your subject. That's the only way you will get to really "own" the words.

But here is an added challenge: often, words that are specific to a topic can actually be used to talk off-topic as well, in ways that are somewhat creative. If you use castle words, for example, to talk about the amount of homework you have been given, you might say something like this:

> I try to build a moat around Friday and Saturday nights and all-day Sunday so they are times that are free of work. But sometimes I get ambushed by assignments I hadn't expected. I'm working to build an armory of excuses so that I can keep my defenses up.

You'll be doing more of this later in the unit in the company of friends, and so it is good practice to get in the habit of adding words to your word bank now. Tomorrow you'll get a chance to share some of the words in your word bank with your partner.

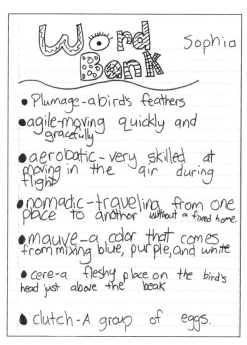

FIG. 6–3   Sophia's word bank

Summary Boot Camp

IN THIS SESSION, you will teach that nonfiction readers create summaries of their reading that include the main ideas and key details of the topic, stated in the reader's own words.

GETTING READY

✔ Ask students to bring the word bank they created for homework last night with them to the meeting area (see Connection).

✔ Display a passage from the "Here Comes the Sun" section of *Everything Weather* by Kathy Furgang to students, or an alternate section that they can use to practice summarizing (see Teaching and Active Engagement).

✔ Chart paper and markers (see Teaching and Active Engagement).

✔ Individual copies of the "Main Idea(s) and Supporting Details/Summary" strand of the Informational Reading Learning Progression, Grades 3 and 4 (see Share).

THIS IS THE FINALE OF BEND I. We think of it, then, as a culminating session, one that caps many days of work and learning. You may be surprised: the title, after all, doesn't conjure up images of an exotic celebration!

But for us, the position of this session is important. For us, summary is no small potatoes. We think the ability to read a nonfiction text and then to be able to consolidate what you learned into a well-organized, abbreviated synopsis of the most important things actually undergirdks any other skill in nonfiction reading. This, alone, is not sufficient, but for a child to read in such a way that he or she can summarize the text, that child has done a lot right—including, in all likelihood, learning from the effort.

Before you closely read the rest of this session we highly recommend you read the "Main Idea(s) and Supporting Details/Summary" strand of the Informational Reading Learning Progression as a good summary requires putting together several strategies. Students have to decide what information to include in their summaries, and what information to leave out. This work of determining importance requires students to identify the author's point—the main idea of a passage, using what they have learned about text structure to support them, and then to sort through paragraphs of supporting details to identify the details that best support the main idea. With their ideas and details in mind, they will have to decide when and if to rephrase information, or if it is important to include a few of the key terms the author used. To top it all off, students will have to decide whether to put information in their summary in a different order from which it was presented by the author.

In some ways, a good summary serves as the bedrock to strong nonfiction reading. In the next bend, students will get into research teams to study a particular type of extreme weather or natural disaster, and you will want kids to practice this summarizing beforehand, so they can use this skill in the future, both orally and in writing. So this session, the final one in Bend I, gives you a chance to teach students to read for the author's point, and to put all that information into a written summary.

You will notice that the format of today's lesson feels significantly different from the other lessons in the bend. Here, we suggest you use guided practice as your teaching method, coaching partners as they participate in what we've come to call a "boot camp." You'll gather students on the rug, introduce them to the idea of summary, and then, instead of demonstrating how you do the work, you will coach them through the process of summarizing a familiar shared text. Across your Teaching and Active Engagement, we suggest you alternate between asking questions and providing tips to lift the level of the work, and asking partnerships to dive into the text and practice the work of summarizing for themselves. We expect you'll find this boot camp energizing and incredibly effective.

"We think the ability to read a nonfiction text and then to be able to consolidate what you learned into a well-organized, abbreviated synopsis of the most important things actually undergirds any other skill in nonfiction reading."

Summary Boot Camp

CONNECTION

Celebrate the word banks students created for homework last night, and invite them to talk with their partner using the new words they are learning.

"I've just been amazed by the word banks you created last night. You filled them with so many important words. Right now, will you take a minute to share your new words with your partner? And, instead of rattling them off like you're reading a list, will you use them in sentences so your partner can start to learn them too? So instead of saying, 'adaptation, predator, habitat,' you could say, "Predators, you know, animals that eat other animals, have really cool adaptations that help them survive in any habitat, any place, where they live. Turn now and give it a try." I gave the students a minute to share, oohing and ahhing at the new words they were using.

Remind readers of the importance of summarizing and let them know that today will be a kind of boot camp to summarize nonfiction texts.

"Readers, almost all of you have finished your challenge book by now, and have had many opportunities to practice the strategies for reading the hard parts of nonfiction. Today I want to tell you about an important skill—the skill to be able to say back what you're learning in a nonfiction text. If reading nonfiction is reading to learn, then nonfiction readers can become experts on what they read. If one part of being an expert is teaching others what they have learned, then it's important for nonfiction readers to hold onto what they've learned and be able to say it back in a clear way.

"When you read a nonfiction text, you need to be sure you have really and truly understood it. Summarizing pushes you to be able to figure out what is most essential to understanding a text.

"Today we will work on how to do that summarizing work for nonfiction texts. Today will be a sort of summary boot camp—you'll jump in and practice it right away."

Word Bank   Rafael

incisors — the two front teeth on a guinea pig

digits — guinea pigs toes

pelts — guinea pigs coats

self — a coat that is just one color

nonself — a coat with 2 or 3 colors

undercoat — layer of soft fur next to a guinea pig's skin which will keep it warm

guard hairs — a coarse layer of hair that protects the body

rosettes — swirls in the fur of a certain breed

popcorning — a guinea pig gesture

quick — the center of a guinea pig's claws

FIG. 7–1   Rafael shares his work bank.

Establish the justification for today's lesson: readers need the chance to practice complicated thinking work that, initially, may seem rather rote.

"On the surface, summary at first seems pretty obvious and easy to do, right? I mean, all you have to do is say back what's in the text, right? But it turns out summarizing is a bit more complicated. To summarize well, you need to know what to include in your summary, how to summarize the author's points in your own words, and how the details support the author's main idea. That's a lot!

"Today I thought we could take one text and practice this work together. I want to give you a gut sense for what it's like to summarize. Instead of a regular minilesson, we'll do some shared thinking and writing, working as a team to craft a summary of a text. As we do this, pay attention to what makes a good summary."

❖ **Name the teaching point.**

"Today I want to teach you that when readers summarize nonfiction writing, you organize your summaries to include what is most important to the writer's topic—the writer's main idea and the key supporting details—all the while being careful to put this into your own words."

TEACHING AND ACTIVE ENGAGEMENT

Remind readers what they have already learned about <u>determining importance</u> and then <u>read a text</u> that the class will summarize together, asking them to listen for what is most important.

"You learned in third grade that after <u>reading a chunk of text</u>, <u>nonfiction readers pause to retell or summarize</u> the author's points in a text—the main idea and supporting details of what they just read. Remember, you practiced doing this using your hand to show boxes and bullets? The main idea in the palm of your hand" (I pressed a finger against the palm of one hand), "and the supporting details across your fingers" (I touched one finger at a time, showing how I could tick off the supporting details).

"Now that you are fourth-graders, you know even more about nonfiction, like the different structures" (I gestured toward the "Common Nonfiction Text Structures" chart) "that a text can take. The structure of your text, whether it is <u>cause and effect</u> or <u>chronological</u>, can guide the way you summarize the main idea and supporting details of the text, so you'll want to be on the lookout for the structure of the text as you read.

"Ready to give this work a try? I'm going to read a text aloud to you. Listen for the main idea and then the smaller supporting details while I read this passage 'Here Comes the Sun' from page 12 of *Everything Weather*."

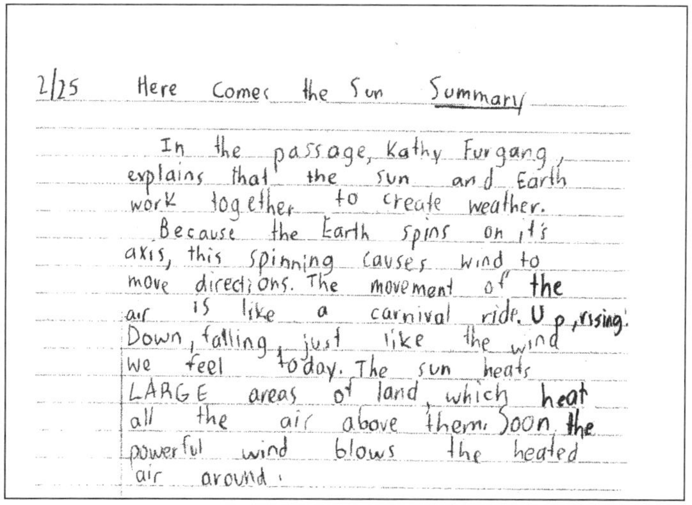

It is no lie to say that summary is complicated work. Nearly a hundred years ago, Jean Piaget studied how children summarized information texts to one another and concluded this is indeed a challenging skill to develop.

2/25   Here Comes the Sun Summary

In the passage, Kathy Furgang, explains that the sun and Earth work together to create weather. Because the Earth spins on it's axis, this spinning causes wind to move directions. The movement of the air is like a carnival ride. Up, rising. Down, falling, just like the wind we feel today. The sun heats LARGE areas of land, which heat all the air above them. Soon the powerful wind blows the heated air around.

FIG. 7–2   Izzy's summary from the minilesson

Here Comes the Sun

The sun is Earth's five-billion-year-old friend. How hot is it? Really hot! The sun has a core of gases that reaches a temperature of 27 million degrees Fahrenheit (or 15 million degrees Celsius). Here on Earth, we are 93 million miles (150 million km) away from the sun, but that's still close enough to feel the burn. The sun provides most of the heat and light for our planet, but it is not the only factor in our weather.

All those millions of miles from the sun, our planet spins on an axis. The rotation causes moving air to change direction. Add more movement to air that is rising, falling, and changing temperatures, and you end up with a wild weather ride.

When it comes to causing weather, the sun, land, and air are partners. The sun heats large patches of land, which warm the air above them. The wind then moves the warm air around, sometimes bumping cooler patches out of the way. The air's constant shifting, rising, falling, heating, and cooling make the weather very unpredictable.

Make sure students can see the text, and channel them to reread to find the author's point, the most important main idea.

"I bet you're already getting some ideas. The first step in crafting a summary is to figure out the author's most important main idea. Right now, will you reread this text with your partner and think, 'What's the main idea? What's this mostly about?' Jot down key sentences to help you, if you want."

Coach with lean prompts. Then convene the class, calling for suggestions as to the next part of the shared summary.

Partnerships dug into the work, rereading, writing, and talking. Meanwhile, I moved around the rug and coached. I stopped first when I saw a partnership sitting quietly, staring at several sentences they had jotted. "I see you two have found some important sentences that you've written. Now ask yourself, 'Which of these sentences go together? How do they go together?'"

To another partnership, I said, "Looks like you found a sentence that popped out for you. Put that sentence into your own words."

After a while I brought the class back together. "Let's hear it: which partnerships have found a way to say back the main idea in their own words?"

I called on Leah. "The sun and Earth work together to create the weather," she said.

I quickly jotted the main idea she suggested in a box on the top of my chart paper:

The sun and Earth work together to create the weather.

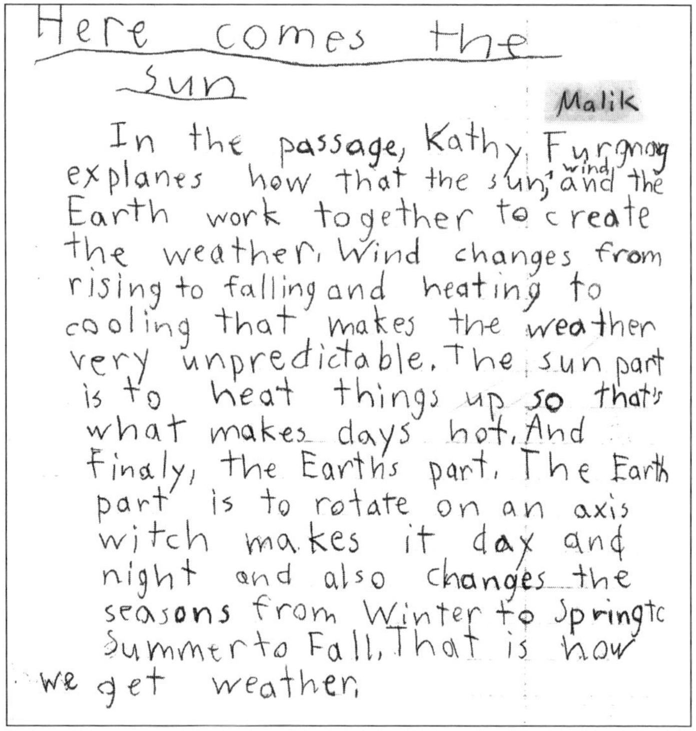

Here comes the sun

Malik

In the passage, Kathy Furgang explanes how that the sun, wind, and the Earth work together to create the weather. Wind changes from rising to falling and heating to cooling that makes the weather very unpredictable. The sun part is to heat things up so that's what makes days hot. And finaly, the Earths part. The Earth part is to rotate on an axis witch makes it day and night and also changes the seasons from Winter to Spring to Summer to Fall. That is how we get weather.

FIG. 7–3 Malik's summary from the minilesson

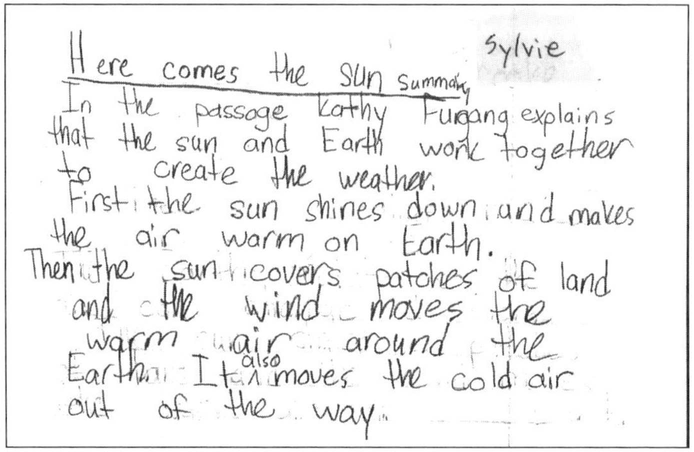

Here comes the sun summary

Sylvie

In the passage Kathy Furgang explains that the sun and Earth work together to create the weather. First the sun shines down and makes the air warm on Earth. Then the sun covers patches of land and the wind moves the warm air around the Earth. It also moves the cold air out of the way.

FIG. 7–4 Sylvie's summary from the minilesson

I said, "Leah, I can tell you and Alyssa put some hard thinking work into developing that. To start our summary, let's tell the main idea and also be specific about who the author is. One way this could sound is, 'In this passage, the author's point is . . .' or 'The main idea of this passage is that . . .' Try out how our first sentence could go." I gave students thirty seconds to try out their first sentence, while midway down on the chart paper, I jotted:

> In this passage, Kathy Furgang explains that the sun and Earth work together to create the weather.

Channel partnerships to identify the text's structure, and then to reread to find supporting details the author provides for the main idea.

"Friends, I think we've got a main idea down in our own words. Now we need to find the supporting details for the main idea. To do this, it can help to think about how the text is structured. When you know how a text is structured, you can choose details for your summary that fit with that structure. Let's look at the text and our main idea: the sun and Earth work together to create the weather. Hmm, . . . What text structure does this passage take?" I gave students a minute to decide, and then I called them back.

"I think it's cause and effect," Jordan said. "Like the sun and Earth work together to cause the weather."

"I think you're right on, Jordan," I continued. "So keep that cause-and-effect structure in mind as you look for supporting details in the text. You might find some details that show causes and some that show effects. Remember again to put them in your own words."

Lean into partner work, coaching with lean prompts to raise the level of their work. Reconvene the class and name out the supporting details you heard partnerships share.

I knelt down to listen in as partnerships sprang into action. "One supporting detail is that the sun is 27 million degrees Fahrenheit," Ibrahim said to Rafael.

I interjected. "That is something that the text says, and is really interesting information, but remember, we are looking for *supporting* details. Does the exact heat of the sun support the idea that the sun and Earth work together to create the weather? Go back to the article and find the specific lines that fit our main idea."

Ibrahim read, "What about this one? 'The sun heats large patches of land, which warm the air above them.' I think it fits with creating weather, and it's got the cause-and-effect thing, too."

"Okay," I said. "Now try the supporting detail in your own words."

Here come the Sun
Summary

In the passage, Kathy Furgang explains that the sun and Earth work together to create weather. Not only does the sun work with the Earth but it also works with the land the air and the wind. The sun heats up the land below it and the heated land and sun warms up the air above. Then the wind blows the warm air to other places in the world to make crazy weather concoctions.

FIG. 7–5 Taylor's summary from the minilesson

As you watch students do this summarizing work, be on the lookout for students who might distort what the author has said or students who bring in irrelevant details instead of supporting details. Another predictable problem is students who bring in their own opinion. Jot down what you notice to inform your upcoming instruction. You can do more teaching into these predictable problems during your small group and conferring across this unit (and year).

After a few moments I called the class back together and shared the supporting details I heard from partnerships, jotting them on the sheet of chart paper underneath where I had written the main idea.

> In this passage, Kathy Furgang explains that the sun and Earth work together to create the weather.

- The sun heats the land, which warms the air.
- Wind moves warm air around.
- The Earth's rotation also causes air to change temperatures.

Direct the class to take the shared main idea and supporting details to "write in the air" their own iteration of a summary to the passage.

"Okay, we have the author's point—the main idea and some supporting details. Now, with your partner, write-in-the-air the summary. It should be a short paragraph that explains the main idea and supporting details in your own words. Start with our first sentence, or write your own, and then give all the details that support the main idea."

Lean in and listen, coaching with lean prompts to lift the level of what kids do and say. Reconvene the class and elicit from students a shared summary. Then coach into writing.

I listened as children recited summaries to each other, many of which went like this:

"In this passage, Kathy Furgang explains that the sun and Earth work together to create the weather. One detail is that the sun heats the land on Earth, which warms the air. Another supporting detail is that wind moves the warm air around. A third detail is that the Earth's rotation causes air to change temperatures.

"Wow," I said. "You are really cranking out these summaries! This hard work is a blast, isn't it? I love that you are taking our shared main idea and supporting details and putting *that* into your own words. Will you try your summary again, and this time try using some phrases like this: In addition . . . She points out that . . . A final detail is . . .'"

After a bit I convened the class and this time, Leo recited his version of the summary to us.

"In this passage, Kathy Furgang explains that the sun and Earth work together to create the weather. One detail that supports this is that the sun heats the land on Earth, which warms the air. In addition, Kathy Furgang points out that wind moves warm air around. A final detail is that the Earth's rotation causes air to move and change directions, which then causes change in temperatures."

Debrief. Show the class what one reader did that you are hoping all readers have learned to do.

"Readers, do you see the way Leo started by repeating the author's point, the main idea in his own words and then explained the details that supported that main idea? He used also some transition phrases to help him link the parts of his summary."

LINK

Send kids off to independent reading, reminding them to push themselves to fully understand a text every time they read. Ask them to try at least one written summary today.

"Readers, summarizing isn't just a one-time deal. This is a skill that you'll use for the rest of your life, when you're sharing a good book, when you're giving a report, when you're teaching someone about a topic. It's important to know that every time you read, you want to be sure you are completely understanding the text, inside and out, and summarizing well can help you to do that.

"As you read today, you'll be tackling the hard parts, finding best ways to capture information, thinking about text structure, and all the rest, but, will you do one more thing? Will you try at least one written summary of a passage or an article you read? Off you go."

Support the Way Kids Are Summarizing with Differentiated Instruction

AS YOU CIRCULATE THE ROOM TODAY, you will likely notice kids are able to summarize with varying degrees of specificity and complexity. You might pull kids into groups that correspond to their ability to summarize, and teach those kids something just above what they are able to do. Carry the Informational Reading Learning Progression with you today, tabbed to the "Main Idea(s) and Supporting Details/Summary" section.

Support kids who are identifying a topic and not an author's point or main idea.

If you notice kids who summarize a text with just a one-word topic, remind these children that summaries generally convey an author's point or main idea in a complete sentence. For instance, if a child is reading a book on cheetahs, and summarizes by saying, *This is about their food*, teach the reader to capture the main idea in a sentence that contains a *who* and a *what*. You might say, "When readers say back what a text is mostly about, they often start with the main idea, which is usually a complete sentence with a *who* doing *what*. For instance, in my book *Extreme Weather*, I wouldn't just say, 'This is mostly about precipitation.' I would say more something like, 'This is mostly about the different kinds of precipitation and how it falls to the earth in different ways. For instance . . .'" In this case you'd have to explain that the *who* would be precipitation, or that it is a *what* doing *what*, and how that may be another way to say a main idea in a complete sentence.

Teach readers to incorporate references to structure in their summaries.

You will also have many readers who are readily able to summarize a text with a main idea and supporting details, and for some readers, you will want to encourage them to keep in mind all that they already know to do, including reading for structure. Perhaps a reader is reading about the history of NASA and the space program. Channel that reader to use the words that align with the text's chronological structure, including *first*, *then*, *next*, *after that*, *finally*. In the same vein, if a reader is reading a book on maps and globes and recognizes a compare and contrast structure, remind that child to use the key phrases *on the one hand . . . on the other hand . . .* so that their summaries, too, mirror the structure of their text.

Push readers to identify multiple ideas across sections and pages of a text.

Some of your readers may already be finding the author's point—or the main ideas—and supporting them with several pieces of evidence from the text. They may also be making references to text structure, summarizing in ways that mirror that structure. Push these readers by teaching them that books and sections of books can hold not just one main idea, but several. For example, if a child is reading about how wolves are compared to dogs and lions, teach the reader that while you could write an overarching main idea that *wolves are similar and somewhat different from dogs as well as lions*, you could also tease each part out as separate main ideas: *wolves are similar to and yet different from dogs* and *wolves are just like but also very different from lions*, and then find details to support those.

MID-WORKSHOP TEACHING   Stop—and Summarize!

"Readers, eyes up for a moment. Since today is a summary boot camp, we should do more basic training in summary. I see that many of you have written down a summary as you've been reading. You might use that written summary as a reference, but for now, will you take a moment to orally summarize to your partner the current bit of text you are reading? Remember to teach the main idea and supporting details, and to keep out the details that aren't important to the summary. Take a minute to look over your text and get ready. I'll let you decide which partner will go first. Turn and summarize!"

Using the Learning Progression to Be Your Own Best Teacher

Teach students to self-assess their work against a learning progression.

"Someone once told me that a teacher's job is to teach you how *to learn*. That is, if I give you tools to teach yourself and show you how to use those tools, as you grow, you may be your own best teacher. Don't get me wrong! I'm not going anywhere, but I wanted to take a moment to share with you a self-assessment tool that I know you're familiar with." I handed out copies of the "Main Idea(s) and Supporting Details/ Summary" strand of the learning progression for third and fourth grade, and enlarged a copy using the document camera.

"Readers, it is important to be able to analyze your own reading skills, being able to talk and think well about what you are working on. Becoming more skilled as a reader requires that you have very clear goals and plans for reaching those goals.

"When you get the progression, read it over, mark it up, notice ways fourth grade is different from third grade. Take a moment to do that now." I leaned in and coached as kids immersed themselves in the document. "Readers, notice, too, the things you already do and the things you don't yet do.

"Turn and talk to your partner: what are some goals you can set for yourself with regard to determining importance in nonfiction reading?"

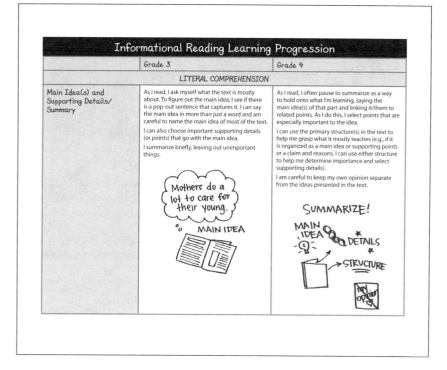

REFLECTING AND MAKING PLANS

Readers, for homework, tonight I am asking you to pause and think about your nonfiction reading work. You have spent more than a week reading nonfiction. Now is a good time to self-reflect. Ask yourself:

- What are things you now do to get ready to read a nonfiction text?

- When you finish reading, are you able to teach someone using an explaining voice, a teaching finger, gestures, intonation?

- What is and isn't working for you? What do you do well, and what are you working on that you could get better at?

Take a bit of time to write some answers to these questions. This writing doesn't have to be long, perhaps a half notebook page. Tomorrow we begin a new bend and we'll begin with these reflections in hand.

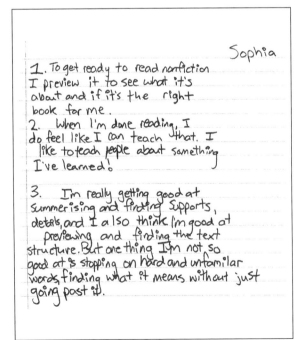

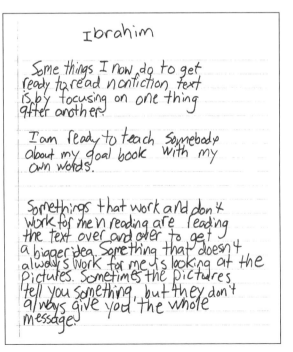

FIG. 7–6   Sophia and Ibrahim's self-reflections

Planning for a Research Project

IN THIS SESSION, you'll launch a whole-class investigation and will get students going in research teams. You'll teach that the first job of a research team is for its members to organize and plan for the journey ahead.

GETTING READY

✔ Create research teams of approximately four students each that will work together for the remainder of the unit. You may decide to place papers in your meeting area with the names of students on each research team so that students can be seated near team members (see Connection).

✔ Cue a few brief video clips of extreme weather and other natural disasters that you can stream from YouTube. Links are available on the online resources. (see Connection).

✔ Gather sets of materials for each research team. The sets should contain books, articles, links to videos, etc. on the team's topic. You should also prepare a set of materials for the class topic, we suggest droughts. A list of recommended materials can be found in the digital resources (see Teaching and Link).

✔ Keep chart paper and markers at hand (see Teaching and Link).

✔ Prepare a chart titled "To Research Well." This will become the anchor chart for the bend (see Active Engagement, Mid-Workshop Teaching, and Share).

✔ Display the "Researchers Take Notes that Follow the Structure of Their Texts" anchor chart from Grade 3, Unit 4 *Research Clubs* (see Share).

THIS SESSION launches the second bend of this unit and a whole-class investigation into different forms of extreme weather and related natural disasters. For reasons that will be clear at the start of Bend III, we suggest you divide the class into research teams that will study these six topics: hurricanes, tornadoes, earthquakes, tsunamis, droughts, floods.

This bend of the unit has not only become a favorite for kids; it's a favorite for teachers as well. On several occasions, teachers attending Teachers College Reading and Writing Project summer institute sections have learned about nonfiction reading by participating in their own version of this unit of study, and each time the teachers have come from this work in high spirits, tickled with the ways in which small groups can conduct parallel investigations of particular extreme weather events, and with the way the work across subtopics can combine and culminate in a deeper understanding of global weather issues. Teachers from our pilot classrooms reported that students' engagement and thinking were sky-high throughout the unit, as well.

Your students will be working in research teams that need to be constituted before today's session. Usually teachers decide to bring two reading partnerships together to form a team, and those teams may not be homogeneous. You'll want to provision each team with a small starter set of books, articles, and links to videos. We have provided many suggestions on the digital resources.

The investigations will be fast-paced—something that is especially important if you do not have a lot of books kids can read on weather. After approximately a week of studying one form of extreme weather, during which they will study several self-selected subtopics, students will teach another research team what they have learned, and then exchange topics. That is, in the third bend, students will be able to compare and contrast different extreme weather events.

Today you'll remind students that when launching a research project, it is helpful to overview resources to generate a list of some of the big subtopics that one expects to study. This need to overview is important at the threshold of a research project, and again once deeper in the research, when one is at the threshold of researching a subtopic, and you'll bring that point home to your young researchers today.

"This need to overview is important at the threshold of a research project, and again once deeper in the research, when one is at the threshold of researching a subtopic . . ."

Students will end up finding that whether they are studying hurricanes or tsunamis or earthquakes, there are some similar subtopics that will merit attention. Encourage your children to investigate those subtopics (the causes of the event, the effects of it, the human story, etc.) because in the end, this will help them think across topics and to derive some bigger, more abstract generalizations from their work. Before this session begins you need to organize your students into teams. You may group them and decide on their topics of study. However, if you want to give students some choice regarding their topics (assuming you have the supply of books to do so), then you might give them a list of topics they can study prior to today's session and ask them to list their top four choices. This gives you some wiggle room when forming research teams and ensures that students have books they can read (though groups are heterogeneous, we suggest that partnerships are not, and you'll still want to ensure that the books students are holding are accessible to them). If students list four choices, odds are you'll be able to give them something from their list.

Planning for a Research Project

CONNECTION

Channel readers to share the reflections they wrote last night for homework.

"Today we're going to launch a really important research project, so will you hurry to the meeting area?" The children came, noting a crude sort of a seating chart in the form of papers dispersed around the carpet, each containing four names, two partnerships on each.

"Readers, one way to start new work is to reflect back on old work. Will you take a moment to share your reflections from last night's homework, the ones where you looked at what has gone well and what goals you have set for yourself in your reading? Quickly turn and share," I said, and leaned into students' conversations. After a moment, I called the class back together.

Rally students to care about the topic you suggest they research for the upcoming bend by showing a few video clips that introduce the topic.

I leaned in close and said, "I have a big question for you. Will you think for a moment about the world events that have made the *biggest* difference in the lives of people over the last few years?"

I left a bit of think time, and meanwhile tried to imagine what they were probably thinking. War? Terrorist attacks? I was pretty sure their answers would not match mine. I gave students a minute to share their answers with their teams and then called for their attention.

"My answer to this question is this: few things have affected the lives of people across this globe more than extreme weather: hurricanes, droughts, tsunamis. I want to show you a few video clips and see if you don't agree that lives have literally been turned upside down."

For two minutes, I showed video footage from a few extreme weather events.

"You see what I mean about people's lives being literally turned upside down? Do you see why I'm thinking that extreme weather might be the most important topic we could study right now? If you are okay with the idea, I'm going to suggest we work in research teams to study hurricanes, tornadoes, tsunamis, droughts, earthquakes, floods, and other

This turn-and-talk is meant to give students a sense of voice as this new bend begins. Having an audience is an important part of keeping their thinking going, but you won't want to drag it on by allowing students to share their answers one-by-one. Instead, give them a quick second to share with their teams and then call them back together.

While piloting, those of us who are less technologically inclined tried to skip this step. The impact was felt immediately. There is nothing as powerful as seeing images of entire villages floating away on the waves of floodwaters, or of cars peeking out from ten-foot snow drifts. The weather videos we recommend will help ensure that you get complete buy-in from your students—and in this case, buy-in means not only excitement, but engagement in the sessions that follow.

There are a few reasons for the drumroll around drought. First, it is probably the most significant topic of the lot, but secondly, it may not initially draw kids in as quickly as the more action-packed topics.

kinds of extreme weather and related natural disasters. And because the crisis around access to water is *such* a huge concern, I am thinking we might study drought (which means a shortage of water) as a whole class."

Explain that the students will work in research teams, which, like a football team, is goal driven. The team's goal is to learn about a subtopic so as to teach it to others in a week's time.

"Each of you will be studying your own topics with your research teams. The goal will be to learn quickly, intensely, and deeply so that in little more than a week, you'll be ready to teach the rest of us about your extreme weather event (and other related natural disasters). In the end, the whole class will want to learn about all these kinds of extreme weather. After this week, you'll have a chance to swap topics so that by the end of this unit, each team will have studied two topics, and also learned about the others from one another."

"I know that when you think of teams, you probably think of football teams, soccer teams, or chess teams. The teams I'm suggesting will work in similar ways. You won't be working to move a ball down the field but you'll be working hard to develop some expertise on a topic. And like a football team, I'm expecting different group members will have different jobs, different roles."

❖ **Name the teaching point.**

"Today I want to teach you that when people are part of a team—and especially a team that has been given a problem to solve—<u>the first challenge is to decide who will do what, when, and how.</u> Although people think of rehearsal as something *writers* do to get ready for writing, rehearsal is actually something *readers* and *team members* do as well, as they figure out a plan for how to get a job done."

TEACHING

Ask students to work with you, imagining the ways you might acquire knowledge about a new topic and make an action plan.

"Imagine something with me: You are all grown up and you are heading to your first day of work at your new job. Depending on where you work, you might be told that your challenge is to work with a team to make sure the city's transportation system runs, or to make sure there are no power outages during the big storm that will hit your city in just a few days, or to find a cure for a serious disease like cancer or Ebola. To solve the problem you are given, you won't pick a book off the bookshelf and start reading page 1, about the topic. No—you'll need to talk to experts, to read lots of books, and conduct internet research to imagine all sorts of solutions and possibilities, and ultimately to decide on a way to fix the problem. Before you can do any of this, though, you'll need to make sure that each team member knows what, when, and how he or she will work to help get the job done.

Note that we deliberately use the term "research team" to differentiate this from a club. In a club, readers usually read the same texts and spend time discussing their shared reading. Members of a research team are more apt to divide and conquer as they work to become experts on a shared topic.

It may seem a distant reality, but in the blink of an eye, your students will be heading into the work-force, and their ability to work well in teams will be an important precursor to the kind of job they are able to acquire. The most important jobs in the world will be for people who are skilled at working in teams. You need to educate students for jobs that involve people going to work, Monday through Friday, to work with a few other people to figure out a problem. For instance, how to keep New York City from flooding during the next hurricane, or how to protect a website from outside attackers. Your students will be given problems to solve, challenges, and a team—and they'll have to figure out how to proceed.

"You won't have to solve the Ebola crisis during this unit, but you *will* be researching some pretty serious topics and will also be responsible for teaching others about them. And you need to do all this efficiently. To do this, you'll want to make a plan for how you will gather information and then what you will do with it.

"Let's roll up our sleeves and try to figure this out together using our class topic: drought. Will you watch as I rehearse for what I'll do as a researcher and reader, making a plan for how I'll learn more about droughts? I'm going to try to make something researchers call an 'action plan.' You can whisper to your partner about whatever you notice me doing, and after a bit I'll stop and we'll collect some notes."

Model getting a "lay of the land" on your topic, familiarizing yourself with the resources you have, and imagining the roles that various team members might take on.

I dug into the bin of materials I had collected on droughts. I picked up an accessible book and began skimming through the Table of Contents and the headings and subheadings. "This is a good overview book," I muttered, and read off chapter titles. "'What Is a Drought?' . . . 'Types of Drought' . . . 'Measuring Droughts' . . . I'm trying to figure out the big parts to the topic," I said. I put that book down and reached for an article called "Dry Times." "Hmm, . . . I'm noticing there is a lot on the causes of drought, and the ways of measuring to see how bad it is . . . What else? There seems to be a lot on drought prevention and safety too." I began a rough list on a sheet of chart paper:

Droughts
- Causes
- How they are measured
- Prevention and safety

"So I'm getting an idea of what we might study, but I also need to figure out what materials each person will read. I'm going to flag places that tell about the causes of drought, and maybe a person or two in our team could study up on that subtopic and teach the rest of us. And let me mark, also, the places that talk about ways to measure drought, because someone could study that subtopic, too. Then maybe a third person could study drought prevention and safety."

ACTIVE ENGAGEMENT

Channel students to function as researchers, naming what they saw you do so as to generate a list of steps for getting started on a research project, especially when working within a team.

I paused, and said, "Will you and your team members talk about what you have noticed me doing that you think you might do as well?" I gestured for students to turn and share and listened in as they did, jotting what I heard on a notepad.

When I called the students back together, I read from my notepad, sharing out the best of what I had heard. "Readers, researchers, you noticed quite a bit about the way I prepared to study droughts. Leo noticed that I began by flipping

You'll want to come to this lesson with a bin of materials that is similar to the starter kit you will give to each research team. You'll probably want to include two to three texts on the topic you are studying as a class. You'll want to survey your books and give the most accessible books and topics to your most struggling readers. You might also consider having students that struggle study the same topic as the class, using some of the same and some different materials. This will help them to build background knowledge on their topic and therefore allow them to more easily access texts. Then too, they'll have the opportunity to have many texts read aloud to them.

Note that these "big parts" of the topic are apt to be equally foundational to a study of tornadoes or tsunamis or any of the other extreme weather/natural disaster events. You deliberately would not mention some of the most obvious "big parts," or subtopics, such as effects and firsthand experiences, because you'll be leaving those for the kids to discover when they set to work. Know that "how the drought/hurricane/ etc. is measured" is less obvious than, say, the effects, and you want to leave this work, these subtopics for kids.

through some of my books and materials, getting to know them. He wondered if I was deciding which feel easiest so that I can read those books first. Very smart thinking!

"Colin and Anthony noticed that as I skimmed through my book and article, I noticed big subtopics that were being addressed (like the causes of droughts, and how to prevent them and stay safe during a drought). I even decided that these could be subtopics that people on my research team take on."

I revealed a chart that captured what the students found were the starting steps to a research project.

ANCHOR CHART

To Research Well . . .

- **Get ready**
  - **Get to know your resources**
  - **Sequence texts, easy → hard**
  - **Figure out the main subtopics, categories, and questions**
  - **Plan for team research roles**

LINK

Give students an opportunity to begin the same process with their basket of resources and research teams.

"As soon as I pass you your bin of resources—just a starter collection—you can get started. Check out the topic I chose for you—I am 99% sure you will end up loving it, but if you don't and want to talk about it, you can do so *after* you spend at least today studying it. I had you sit in your teams today because I wanted to give you a chance to make the action plan for your research. Right now, while you are still in the meeting area, decide who will research which subtopic (in ones or twos) and where that person will go to learn. I'll give each team a sheet of chart paper and some markers to use to record your research plan."

As research teams dug into their bins, I interjected: "As you look through your resources, remember to look for easier overview texts first, and to try to get a quick sense of the big parts, the big subtopics, that will be important to learn about."

I listened as Izzy, a member of the earthquakes group, found a chapter called "Quakes to Remember" and started to add that to her group's list of subtopics. I coached her to keep those subtopics general, and soon she'd crossed that out and instead added "Important Events" to her group's list of subtopics. Izzy also found a chapter that she called stories of survival. "Like here," and she said, pointing to a specific page. "It says 'I Was There!' That means there is going to be a story about a person who was at this earthquake in Haiti."

I moved on to a second group and found myself listening to a similar conversation. Standing in a central place, I asked for children's attention. "Researchers! Something really interesting is happening. Since I am the only person who is traveling among your groups and listening in on your conversations, I want to tell you what I'm hearing. The subtopics that are important to a drought are turning out to be important subtopics for pretty much *any* extreme weather event." I used a sentence strip to cover up the word "droughts," replacing it with "Extreme Weather and Natural Disasters," to show that the chart encompassed all the research topics in the class.

"I saw that a bunch of you have added 'effects' and also 'personal stories.' What other general subtopics are teams coming up with that could work for any kind of extreme weather and natural disasters?" Soon we had compiled a list of subtopics that are important to earthquakes, floods, droughts, hurricanes, tornadoes, and so forth. Each group, of course, knew it could also develop its own categories.

~~Droughts~~

Extreme Weather and Natural Disasters
- Causes
- How they are measured
- Prevention and safety
- **Important events**
- **Effects**
- **Firsthand experiences**

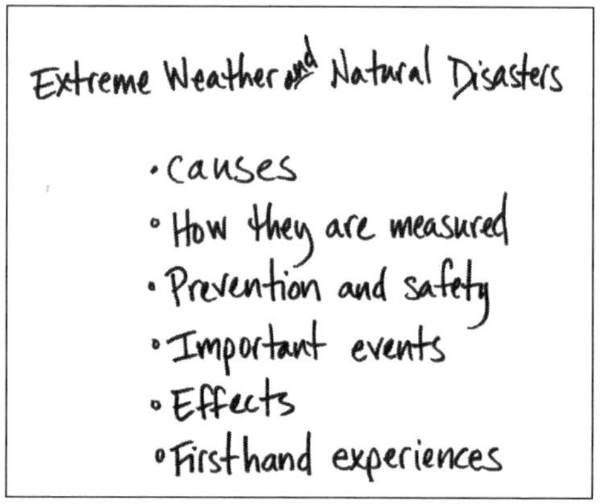

After a bit, I said, "Teams, you have just two more minutes before it is time to read. For now, make sure you have given yourselves assignments. Will you work in teams or alone? If you are going to each tackle one subtopic, who is going to focus on which subtopic first? In a day or two, then, you might swap subtopics. Get started!"

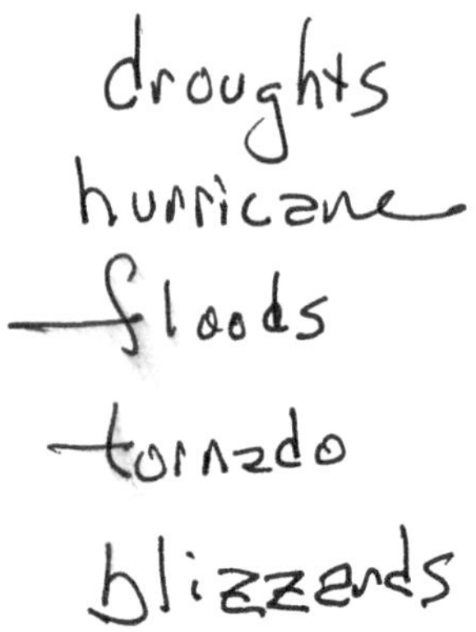

droughts
hurricane
~~floods~~
~~tornado~~
blizzards

You won't be surprised to hear that although I suggest it is odd that the list of subtopics pertaining to drought also works as subtopics for other groups, that actually has been part of the plan all along. The consistent subtopics will make it easier for kids to do some cross-topic compare-and-contrast work later on.

Extreme Weather and Natural Disasters
- Causes
- How they are measured
- Prevention and safety
- Important events
- Effects
- Firsthand experiences

Supporting Critically Important Work, Reading with Awareness of Text Structures

YOU'LL WANT TO GO INTO TODAY'S WORKSHOP with a clear picture in mind of the sort of work your students will be doing. Chances are good that at the end of the minilesson most research teams stayed together for a bit, rummaging through bins of resources, and scanning those resources. Before long, the teams will each have a revised version of your list of subtopics, and they'll begin making a plan for who will read what. Given that the research teams are heterogeneous, it's likely that one partnership will not be able to read all the books in the bin, so you probably will want to subtly steer some of the partnerships containing less proficient readers toward subtopics that are featured in many online links to videos and in more accessible books.

In any case, after about five more minutes for planning, it will be time for every team member to settle down and begin reading to learn about his or her assigned subtopic. Some children will be doing this reading in a partnership, and it may be that one partner literally reads to the other. In any case, as kids settle in to read, you will have just a small window of time in which to make sure that your students draw on all they learned in the first bend about overviewing a text before launching into reading it, while also keeping the larger subtopics and text structures in mind as they read. Research not only *whether* but also *how* kids preview texts. It will help if you carry with you an internalized continuum of proficiency in this skill, or even a physical copy of the "Orienting" strand of the Informational Reading Learning Progression.

I did this work with Alyssa, who was reading the back blurb of a book titled *Tsunamis*. When I asked her what she thought the book was going to teach her, she said, "Hmm, . . . I think this book will teach me about tsunamis." I knew Alyssa would benefit from learning how to generate more specific expectations. I complimented her on her use of the front and back cover to help her preview, and then I shifted into teaching mode. "If the text contains a Table of Contents, you can be even more specific when you preview and say 'I think this book will first tell about . . . and there will also be a part about . . .'" We then tried it together.

Alyssa opened her book to the Table of Contents and began. "I think the book will first tell about what tsunamis are, and then there will be a part about how they happen, which is what I'm studying." I left Alyssa a cue card with some prompts that remind her to think, "In specific, I think it'll say . . . Then it will also tell about . . ." I knew that sort of orientation to the text would help her read with big mental containers.

It is essential that you help students refrain from inching through a text, recording each factoid in ways that make it hard for them to think about the big ideas the text is conveying (and *then* about the specific examples of those big ideas). If students are conscious of organizational structures in the texts they read, noting the words that signal those structures, this can help them keep the big picture of a subtopic and a text in mind. The easiest structure to discern is that of main ideas and supporting details. One peek at their notes will give you all the data you need. Are they organizing their notes by structure (whether it is the structure of the text or the category of research they are doing)? Or are they simply filling a page with fact upon fact? It is certain that you'll find that some readers need help recognizing the author's points, or main ideas.

Help students move from collecting facts to organizing information into the author's points—the main ideas and supporting details.

In some instances, especially with some of your struggling readers, you may find that the work you need to do is pretty foundational. For example, we all know the student who reads and reads, only to conclude that the entire section he or she has just read was about one, very cool fact. Then there is the factoid collector. His or her notebook will be filled with facts from the text, often copied verbatim. Often these students spend more time writing than reading, and feel their job as a nonfiction reader is to collect all that they learn in writing.

In either instance, you'll want to help these students step back from a text, identify the main idea of a section, and collect corresponding details. It often helps to start this work by asking students to attend to text features. "Let's look at the pictures and the

Readers Take Stock of Their Reading Behaviors

"Researchers, will you pause to take stock? What I mean by this is: will you assess your overall reading situation right now? You have learned a lot about how to approach a research project, and the one thing you have definitely been taught is that you *don't* just open up one book and read, read, read. You first do some orienting, you figure out the big subtopics, categories, questions.

"So—you just started researching your own particular corner of your topic. Will you think for a moment about whether you are approaching your particular subtopic (say, the effects of the drought, the science of a tornado) in the way you have learned to approach a research topic? Think about how we approached the more general topic of weather." I gestured to our chart.

ANCHOR CHART

To Research Well . . .

- Get ready
  - Get to know your resources
  - Sequence texts, easy → hard
  - Figure out the main subtopics, categories, and questions
  - Plan for team research roles

Gesturing to the final bullet, I acknowledged, "Okay, so when you're planning your own work, you don't plan for *other people's* research roles unless there are two of you on a subtopic, but you *do* make an action plan for yourself. What will you read first, and how will you read it? Have you been following this chart or have you already (within fifteen minutes!) forgotten everything I taught you? If so, correct your ways quickly before I see and worry that my teaching isn't working!"

headings," you might say. "Does this give you any clues about what this section might be about?" Of course, depending on the level of the text a student is reading, the features may or may not be supportive. From there, you might teach students to attend to the topic sentences at the beginning and end of sections of texts, checking to see if the author sums up what the section is about. Looking for repeating words or phrases can also be helpful. Seymour Simon, for instance, who is famous for his enthralling text and gorgeous photographs, does not use headings or chapter titles in most of his books. It is up to the reader to ask: "What is this page about?" While Seymour Simon does not use headings, he *does* give many other clues as to the main idea of each section. In his book about lightning, for instance, he writes about the different kinds of lightning. He begins one particular page with the sentence: "There are three main kinds of lightning." Then, throughout the text, he repeats the word "kind." When writing about cloud-to-ground lightning, he writes: "It is the kind we know most about . . ." "The third kind . . ." the next sentence begins. When a reader reads attuned to repeating words and topic sentences, one can discern that this page is about the different *kinds* of lightning.

Still, there are students who will argue that this section of text is about how lightning "leaps across a gap of clear air between two different clouds" or other cool facts. For those students, testing potential main ideas is often helpful. In order for something to be a main idea, there must be several corresponding details that relate to it. "Can you find two or three more details about how lightning jumps from cloud to cloud?" you might ask. (They won't be able to.) "When something turns out to be a detail, not a main idea, we try again," you'll suggest. Harken students back to any of the strategies above and try again, testing the proposed main idea by checking to see if it has corresponding details. Many teachers find it helpful to remind students to make a "small" sign by holding their thumb and forefinger half an inch apart for details, and a "big" sign by stretching their arms apart for when they find a main idea.

Rereading and Revising Notes so They Match Text Structure

Channel research teams to reread their notes through the lens of text structure.

"Researchers, I know you are dying to meet with your research team and start teaching each other what you have learned, but I'm going to ask you to do one more day of reading and research before you bring what each of you has learned to the entire team. And for now, I need to teach you something super important, so will you come to the meeting area with the text you're reading and your reader's notebook?"

Once the kids had gathered, I said, "Earlier today I asked if you had remembered to orient yourself to your topic and your materials before diving in, to read a more accessible text first, and so forth. You'll remember watching that video a week or so ago about the oryx, a threatened species that is being saved by the Phoenix Zoo. Remember that we found the video was organized into a problem-and-solution structure? (The problem was the animals are nearly becoming extinct, the solution is that the zoo is trying to save them.) The point of that work we did together, you'll recall, was that it can help to think about how a text is structured, as you read. What structures do you remember?"

The kids called off various kinds of structures and referenced the "Common Nonfiction Text Structures" chart that listed signal words that cued them in to the presence of one text structure or another. I nodded. "And you recall my suggestion that it often helps to take notes on nonfiction reading that echo the text structure of the texts you are reading, right?" Kids nodded.

"I'm glad you remember that instruction because my goal in teaching is always to teach stuff you will use for life. So now my question is this: will you look back at the text you have been reading, and think about how that whole text is structured? Then will you look at your notes, and think about how your notes are structured? In a few minutes, you'll talk to someone from your research team about that."

After just a few moments I asked children to talk. Many agreed that their notes weren't actually structured at all. "If your notes aren't structured, go back and reread them. Star the parts that should be in capitals, and find a way to link things that should go together. While you do that, I'm going to add on to our anchor chart."

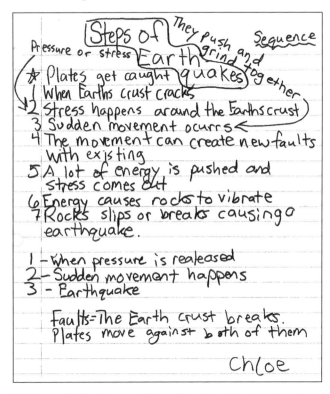

FIG. 8–2   Notice the way Chloe attends to the text structure in her notes

Researchers Take Notes that Follow the Structure of Their Texts

BOXES AND BULLETS

Main Idea or Subtopic

- Supporting detail
- Supporting detail
- Add more bullet points if your text includes them

SEQUENTIAL

Main Idea or Subtopic

1. First thing that happens
2. Second thing that happens
3. Add more steps if your text includes them

COMPARE AND CONTRAST

Similarities between two things

- First similarity
- Second similarity
- Add more similarities if your text includes them

Differences between two things

- First difference
- Second difference
- Add more differences if your text includes them

CAUSE AND EFFECT

| An action that happens first; the reason something else happens | → | What happens as a result; the consequence of the first action |

Detail about the action; add more details if your text includes them

One result of the action; add more results of the action if your text includes them

PROBLEM AND SOLUTION

| A problem | → | A solution to the problem |

- Detail about the problem
- Detail about the problem
- Add more details if your text includes them

- Detail about the solution
- Detail about the solution
- Add more details if your text includes them

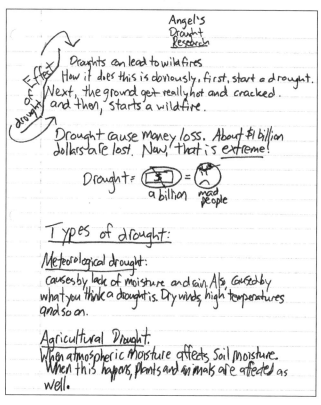

FIG. 8–3 Angel's notes show multiple text structures: effects of droughts and types of droughts

GATHERING MATERIALS TO SUPPORT RESEARCH PROJECTS

Readers, for homework, begin to collect information and materials to support this research project. You might find materials for your own team, or you might find materials that support other teams, but either way, your help is important. This effort may take more than just this evening, but get started doing this.

If any of you want me to set you up to work at our school library before school starts tomorrow morning or during recess tomorrow, I can do that.

Here are a few suggestions for gathering materials:

- Ask an adult if they will take you to the public library, our school library, or a bookstore to get a book or two on your topic.
- Conduct Internet research using a kid-friendly search engine like awesomelibrary.org, kids.gov, or americaslibrary.gov.
- Be on the lookout for articles that have to do with your topic. Ask adults to help you look through magazines and newspapers.
- Check out kids' magazines like *Time for Kids*, *Scholastic*, *National Geographic*, and others. Most of these magazines also have websites.
- Look at any newspaper and you will find a section on the weather. You may even find articles that relate to weather events around the world.

Then, of course, begin learning from that material or from whatever you brought home from school. As you learn, remember to orient yourself to a text, to think about what the big parts of the topic seem to be, and to take notes that show you are working with some awareness of text structure. As you start to take notes from a variety of books and articles, it's important that you keep track of which source your notes are coming from. As you gather more information, you may find that some of the information conflicts, or builds on another bit of information, and you may want to cross-check your sources. When you are taking notes, be sure to jot down which source you are getting your information from. The title and author will do.

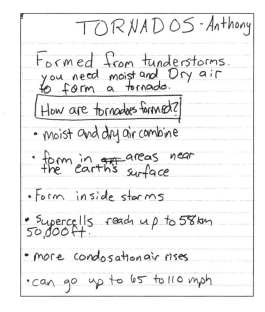

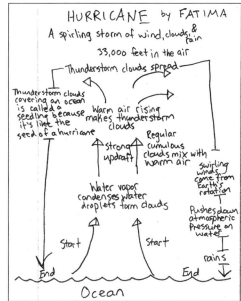

FIG. 8–4 Anthony and Fatima's notes demonstrate the way students should make decisions about the format of their notes.

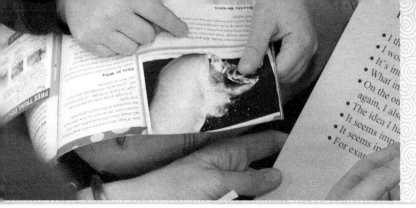

Synthesis

IN THIS SESSION, you'll remind students that as researchers read multiple texts on a subtopic, they read the second (and third, and so on) texts differently than the first. They read subsequent texts asking, "Does this add to what I've already learned? Change what I learned?"

GETTING READY

✔ Ask students to come to the minilesson with any resources that they gathered for the previous night's homework.

✔ List of Extreme Weather and Natural Disasters subtopics that was created in Session 8 (see Teaching and Active Engagement).

✔ Cue the video "Droughts 101" (see Teaching).

✔ Gather white boards and markers, one for each research team (see Teaching and Active Engagement).

✔ Keep chart paper and markers at hand (see Teaching and Active Engagement).

✔ Provide copies of the transcript of "Droughts 101," one for each research team. The transcript can be found on the online resources (see Teaching and Active Engagement).

✔ Locate a second resource for information on your subtopic. We chose a passage from *The Big Thirst* by Charles Fishman (see Teaching and Active Engagement).

✔ Prepare to display "To Research Well" anchor chart (see Link).

✔ List several transitional phrases on a sheet of chart paper that students can use to show they are citing information directly from a resource. You will also want to distribute individual copies of the "Transitions: From Main Ideas to Citing a Text" chart to students (see Share).

✔ Before tomorrow's lesson, you will want to have read one of the two articles you could choose to use in the inquiry. Links to these articles can be found on the online resources.

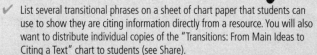

YOUR STUDENTS have prior experience with synthesis, and you will want to draw on and make explicit connections to this learning as you support your researchers across Bend II. The first third-grade unit that supported reading nonfiction, *Reading to Learn*, helped students to not just think about the part of the text they were reading in the moment, but also how that part of the text fits into the context of the entire text. They worked first to fit parts of a text together. In the second third-grade nonfiction unit, *Research Clubs*, students worked to synthesize across texts, as well.

Today you will teach them that after they have read an initial text on a subtopic, they can read two subsequent texts on the same subtopic and they will come to those subsequent texts differently because of their earlier readings. Across the lesson, you will support students in considering how the new text they are reading adds to or changes what they already learned, and you will demonstrate for students how to revise their writing about reading to incorporate their new learning. Today's world-class standards ask fourth-graders to "integrate information from two texts on the same topic in order to write or speak about the subject knowledgeably," and this lesson supports students in meeting that challenge.

You may worry that this lesson occurs too early into the second bend of this unit, with students only two days into researching their topics, having studied only a small number of texts. Perhaps you are concerned that students will not have read enough or know enough to engage in this complex work. Be assured that teachers who piloted this unit felt strongly, and we certainly agree, that starting synthesis early helps develop the expectation that anytime researchers pick up a second (or third, or fourth) text on a topic, they read that text differently because of their experience reading the first text. The texts your students are reading are dense and filled with information, and later in the unit, your students' brains will be overflowing with information. We think it is helpful to equip them now with the tools to determine how the new information they are reading links to what they already know.

Know that in classrooms that piloted this work, the synthesis work that students engaged in today took on a variety of forms. It is likely that some students will be synthesizing within a text, noticing when the part of the text they just read fits with something they encountered earlier in the same text, and thinking about how those parts could fit together. With your support, other students will read the sections from several texts that address a particular subtopic and they will be synthesizing across those related passages, noticing how the second text on their subtopic adds to or changes what they learned earlier. Students, too, can develop their synthesis skills through conversation, as they discuss the various sources that different researchers encountered on a topic, considering how those sources fit together. Celebrate (and note) the multiple entry points your students will have to this work. The Informational Reading Learning Progression will be useful to you and your students as a means of assessment and determining the next steps.

Consider how you can use some of your read-aloud time to support and extend synthesis work for your students. Up to this point, you may have been reading through sections of texts and talking about what authors taught in isolation. Start looking at ways to bring cross-text work into your read-aloud, so students have regular opportunities to synthesize information across subtopics in a text. You might read aloud a part in *Everything Weather* by Kathy Furgang, ask students to turn and talk and recall parts where the same subtopic was addressed within another text, and then reread the part students identify, helping the class to consider how the information in two parts of the text fits together. With this new information in mind, support students in returning to the shared class notes you have been taking during read-aloud, and model how you revise with the new information you learned in mind. Be sure during your synthesis work you are alert for times when the text changes what you learned, as the work of letting go of earlier ideas tends to be particularly difficult for students.

Synthesis

CONNECTION

Invite students to share the resources they brought from home and to begin thinking about which team member will read which of those resources today.

"Readers, as you come to the meeting area, will you bring any new sources of information that you found last night that you can add to your team's bin (or to another team's bin)? Take a second to show each other what you found and to think about which team member might want to read what materials first." As students shuffled through the materials, I moved among them, exclaiming with excitement over the new resources. I posed questions: "Which of these materials do you think will be especially relevant to your research? What parts of this do you think you'll study?"

Remind readers of the synthesizing work they did last year, and explain to them they will be doing it again with a new layer of complexity.

"Researchers, let me bring your minds back here for a bit. Let me ask a question that may seem off-topic, but that actually isn't. How many of you, when you were younger, studied animals? Maybe one group in your class studied the elephant and another group, the shark, and other groups studied other animals. How many of you did that?" Lots of thumbs went up.

"For those of you who did that research, am I right that you learned you could take one subtopic—like elephant babies—and read a section about elephant babies in one book, and then read about elephant babies in another book, and then take what you learned from one book (and I spread out one hand) and what you learned from another book (and I spread out another hand) and bring that information together (and I clasped my hands)?" Many kids started talking at once as they recollected the work they'd done studying animals.

Quieting them for a second, I said, "I gather you have a lot to say about that research! Right now, all those who studied that sort of synthesis last year—will you tell people around you what you learned that might be relevant to the research you'll be doing now as you each develop expertise on another topic—like, say, on early warning signals for earthquakes or on whatever else it is you are studying?"

The room erupted into conversation, as children talked to each other about how they could work across texts on their new subtopics.

You are not only following up on the home-work—reminding kids that you expect them to do it—but you are communicating a shared ownership of this endeavor. Then, too, you are highlighting one of the ways in which this year's research project is more challenging than last year's. When students were third-graders, the materials were handed to them. It is important to teach youngsters to search for resources and to examine them for relevance.

If you know your students did—or did not—experience the third-grade curriculum, you can adjust your wording accordingly. Although third-grade teachers will think of that as a unit on synthesis, your kids will remember it as a unit on animals. When possible, it is always a good thing to help students understand that their fourth-grade studies all build upon what they learned in previous years.

⚜️ **Name the teaching point.**

"Today I want to remind you that when a researcher reads many texts about a subtopic, the researcher must read the second (and third) texts differently than the first. The researcher keeps notes and information from the first text in mind and reads the second text, asking, 'Does this add to what I've already learned? Change what I learned?' The new text gets filed into mental files (or notes) from the first text."

TEACHING AND ACTIVE ENGAGEMENT

Show how to synthesize two texts on the same topic. For the first text, show a snippet of video, asking students to cull out the portions relevant to the topic of causes of drought. Do this twice.

"You'll remember that we've looked over our sources enough to have a flash-draft plan for some of the big subtopics we expect we'll learn about in our research." I referred to the list of subtopics we had made the day before.

Droughts

- Causes
- How they are measured
- Prevention and safety
- Important events
- Effects
- Firsthand experiences

"We *could* just read stuff and get more information on each of these subtopics (and in a way, anything we read on drought will probably teach these), but remember that when studying animals, we zoomed in on just one of the sub-topics (like the animal's young) and read about that subtopic across several texts. Let's do that again, this time with a subtopic related to our class topic of drought.

"Are you okay researching *causes* of drought first, as that logically seems like it comes early in a study? We're going to need to read and take notes on one text, then go to the next text and read it asking, 'Does this add to what we've already learned? Change what we learned?'"

Ask students to watch a snippet of video through the lens of causes of drought. Play the clip twice, the second time alongside a transcript, channeling kids to jot notes while you jot as well.

"To get the hang of this, we'll study just tiny texts, though when you go off today to do your research, the texts you study won't be so tiny. Let's first watch just two minutes of a National Geographic video on drought. This video clip is not specifically on the *causes* of drought, the subtopic we are thinking about right now, but instead it is all about drought. So as we watch we'll need to cull out information that helps us understand the causes of drought. Let's just listen for as long as 'the causes' is the focus. Don't worry about taking notes yet. Just watch and listen, I'll play it a

If it is technically hard for you to show a video during the minilesson, you could choose instead to display the transcript of the video for students and read it aloud, which could be one of the two texts in your text set.

second time for note-taking." I played the first one and a half minutes of the video—the portion of it that focuses on causes of drought.

We watched it once, then I addressed the class. "We'll watch it again, and this time, work with your research team to take notes. You might want to designate one person to take notes on a white board, while the others help out, or perhaps you will all take notes in your notebooks. Don't forget to jot down the source of your notes. Something like 'Nat Geo drought video' would be sufficient. In case it helps, I'll give one member of each research team the transcript for the first part of this video. Everyone ready? Let's watch this again and this time, be ready to capture notes."

Transcript of 1:30 of "Droughts 101"

Its signs are subtle and slow. The earth dries, water levels fall, the rains do not come, and the land is ripped by drought. At its most basic, a drought occurs when more water is used than is replenished. It is a balance between supply and demand with both natural and human factors in play.

The weather is constantly in flux. A low-pressure system allows moist air to rise, cool, and form rain clouds. A high-pressure system traps the air beneath it and banishes the clouds. Droughts form when changing wind patterns cause high-pressure systems to last for months, or even years.

Aggravating the problem is society's demand for water. Farms are heavily dependent on water to irrigate crops and provide pasture for livestock. Urban areas also place huge demands on available water supplies.

If the demand can't be reduced, the drought begins to take its toll.

As the children took notes, I did as well, recording them on a sheet of chart paper while students did the same. I left lots of white space throughout for notes that I planned to later bring in from a second or third source. My notes, once the video had been played twice, looked like this.

> Drought causes—more H$_2$O used—more demand than supply. Human and natural causes.

- Weather—high-pressure systems.
- Farms use a lot of H$_2$O (crops).
- Cities use a lot of H$_2$O.

So: If demand can't be reduced . . . result is drought (and then . . . see effects!).

The transcript of this portion of the video can be found on the online resources. If you don't have the ability to show the video, you can distribute the transcript instead, and even if you do have a way to show the video, you may want to give students the transcript for additional support.

We suggest you take notes in a format we refer to as boxes and bullets, jotting down the author's points and main ideas in a box and recording the supporting details as bullets underneath.

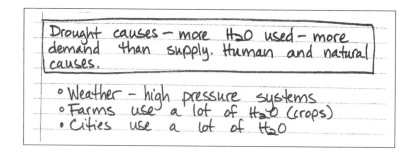

Read an excerpt from a second text on the same subtopic.

"Now let's read a second text and again, we'll read this, noticing especially the parts of it that have something to do with our subtopic, the causes of drought. I'll read a bit and then pause, so we can summarize this new text, and then figure out how it fits with what we've already learned on the topic. Remember, when researchers approach a second (or third!) source, they always ask themselves 'Does this add to what I've already learned? Change what I learned?' Keep these questions in mind as I read to you from our second source. Then we'll go back to my notes and add to those together." I opened the book *The Big Thirst* by Charles Fishman, projected it on the document camera, and began to read.

The Big Thirst: The Secret Life and Turbulent Future of Water

by Charles Fishman

We live very wet lives but we have no idea just how wet. The effortless way we have come to manage water is a testament to both water's moment-to-moment utility and to our own ingenuity. But unlike the time we spend at the gas pump—where we can see the gallons as they are pumped, and the instant impact on our credit card—the way we handle water use insulates us not just from the wonders of water, but from any sense of how much water daily life requires, or the work and expense required to deliver that water.

. . . The bad news is that the invisibility of water in our lives isn't good for us, and isn't good for water. You can't appreciate what you don't understand. You don't value and protect what you don't know is there.

Back in 1999, a team of researchers recorded . . . every water event in each of 1,188 homes for four weeks . . . The study's overall conclusion can be summed in four words: We like to flush.

For Americans, flushing the toilet is the main way we use water. We use more water flushing toilets than bathing or cooking or washing our hands, our dishes, or our clothes.

Pause to summarize with the students what you just read.

"Readers, that's already a lot to think about. Let's summarize what this book is saying, and remember, you have to use your own words to do so. Take a minute to come up with a summary, and then we'll come back together." I gave the students a moment, then called the group together and asked for a volunteer to share their summary with the group. "Jack, can you tell us what you and your team came up with?"

Remember, as you read this or any text aloud, you want to be sure that you demonstrate fluent reading for your students. This means using your voice to add meaning, emphasize points, and link information and ideas.

Jack began. "Well, we thought the author's main point is that water is everywhere but we don't really notice it. We notice how much we use gas because we pay for it at the gas pump but when water is free to us, like when we flush the toilet, we don't have any idea how much it costs or how important it is."

I turned to the class. "Is this along the lines of what the rest of you were thinking?" Heads nodded; murmurs of, "Yeah, we thought so, too," rippled throughout the group.

Channel partnerships to discuss how the information in this text adds to or changes what they have already learned.

"We don't need to read much before we pause to think, 'Does this add to what I've already learned? Change what I learned?' What do you think?" I gave students a minute to think and then said, "Turn and discuss."

I knelt down next to Madison and Taylor. "It's sort of both. It sort of goes with what we've learned about people causing drought," Madison started. "Like the video talked about farms and cities using so much water. This kind of adds to that idea and maybe changes it a little."

Taylor jumped in. "Yeah, like people might be using so much water not because they are greedy but because they have no idea how much it costs. So they just use, and maybe waste, a ton."

"Great point! Let's add that to our chart."

> Drought causes—more H$_2$O used—more demand than supply. Human and natural causes.

- Weather—high-pressure systems.
- Farms use a lot of H$_2$O (crops).
- Cities use a lot of H$_2$O.
- <u>Water seems free so people use a lot and waste.</u>

Pause students after a few minutes of talk. Model revising notes on the subtopic based on the new information.

"Readers, I heard many of you talking about how water seems free to people and that leads to waste, so I added this to our chart. Now, will you listen to what Chloe noticed as she was synthesizing across subtopics? While she talks, I'm going to add the new information she found to our class notes." I gestured to Chloe to begin.

As in any active engagement, you'll need to keep the pace of the lesson going, while also assessing and coaching students. Be sure not to spend too much time with one group of students—move from group to group.

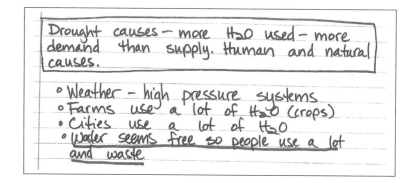

"Well, the article said people aren't wasting water the way we would have expected, like filling pools or taking lots of showers and baths," Chloe explained. "Instead, we're using water and wasting water by flushing the toilet. Which is sort of different than the National Geographic video. I mean, both sources said that people are contributing to drought. But the video showed a hotel pool, with a waterfall. Sort of made you feel like people are wasting water on silly things, things for entertainment and having a good time. But really, most of the water use comes from flushing the toilet!" Soon our class notes looked like this.

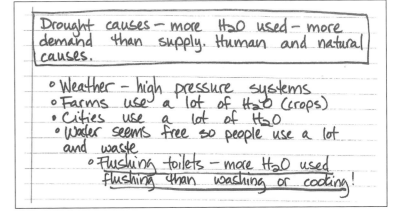

Drought causes—more H_2O used—more demand than supply. Human and natural causes.

- Weather—high-pressure systems.
- Farms use a lot of H_2O (crops).
- Cities use a lot of H_2O.
- Water seems free people use a lot and waste.
- Flushing toilets—more H_2O used flushing than washing or cooking!

LINK

Recap the work you've done together, providing concrete examples of synthesis. Set students up to continue their team research.

"Readers, do you see how using both the video and the Fishman text contributed to our growing understandings of the causes of droughts? The video gave us a broader sense of the causes. And the text focused in on one of those bullets, human causes of drought. So the second source deepened our understanding of one of the bullet points. Do you see how this synthesis work can help you think across texts? I'm hoping you take some time to do it in your own research team topic, today. I'm going to add this synthesis work to our anchor chart, as to research well, it's important that we do this."

To Research Well . . .

- Get ready
  - Get to know your resources
  - Sequence texts, easy → hard
  - Figure out the main subtopics, categories, and questions
  - Plan for team research roles
- Take organized, structured notes
- **Synthesize what you are learning across texts**

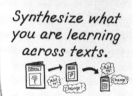

Synthesize what you are learning across texts.

"So researchers, take a minute to caucus with your research team to revise your action plan. Will you each continue studying the subtopic you took on yesterday? If so, chances are you'll be moving to another source on that same topic, and today's minilesson will be relevant to you. Some of you may find it helpful to stick with the one text you've been reading a bit longer. Some of you may decide your subtopic doesn't require another day of study and you may want to assign yourself a second subtopic. You have three minutes to plan all that out, knowing that at the end of today, members of your research team need to be ready to teach one another."

Although you hand over the reins to each research team to choose its own action plans, know that as students work and you confer today, you may need to steer clubs toward alternate plans. This would certainly be the case if the plan a group chooses doesn't set individual members up either for deep engagement with a subtopic, or for reading across enough subtopics.

Transition Students from Planning to Previewing to Getting to Work

AS ALWAYS, you'll need your own action plan to use every minute wisely. The first thing you'll do will be to listen in to research teams as they make their plans. Notice if the tendency on some teams is to race around from one subtopic to the next, scooping up just the surface layer of information on each topic. If you see that, you might encourage readers to slow down and work more zealously to develop more depth on one subtopic. You might remind students that after all, part of the reason to do this research is so they become more skilled as readers of nonfiction texts, and if they just race from one subtopic to another, skimming off the obvious facts, they won't be giving themselves chances to do new and higher-level work. Having said that, there will be some kids who got started in the previous session on a research tangent that isn't going to bear fruit for them, and it is also important to help those kids make the early adjustments so their work pays off. They may need to come up with bigger subtopics, or make a new plan to switch subtopics sooner rather than later.

After a few minutes, use a voiceover to remind kids that they need to shift from talking and planning to reading. You'll probably find that most kids are continuing to read their first resource. This material is dense and children will tend to read around their focal topic rather than homing in on it (which makes sense), so many of them won't be reading a second source at the start of today. That's just as well because children will need help gleaning well-organized summary notes from their reading. As they work, voice over. "Remember to stop in certain places, maybe at the end of a section or page, to take notes. That works better than reading three lines and then recording information, then reading a few more lines and stopping again." You might also say, "I love the way you are asking yourself, 'What will this *mostly* be about?' It really works to take notes that are sort of boxes and bullets. You'll get the specifics down, the facts, but they'll be tucked under umbrella ideas."

When students do begin a second text on their subtopic, this will be a time to remind them to preview the text. They'll need to preview it first to identify the portion of it that is relevant to their topic, so you may need to teach skimming. Once they locate that part of the text, you'll want to remind them to preview it to notice the big things it

MID-WORKSHOP TEACHING
Synthesizing Contradictory Information across Texts

"Readers, eyes up here. You know that one way researchers synthesize information across texts is by reading a new text differently than they read a first text on their subtopic, and asking themselves, 'Does this add to what I've already learned? Change what I learned?' Then, they revise their notes to reflect their new learning. Right now, wherever you are around the room, scan your notes looking for one place where you tried this work." I gave students a minute to scan. "When you turn to your partner, say, 'This text added to . . .' if the text added to what you already knew, and say, 'This text changed . . .' if the text changed your thinking. Quickly share!" I knelt down and listened in. Predictably, conversations began with 'This text added . . . ,' and I heard few students acknowledging and synthesizing contradictory information.

"Thumbs up if you started with 'This text added to . . .' It is certainly powerful work for researchers to read new texts and notice ways they add to texts that were read earlier. I'm delighted to hear you're doing this work already. I'm thinking, though, that now that you're in fourth grade, you're ready to take on that second question: 'Does this change what I learned?' By that I mean you will need to read thinking not just what fits together, but what contradicts. Sometimes the contradictions might feel huge, like if two articles report different numbers of people who died from natural disasters, but others will feel smaller and subtler. When you encounter these, you have to pause and think, 'How does this new text change what I learned?' To do this, you'll sometimes have to turn to a third text to check and see what information is correct.

"Do any of you already have a place in mind where you could try this work? Great! Keep reading and synthesizing, thinking not just 'Does this add to what I've already learned?' but also, 'Does this change what I learned?'"

seems to teach. Coach them to look at headings, topic sentences, and to say, "I think this upcoming part seems to be mostly about . . ." and tell them that as they keep reading, they should be adding on to that thinking. "It looks like this text is mostly about . . . It seems to start with . . . , and then I think it . . . and later, it . . ."

Remember there will be instances when the titles and subtitles do not explicitly tell readers what the text will be about. Instead of "Causes of Hurricanes" the title might be more artsy: "Sounds from Afar" or "Red Flag Alert!" Show children that in those instances, they may need to conjecture a few possibilities, using words such as, "Perhaps it will be about . . ." Remind students that when they take guesses, they need to be ready to revise. That is, if the section turns out to be about something different than what a student expected, you'll want to ensure that the student has an "Ahah, I need to change my idea!" moment.

Focus in on students synthesizing within and across texts.

Finally, you'll want to help students with synthesis work. If two children are working together—be glad! It will help if one child reads the new text aloud, and then they pause after chunks of reading to talk about how the new text connects to the old text, and to insert new notes into the original set of notes.

If children are reading aloud to each other, you may need to coach them to read in ways that make it easy to listen. For example, when I observed Sophia reading *Twisters* to her partner in a monotone fashion, I told her, "You are reading all the words correctly, without a stumble, but your partner and I are having a hard time figuring out the important information. I'm wondering whether you might have missed the importance of that passage while you read it out loud." Reassuring her, I added, "It happens to all of us. It's easy to just say the words, but not really express their meaning. One thing nonfiction readers do is use their voices to highlight the most important parts of a text. You know how authors sometimes use bold letters or a large font to show super-important information? You can 'bold' your voice to show the sentences that hold bigger ideas, to pop out the important stuff."

It is a very big deal to teach readers that the page they are reading is related to other pages. Those intratextual connections are complicated. Perhaps the first page states a big idea, and a later page qualifies that idea, or provides an example of that idea, or extends that idea. You might say: "Readers, I want to point out that experienced nonfiction readers synthesize automatically as they read, doing this in their minds. As you read across related subsections, try to always think about how the information you are reading fits with what you just read. In your brain you should be calling, 'Fill in!' or 'Add on!'"

It's important for you to pause and realize the importance of the minilesson you have taught today, and of the skills you are highlighting. One of the biggest problems one sees in students' reading—all of it, not just their nonfiction reading—is a tendency to read with blinders on, unaware of how one page relates to those that went before it or to other pages from other texts.

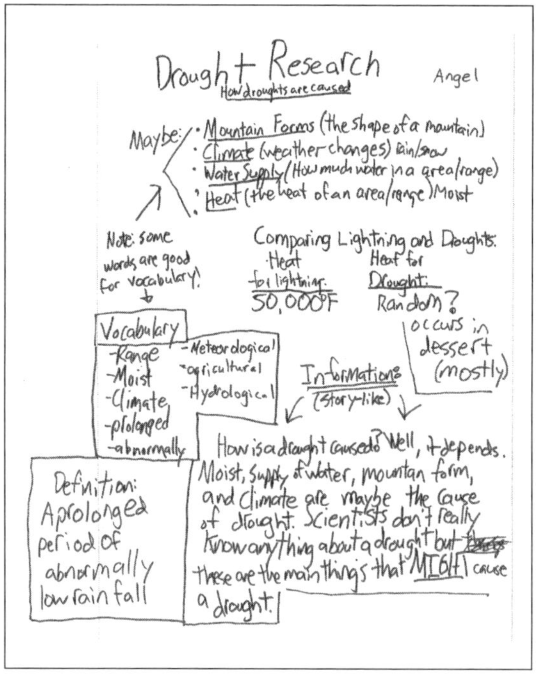

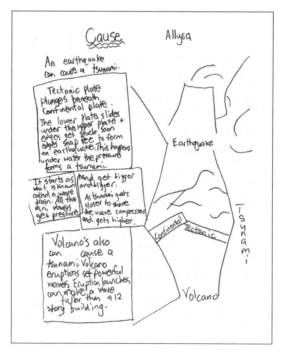

FIG. 9–4   Angel's notes show the way he is working to synthesize information and vocabulary as he conducts his research.

FIG. 9–5   Allysa's notes show the way she synthesized information, in this case using a graphic to represent her learning.

Using Transitional Phrases to Synthesize and Teach

Invite students to take a few minutes to rehearse for teaching their research team about their topic, reminding them to plan main ideas and supporting details and to use key words.

"In two minutes, I'm going to ask you to begin teaching the other members of your research team what you have learned. When you do that teaching, you'll be talking about a main idea, and drawing on several sources to fill in information about the author's main points. You'll want to be ready to cite passages from your sources, so make sure you have marked those passages with Post-its. Take just a second to get ready for that—either working alone, or with your partner if two of you studied one subtopic together."

I gave children time to do that. As they worked, I distributed a list of transitional phrases they might use to go from talking in general to citing an author's words in specific, or from talking about what you learned from one source to talking about what you learned from another. I had also listed these transitions on a sheet of chart paper, which I displayed at the front of the meeting area.

Transitions: From Main Ideas to Citing a Text

[Author's name] tells more. She writes . . .

[Author's name] provides more detailed information. This text says . . .

[Author's name] describes that. She writes . . .

[Author's name] explains that. She says . . .

[Author's name] gives an example. She writes . . .

[Author's name] tells something that sort of builds on this . . .

Channel kids to teach their research team members. After one person teaches, encourage team members to talk more about the topic, adding on, connecting to what they learned.

After a few minutes for frantic preparation, I said, "Will one person or partnership begin teaching the other members of the research team all about the subtopic you have been studying? Keep your notes and your texts front and center."

Angel, a member of the drought research team, began talking to his group. "That video by National Geographic says that droughts are about supply and demand. In the video, it tells us . . ." Angel paused, glanced at his list of transitional phrases and the transcript of the video, and then continued. "The video explains that '*a drought occurs when more water is used than is replenished. It is a balance between supply and demand with both natural and human factors in play.*' It seems like National Geographic is trying to teach us that droughts can be caused by nature and by people. And I read this other article, by Natalie Wolchover, and she says this, too." He glanced at his transitional phrases list again. "She tells something that sort of builds on this when she describes the four types of drought, and how scientists define what kind of drought it is, based on what the cause of the drought was."

As teams talked, I voiced over, "Listeners, take notes, and after your team member teaches you about his or her subtopic, be prepared to talk about that topic, too. Do you know anything more about the topic, maybe information you've come across while researching your own subtopic? Do you have examples to add? Questions to ask? Your talk might go like this: 'When you said . . . I have another example of that. I learned that . . .' or, 'When you said . . . I think that connects to something I learned . . .'"

 # REORGANIZING YOUR LEARNING SO IT'S EASIER TO CARRY

Researchers, I think you are realizing that as you learn more, besides collecting more, you also need to reorganize. Here's one way to think about it. Imagine you were going on a long hiking trip and carrying a backpack full of stuff. You stop at a store along the way and see things for sale in that store which you *really* need. You buy that new stuff but before you sling the backpack onto your back, what do you need to do? To reorganize. You need to empty out what's already in your backpack and decide whether there is anything you've been carrying all along that you now may not need. So you leave it behind. And perhaps you realize you can organize things differently so stuff fits together, and takes up less space in your backpack.

That's essentially the process a researcher does all the time. You aren't going on a hike, but you *are* traveling . . . to new books, new conversations, new parts of your topic, new sources. You can't just carry more and more. Your brain won't hold it—and your fellow students won't want your teaching to take ten hours either! So as you learn more, you need to think, "What of this stuff is worth carrying? Why is this important?" And if you decide something is important—then you decide how to make it fit with all you are already carrying. The new pot can get fitted right alongside the stack of other pots.

Tonight, learn more—and do the organizing that is necessary so you figure out what to carry. You may tape spider-leg notes off your existing page of notes, or scissor notes up and insert new bits of notes, or cross things out (even cut them out). You might find ways to start new main ideas, and to tuck smaller stuff under the author's points. Soon, we will all admire each other's notes.

Session 10

Reading Various Types of Texts

ear Teachers,

We have placed this session in between a session where students are reading across multiple texts to synthesize their learning, and a session where they are growing and grounding their ideas in the research that teams are embarking on together. If we think about a lot of the reading we do as adults, we are constantly inundated with information from multiple sources. Think about your own nonfiction reading and about the variety of texts you read. Some will be print texts, some will be tweets, blogs, video clips. You no doubt gather information from a great variety of texts, and put what you learned from one source alongside what you learned from other dramatically different sources. It is important to teach students how to navigate different sources of information, too.

The hope is that this session provides students with more time to research in their teams, and that they draw on everything they have learned as they research. Already, each team has divided its larger topic into several subtopics, and students are working either individually or in pairs to tackle their chosen subtopics—which may be a second subtopic by now. For example, in the hurricane group, you might have one or two students studying the causes of hurricanes, while another student (or partnership) might be studying the effects of hurricanes, and still another student might be looking at the ways scientists are able to measure the strength of or predict hurricanes. To do this research, your hope is that students are drawing on instruction they have received across this whole unit. Certainly, they'll use the most recent instruction in synthesizing across texts, but ideally, they are also drawing on all you taught prior. Are they previewing texts? Are they using a knowledge of text structures to help them differentiate unimportant and important information, and to help organize their notes? Are they drawing on a repertoire of strategies for tackling trickier words?

Before teaching this lesson, you will want to have read one of the two articles we are suggesting you use in an inquiry into the ways nonfiction articles are similar to and different from nonfiction books. Links to these articles, "A Summer Scorcher" by Jennifer Marino Walters and "In the Grip of Epic Drought" by Alysa Goethe, can be found on the online resources.

It would also be helpful to reflect on the different kinds of texts that your students will have access to so you can make sure you help them anticipate ways in which their reading might change somewhat based on the genre in which they are reading.

MINILESSON

For your connection, you might start out by reminding students that earlier in the unit, they learned that one of the challenges when reading nonfiction texts is that many of them are structured in hybrid ways. An article might open with a long story, then shift into a main idea and supporting details format, and readers who are using the structure of a text to help them glean what is most important will need to follow the cues in the text to notice that the structure is changing.

For review, you could display the "Signals Authors Use to Let Us Know When to Read with a Certain Lens" chart you created earlier, and ask students to discuss with their partner what they already know about reading narrative nonfiction differently than reading expository nonfiction. Their books will be studded with anecdotes, and your hope is that when readers see these, they are reading with an awareness that this will tell the story of a character (or subject) who probably has some traits and some motivations, and who probably encounters difficulties (that is especially likely because they'll be reading about extreme weather, so difficulties may actually be an understatement). Then, you could suggest that this session takes that work a step farther.

To lead into your teaching point, you might say, "Readers, the nonfiction texts you are reading now are coming in a huge variety of shapes and sizes, genres and structures. Readers are wise to take a moment to think about the kind of text they are reading, so they can figure out how to read the text they are holding."

Then, you might state your inquiry question. "I thought we could investigate these questions together: in what ways do authors write nonfiction articles differently from nonfiction books? How do you read differently when you read a nonfiction article as opposed to when you read a nonfiction book?"

Since your teaching method is inquiry, you are going to blur the lines a bit between the teaching and active engagement portion of your minilesson. You could choose to distribute copies of a familiar article on drought that you previously used for read-aloud. You might choose from one of the two articles on drought: "A Summer Scorcher" by Jennifer Marino Walters and "In the Grip of Epic Drought" by Alysa Goethe, found on the online resources. Then you might say, "Readers, will you study this article with your teams, thinking, 'In what ways do authors write nonfiction articles differently from nonfiction books, books like *Everything Weather*?'" Remind them that while they are definitely going to see similarities between this article and their nonfiction books, it's important to look closely at how the article is written differently from nonfiction books. You might choose to project a page from *Everything Weather* that can aid students in their comparisons.

As students talk, you can coach into their conversations and jot down what you are hearing on a chart.

The chart you co-construct with your students might look something like this.

In What Ways Do Authors Write Nonfiction Articles Differently from Nonfiction Books?
- Articles tend to be much shorter than nonfiction books.
- Articles tend to talk about current events or events that happened close to when the author wrote about them.
- Most articles seemed to start with the most important newsworthy information, then gave some details related to the news, and ended with other background information.

For the last bullet, you might introduce what journalists call the inverted pyramid to show how they often structure news articles. Spotlight how Alysa Goethe, the author of the Scholastic article "In the Grip of Epic Drought," used that structure to organize information.

After providing students with a chance to think and talk around the first inquiry question, shift the investigation to the second inquiry question. "Now that you have ideas about how authors write nonfiction articles differently from books, you have to consider how this information will change the way you read. Will you and your team investigate our second question: 'How do you read differently when you read a nonfiction article as opposed to when you read a nonfiction book?'" Again, as students talk, coach into their conversations and use this information to create a chart, similar to the one that was crafted for the first question.

In the link of your minilesson, you can remind readers that they are going to encounter several different kinds of texts while researching their topic and that when you encounter a new *kind* of text, it is helpful to ask yourself, "How is this different from other kinds of texts? How will I read this kind of text?" When you send children off to read, you might remind them, too, to switch to a new subtopic, if they haven't already done so.

CONFERRING AND SMALL-GROUP WORK

During conferring, you may want to suggest students consider the challenges posed by other nonfiction text types. For example, they may note that some texts revolve around charts or graphs, but find themselves unsure how to read and learn from those texts. To address this, you might gather together several students and lead a small group to help them navigate complex numbers. Demonstrate how you make sense of quantities and comparisons in a read-aloud text, and provide students with some helpful prompts for thinking about numbers:

Numbers Help Readers Think of Quantities and Comparisons

- Is that more or less than . . . ?
- That seems like a lot because . . . That seems like a little because . . .
- If I were to picture that, what would it look like, how much is it really?
- How does that compare with . . . ?

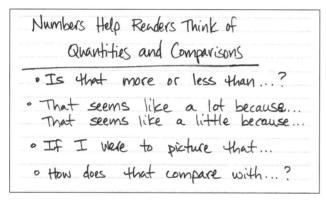

FIG. 10–1

Then, set students up to read on the lookout for quantities and comparisons in their texts, and coach them as they make sense of those numbers. You might choose to send students off with their own copy of the "Numbers Help Readers Think of Quantities and Comparisons" chart.

Mid-Workshop Teaching

In your mid-workshop teaching, you might teach students that another type of nonfiction they will encounter in their research is websites. Depending on the needs of your students, you might warn readers of some of the predictable pitfalls of Internet research, which include clicking on links that can cause researchers to tunnel too deeply and to lose track of their sources. Or, you might show kids on a Smart Board or projection screen how to organize these sources by opening a new tab or new window and cutting and pasting important websites into a new document.

SHARE

For today's share, you might ask research teams to share the work they did reorganizing their notes as part of last night's homework. Give suggestions for how this work could go. Perhaps research teams will lay their notebooks on desks and do a gallery walk, moving from exhibit to exhibit to take notes. Or, maybe they'll choose to lay one notebook out in the center of the group at a time and all study it for a minute or

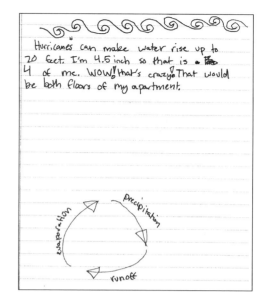

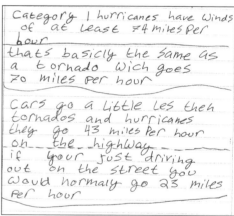

FIG. 10–2   These notes show the way students make quick jots about information, in this case numbers, to understand the information better.

two before moving onto the next. Whatever they decide, be sure they are not only looking, but also getting ideas for how to structure their own notes moving forward.

Homework

For homework tonight, you might ask students to continue researching their subtopics, synthesizing across sources of information as they do so and taking notes that reflect their new understandings. If students are beginning a second subtopic, remind them to bring all that they learned today (and in prior instruction) to the sources they read on that topic. You will likely remind students to think about the type of text they are reading, pausing for a moment to notice how it is different from other kinds of text and then making a plan for how to read that kind of text.

Good Luck!
Emily and Mike

Writing to Grow
Research-Based Ideas

IN THIS SESSION, you will teach students that they can use writing to grow their ideas about their research topics.

GETTING READY

✔ Students will need all of the notes they have taken on their topic for the bend, displayed on their tables for a gallery walk (see Connection).

✔ Prepare a series of notebook entries to share with students that capture the dos and don'ts of writing about reading (see Teaching).

✔ Have a chart titled "Writing to Grow Ideas: Dos and Don'ts" to add to during the minilesson (see Teaching).

✔ Be sure students bring their reader's notebooks with them to the rug (see Connection, Teaching and Active Engagement).

✔ Prepare to display "Ways to Push Your Thinking" chart (also shown in Session 4 of *Boxes and Bullets: Personal and Persuasive Essays* in Units of Study in Opinion, Information, and Narrative Writing, Grade 4) (see Mid-Workshop Teaching, Share, and Homework).

YOU'LL FIND that your teaching often needs to shift from emphasizing one thing for a few days, to emphasizing something different—even opposite—for the next few days. The goal is to help your teaching achieve a bit more balance. For days you have helped students read nonfiction, intent on extracting the main ideas and supporting details from the text. You've talked to them about creating comprehensive and responsible notes and summaries of a text, and about synthesizing several texts.

The skills you have taught are necessary—but they are not sufficient. For your students to grow up to be skilled researchers, they also need curiosity, enthusiasm, passion. They need to question and connect and wonder and imagine. They need to not only hunger for information, but to digest that information and grow their own ideas.

This session makes a start toward supporting those qualities. Your emphasis is on the fact that researchers need not only to collect information but also to grow ideas, and you especially stress that the ideas that matter most will be those that are developed in response to information. That is—the goal is not fluffy blow-in-the-wind feelings about a topic, but instead, the comparisons, connections, observations, and insights that come from thinking deeply about information.

You may find that some of your students struggle to write and talk about their ideas. I've come to believe that many children are more comfortable talking at great length about *objects* and *activities* rather than their own *ideas*.

Joan, a woman I know well, adopted an eight-year-old boy from Siberia. When the child had been in the States for just a year, I asked Joan how life here compares with life in Siberia. She thought for a moment and then said, "I don't think he has the English to talk about that."

I pressed on. "When he goes to the translator—when he talks in Russian—what does he say about how life here compares with life there?"

Joan answered. "I don't think he has *the Russian* to talk about ideas like that. When he was there, I don't think anyone talked to him about his ideas, and I don't think he would be able to put that sort of thinking into words."

That conversation got me thinking. I don't think that child is alone. In many schools, kids talk during social studies and science classes about people and actions and objects—about magnets and stars, and Ellis Island—but they do not tend to talk about magnetic attraction or the rotation of the planets.

"Readers are expected to compose the big ideas from a wealth of factual detail."

This matters. When a child is unaccustomed to using language to talk and think about concepts, about abstractions, when that child is finally asked to handle ideas, it can almost be as if that child is wearing ski mittens hardly able to grasp an idea. When students are unaccustomed to using abstract terms such as pollution, erosion, and evolution, this will have important consequences because they won't, then, have access to the highly academic *ideas* that academic language carries.

So in this session, you will nudge kids to talk about ideas. This becomes especially important as kids progress to more and more challenging texts because as texts get harder, often the specific facts—the statistics, the dates, the names—are meant to be illustrative of the bigger principles that may never even be explicitly stated. The author expects the reader to infer—to state—the big idea that the specifics suggest. Readers are expected to compose the big ideas from the wealth of factual detail. Today's session nudges students to do this important work.

Writing to Grow Research-Based Ideas

CONNECTION

Channel readers to grow a few ideas off their current nonfiction topics using some predictable thought prompts. Tell them that today they'll be growing more ideas in their nonfiction reading.

Once students had made their way to the meeting area, I began. "Readers, I'm wondering what's on your mind about the topic you are studying—drought, hurricanes, tornadoes—whatever it is. Let's do some thinking on paper, just to get those ideas out. Open your reading notebook, and do some thinking with your pen."

I turned to a blank page in my notebook and started writing intently, resisting the urge to eyeball the kids, knowing that my example would probably serve as the nudging they needed.

After a bit, I stopped. "Here's the really important question. What was that like for you? Was it easy for you? Hard? Do you think you wrote something that is helpful, valuable . . . or just blah? Turn and talk about what that was like for you."

The room erupted into conversation, and I listened in. Some students felt writing was helpful, others said they just sort of rewrote what they'd already learned and taken notes on. I reconvened the class. "My goal is for today's minilesson to give you pointers enough that after this, you can count on the fact that your own writing about your research topic can provide you with a reliable way to generate ideas—ideas that are critical to your learning. It is not just important for you, as a researcher, to synthesize information from one source and another, it is also important to synthesize your own thinking.

❖ Name the teaching point.

"Today I want to teach you that writing is a good way to get yourself thinking about what you are reading and learning. It helps to think about parts of the topic, to ask, 'What seems important about this?' 'How does this connect to what I know?' and to write to explain things to yourself and others."

It's important to keep your workshop feeling lively. This connection asks kids to try something—writing about their ideas—right away, and provides some nice variety for your students.

As always, pacing and assessment are crucial and you'll need to be sure that you give students enough time to give this a try, but not so much time that they become disengaged.

TEACHING

Tell kids that you will be giving "Dos and Don'ts" of writing about reading, then proceed to demonstrate a "don't" (writing in ungrounded generalizations) and a contrasting "do."

"Researchers, the goal of today's minilesson is to make it likely that you use writing not only to record what other people have said about a topic, but also to do some thinking about the information you are learning. I watched the writing you just did, and have studied writing that kids do when asked to write about their thinking, and I want to give you some tips about what doesn't work—and what does.

"Let's start with what doesn't work, then move on to what does. As I run through a few tips, will you record a chart of 'Don'ts and Dos'?

"First, when you go from taking notes full of information to thinking about those notes, don't leave behind all the facts, all the specific information, and write in blowin'-in-the-air ways. I shouldn't write about the causes of drought like this." I placed a notebook entry under the document camera and read it aloud.

> Drought is a problem and we have to change our ways and be good to the earth. Humans will have to take better care of our planet. If we live in a drought area, we probably have ourselves to blame.

Don't

Drought is a problem and we have to change our ways and be good to the earth. Humans will have to take better care of our planet. If we live in a drought area, we probably have ourselves to blame.

"No way! It'd be better to write like this," I said, placing a stronger notebook entry under the document camera.

> *Natalie Wolchover says, "Population booms can trigger droughts almost by themselves." I think the important part about that is she thinks people can prevent droughts from happening. I don't know if I agree. I mean, is it okay for governments to control the population to prevent drought? Imagine if someone told you how many children you could have?*

Do

Natalie Wolchover says, "Population booms can trigger droughts almost by themselves." I think the important part about this is she thinks people can prevent droughts from happening. I don't know if I agree. I mean, is it okay for governments to control the population to prevent drought? Imagine if someone told you how many children you could have?

I looked expectantly at kids' notebooks and nodded, urging them to jot their own list of dos and don'ts. While they jotted, I added a few tips to a class chart of Dos and Don'ts.

Writing to Grow Ideas: Dos and Don'ts

Don't . . .	Instead, do . . .
• Skip the facts and write blowin'-in-the-wind ideas.	• Cite the text or specific information, and write your ideas about that.

"On the other hand, when you go to write about your notes, *don't* be so factual and information based that you just repeat the facts. Don't write something like . . ." I displayed the next entry and read it aloud.

> People need water. We are made of 55% of water. But we don't have enough water. Forty percent of the world doesn't have good access to water. A typical person needs three liters of drinking water a day. Five thousand kids a day die from lack of water.

"Instead, go out on the thin ice of having ideas, even though those ideas could be wrong. Check out this entry."

> IIn *The Big Thirst*, by Charles Fishman, readers learn that forty percent of the world doesn't have good access to water. Forty percent is big—almost half the world's population. If we thought about that in terms of our classroom that would be scary! It would mean that almost half the kids in the class wouldn't have access to water every day. How would we survive?

> Why aren't we all talking about solutions to this horrible problem? Could it be that we just aren't aware of it because it's not happening to people we know—it's not happening to us? Maybe it's hard to understand because it's happening more in faraway countries.

"Readers, did you notice what I did? The first version was *all facts*, with no thoughts. When you want to write in order to think, it helps to rank or compare or categorize or question or connect. Make sure you are adding this to your chart of 'Dos and Don'ts.'" I added additional ideas to our chart.

Don't

Dos

> People need water. We are made of 55% of water. But we don't have enough water. Forty percent of the world doesn't have good access to water. A typical person needs three liters of drinking water a day. Five thousand kids a day die from lack of water.

We realize that this is a very sensitive topic. If you feel that this subject is too sensitive or inappropriate for your classroom, please feel free to choose another statistic for comparison.

> In *The Big Thirst* by Charles Fishman, readers learn that forty percent of the world doesn't have good access to water. Forty percent is big—almost half the world's population. If we thought about that in terms of our classroom that would be scary! It would mean that almost half the kids in the class wouldn't have access to water every day. How would we survive?

> Why aren't we all talking about solutions to this horrible problem? Could it be that we just aren't aware of this because it's not happening to people we know—it's not happening to us? Maybe it's hard to understand because it's happening more in faraway countries.

Writing to Grow Ideas: Dos and Don'ts

Don't . . .	Instead, do . . .
• Leave behind the facts and write blowin'-in-the-wind ideas. • Write only a list of facts.	• Cite the text or specific information. • Write your ideas about facts and specifics—ranking, comparing, categorizing, questioning, or connecting to grow ideas.

ACTIVE ENGAGEMENT

Channel kids to assess the writing they did earlier in the minilesson based on their list of "Dos and Don'ts" and to imagine how they'd revise it to improve it.

"It's easy to name some 'Dos and Don'ts' and harder to actually keep them in mind when you write about reading. Would you look back at the writing you did at the start of today's minilesson and think about how you would assess that writing? See if you can put your finger on a part of your Dos and Don'ts chart that could help your writing to get better." I left time for them to do this.

"How would you revise your writing based on the 'Dos and Don'ts'? Turn and talk with your partner."

I leaned in and listened to conversations, lifting up the level of individual work as students moved from talking about their revisions to revising their notes. I whispered prompts such as, "Don't forget to use those transitions before you cite the text," I said to one. "How will you think about what you have learned?" and "Are you going to question, connect, rank, or categorize?"

I crouched close and listened in as Colin and Anthony talked about their notes on tornadoes. "I found a ton of facts, like tornadoes can go fifty miles per hour and then can leave a path of damage a mile wide and fifty miles long," Colin said.

I gestured to the "Writing to Grow Ideas: Dos and Don'ts" chart and looked at Anthony, signaling that this was a good time for him to chime in. "Maybe you could add in some ideas to make it better, ideas you have about all those facts," Anthony said.

"Yeah, maybe I could compare the damage from the tornado to the damage from other things, like droughts, and I could have some ideas off of that," Colin replied.

Be sure to move from student to student, offering compliments, prompting and questioning with the "Dos and Don'ts' chart as your coaching tool.

LINK

Urge readers to try today's strategy anytime they research nonfiction texts, and also urge research teams to draw upon a repertoire of strategies they have learned in the unit thus far.

"Readers, before your research teams meet to make a plan for the day, remember this: one way to think off a text is to write off it. Use the Dos and Don'ts chart to help guide your thinking. I expect to see a lot of idea growing today—and all days.

"As you read and grow ideas today, I know your team will be drawing from everything you've learned in this unit. Some of you I know will continue to synthesize from different texts on whatever subtopic you are now studying. Others of you will likely be looking in and around words to figure out their meaning, or tackling the hard parts as you read. In fact, before you go off to make your research team plan, take a moment to scan the charts in the room and think, 'What can I deliberately practice today to make myself an even better reader?'

"Meet with your clubs to make a plan." While students met with their teams I quickly added today's learning to our anchor chart. Write your ideas about facts and specifics—ranking, comparing, categorizing, questioning, or connecting to grow ideas."

The more you make use of the charts you introduce, the more your students will be aware of these valuable tools for independence.

ANCHOR CHART

To Research Well . . .

- Get ready
  - Get to know your resources
  - Sequence texts, easy → hard
  - Figure out the main subtopics, categories, and questions
  - Plan for team research roles
- Take organized, structured notes
- Synthesize what you are learning across texts
- **Write to grow your own ideas about a topic**
  - **Cite specific information from resources**
  - **Ask questions**
  - **Make comparisons and connections**
  - **Rank and categorize information**
  - **Write your own ideas about the information you have gathered**

Nurturing Thoughtful Responses to Nonfiction Reading

AS RESEARCH TEAMS MAKE THEIR PLANS TODAY, keep an eye on kids' motivation and enthusiasm. Do all you can to sustain interest and excitement. Today you might confer with research teams and individuals to bring kids talents to the surface, and to allow them to be surprised when they set new information alongside the information they already know. Of course, you will probably want to make use of the Informational Reading Learning Progression. Today's minilesson focused on growing ideas so this strand may be particularly helpful, but the entire learning progression should support you as you confer and lead small groups.

Channel research teams to recall and draw upon strengths from previous lessons and units.

You may decide to confer with research teams today, asking each group to consider ways they can maximize the efficiency and power of their work by bringing individuals' strengths to the group. You might say, "Every team has players, and players often bring their own talents to a team to improve the team as a whole. The members of a soccer team don't all have the same role—instead their roles are tailored to their strengths. The same can be true for a research team. Start by scanning the charts in the room and thinking to yourself, 'Which of these skills are strengths of mine? Am I bringing those strengths to the team?'"

Before you leave any one research team, you might channel them to talk to each other about how each team member can help the larger cause—with an eye to a fast-approaching publication date. If one person is strong at reorganizing notes—in boxes and bullets, or in ways that mirror the text's structure—then that person could coach others in note-taking. Maybe one person is strong at figuring out what words say, and could be in charge of a team word bank. Or perhaps one team member is the next Michelangelo—and is willing to sketch and diagram important information. Perhaps one team member is willing to take on an operational leadership role, helping remind others of homework and helping to plan toward the future publication.

Teach research teams the importance of being surprised and assimilating new information with prior knowledge.

If you have a team that seems to be collecting facts but not digesting those facts to grow insights, you'll probably want to address this head-on. It is possible that such a team will also be characterized by a lack of intellectual engagement, because that engagement comes from learning, from ahahs! When I felt the blizzard group was plowing along without developing ideas or energy, I gathered them together for a pep talk.

"I've been worrying about you and want to give you a bit of a pep talk. You know that I don't usually read you quotes by famous people, but there is a writer named Jean Fritz [Surprising Myself, 1992] who could help you, I think. Fritz thought about what makes for a good nonfiction book—or book talk—and she said this: 'Whenever education glides over surprise . . . it is weakening the power of nonfiction . . .' (164). She goes on to add, 'As human beings, we thrive on astonishment. Whatever is unknown quickens us . . .' (185).

"That's on my mind because I haven't seen your group being surprised. You gather information and just pile it up, but I'm not sure you are thinking about how the new thing you learn fits with what you already knew. It almost seems like nothing surprises you.

"I worry that you aren't being surprised. You need to be able to read new information and think, '*Really?*' or '*Wow*, really!?' As you go back to your reading today, try using a Post-it note to flag the information that makes you stop and say, 'Really?' Then, figure out whether this new learning fits into what you already know or needs its own space, because it is new information."

"Readers, this might seem like it is off-topic, but it is not. Have you ever heard of a metal detector, you know, the device that some people carry around when they are searching for precious metals? Like on a beach? People walk around like this?" I held my imaginary metal detector in front of me, pretending to steer it back and forth, then said, "All of a sudden it will start beeping like mad when it detects a precious metal like gold or silver. And that's the spot that the person will dig into to find the precious metal—the gold coins or the silver necklace.

"I'm talking to you about that metal detector because I hope that as you read today, you are holding an imaginary gold detector, and that you read in such a way that it often starts beeping like mad. If you can't find bits of intriguing, surprising, noteworthy information in the texts that you are reading, then you will never be able to think in response to what you are reading. The first step is to read with that metal detector going off.

"If you are just gliding past the text, with nothing really making a big impression on you, stop! Either reread, or shift to a new text. But one way or another, make sure as you read, you are finding gold.

"And when you find gold: write in response. Write to think about parts of the topic, to ask, 'What seems important about this?' 'How does this connect to what I know?' Remember the things you can do to write to grow your own ideas about what you are learning." I gestured to the anchor chart. "And, see if you can use these prompts you know to help you push your thinking further." I referred to a chart we had been using to grow ideas in writing, in the *Boxes and Bullets: Personal and Persuasive Essay* writing unit of study.

Ways to Push Our Thinking

- In other words . . .
- That is . . .
- The important thing about this is . . .
- As I say this, I'm realizing . . .
- This is giving me the idea that . . .
- An example of this is . . .
- This shows . . .
- Another example of this is . . .

- This connects to . . .
- I see . . .
- The thought I have about this is . . .
- To add on . . .
- I used to think that . . . but now I think that . . .
- What surprises me about this is . . .
- Many people think . . . but I think . . .

"Do some thinking on the page, and be prepared to share it with your research team in a little while."

Ways to Push Your Thinking

- The important thing about this is...

- I'm realizing...

- This is giving me the idea that...

- This connects to...

- The thought I have about this is...

- What surprises me about this is...

- This makes me think...

Teach readers to rank the most important information.

There are some predictable problems to watch for as you confer and lead small groups. For example, be alert for readers who may be growing ideas off of any information without regard to determining what's most important. Teach these children that readers rank and sort information, and grow ideas off the information that is most pertinent to the big ideas of the text.

I noticed members of the tornado team having trouble with determining importance. To them, I said, "Readers, let me give you a tip: researchers don't just grow ideas off any ol' part of the text. Instead, you think about the information that seems *most important* to the big ideas of your topic. One way to do this is to rank some of the information

FIG. 11–5 Lila's notes show the way she is growing ideas by comparing, contrasting, and connecting.

you are learning, and grow your ideas off the information you've ranked at the top. Some prompts to help you with this include, 'This is most important because . . .' and 'This fits with the overall topic because . . .' and 'This information is *so* crucial to know, because without it . . .' and the like."

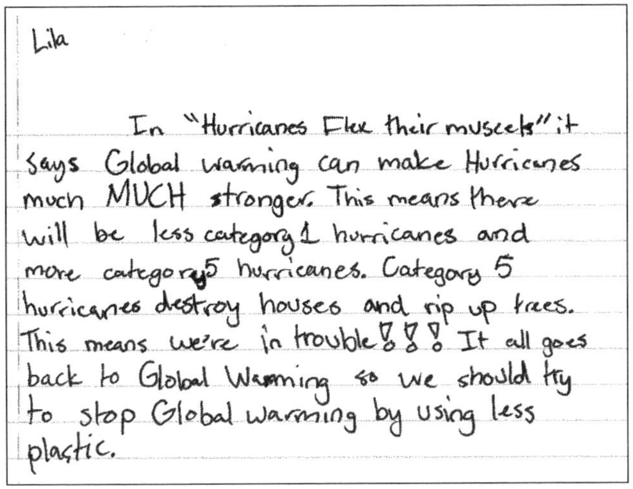

We tried it together. "Well, I think the stuff about the effects of tornadoes is most important," Colin said, "because when homes and buildings are destroyed, people might have a hard time rebuilding their lives—that is kind of a sad thing to think about."

"I agree," said Anthony. "I think maybe the information on ways to prepare for a tornado fits with the overall topic, too. Because if you're ready for what to do when the storm sirens blow, you can stay safe and maybe help other people rebuild if their homes get damaged."

I nodded and linked my teaching. "As you do this ranking work, you'll also want to determine what is less important and why. Remember you can do this anytime you are reading nonfiction, whether you are growing research-based ideas or summarizing a text."

Meanwhile I listened to the small group that was researching the class topic, drought. Angel seemed to have grasped the idea of "supply and demand" and was seeing examples of this everywhere. I supported this. "It is like you have made supply and demand into a main idea of your teaching about drought, and your teaching has a boxes-and-bullets shape. You give lots of examples of supply and demand in relation to drought. Good going!"

Jasmine seemed to be onto the idea that it's important for people to do a little more to help those devastated by drought so that the worst consequences like famine, war, or migration never happen. I challenged her to find specifics to go with her main idea.

Having Collaborative Conversations

Coach research teams to have collaborative conversations by guiding them to talk off of each other's ideas, using thought prompts as a scaffold.

"Researchers, I know you are going to want to meet with your research teams and to pool your knowledge. You can start with one person sharing the gold information he or she read today—actually read a bit of the text aloud. Then that person will want to share, too, the ideas you developed from that information.

"But here is the thing. A good conversation is just that: a conversation. Your research team has all been learning-related stuff. So when one person talks, it will spark ideas in the rest of you. So butt in.

"A good strong conversation doesn't feel like one person making a report while others yawn and wait their turn, then the next person gives a report. Instead, one person starts. That person talks for a bit, then the team jumps in, with lots of people saying, 'That reminds me of . . .' and 'The part I don't understand is . . .' and another saying, 'Wait, my book says something about that too.'

"Use the thought prompts on the 'Ways to Push Your Thinking' chart, if that helps, to develop what one person says so that your research team is excited by all your new thinking."

As you move from group to group, watch and listen for the ways your students are using information, coming up with their own ideas, and talking to one another. If you don't see students doing these things, by all means prompt them to do so!

REVISING NOTES AND GROWING IDEAS

Researchers, for your homework tonight, continue reading and writing about your topic. Also, take some of your homework time to reread your notes and to think off of them. Rereading, revising, and reorganizing notes can help you to grow even more ideas. Some ways to do this might be to:

- Star, box, or mark notes that seem important.
- Draw arrows between notes that go together.

After you reread your notes and mark them up, take a few minutes to write long. Use these prompts below for help getting started.

Ways to Push Our Thinking

- In other words . . .
- That is . . .
- The important thing about this is . . .
- As I say this, I'm realizing . . .
- This is giving me the idea that . . .
- An example of this is . . .
- This shows . . .
- Another example of this is . . .
- This connects to . . .
- I see . . .
- The thought I have about this is . . .
- To add on . . .
- I used to think that . . . but now I think that . . .
- What surprises me about this is . . .
- Many people think . . . but I think . . .

Ways to Push Your Thinking

- The *important* thing about this is...
- I'm realizing...
- This is giving me the idea that...
- This connects to...
- The thought I have about this is...
- What surprises me about this is...
- This makes me think...

Don't Skip the Hard Stuff

IN THIS SESSION, you will teach students that readers tackle complex, technical passages head-on by reading and rereading small parts, thinking about what those parts are teaching, and using talk and writing to explain their ideas.

GETTING READY

✔ Inside each research team's book bin, you might place a few extra maps and graphs that fit each group's topic.

✔ Be ready to project pages 18 and 19 from *Everything Weather* (see Teaching and Active Engagement).

✔ Have your reader's notebook ready to sketch and write (see Teaching and Active Engagement).

✔ Have your "To Read Nonfiction Well . . ." chart handy (see Link).

✔ Display the "Cross Text(s) Synthesis" strand of the Informational Reading Learning Progression (see Mid-Workshop Teaching).

✔ Prepare a chart titled "When Preparing for a Group Presentation, Think About . . ." and be ready to share it with students (see Share).

THIS SESSION RETURNS TO A THEME that was important earlier in this unit—embracing the challenges of difficult texts. At this point in the unit, you've taught your readers to look out for ways that nonfiction texts can be hard—with misplaced headings, fact overload, confusing beginnings, and long detours—and you've empowered them to tackle these challenges with zeal. This session offers another opportunity for you to infuse enthusiasm into reading the hard parts.

Because your class has undertaken a research project that is scientific in nature, it is predictable that they'll encounter dense descriptions of processes and procedures that will raise challenges for them. To explain a scientific process, a text may put forth several ideas that readers have to make sense of and hold onto while they're reading. Within these dense descriptions, readers will also find difficult vocabulary that they will have to learn and process as they are taking in the complex material. Finally, students will have to tackle the text features that portray these scientific processes and procedures—the graphs, diagrams, charts, and so on. In easier texts, these features help readers understand the text. But as texts become more difficult, the text features begin to hold essential information that readers need to decipher to fully comprehend the text.

Reading dense material can feel daunting and make youngsters feel like their brains are turning to jelly. Your goal in this session is to teach students to expect hard parts to come up in their reading, and then, rather than skipping over those parts when they encounter them, to read them extra closely. You will suggest that one way readers do this is by breaking challenging technical sections into parts and pausing after each part to say, "What is this teaching?" Then, too, you will show your students that to understand these parts, the reader has to synthesize across all information on the page, reading both the text itself and the text features closely. Finally, you will demonstrate how you can use writing and talk as tools to understand a text more deeply, and you'll expand students' notions of what that writing can look like by sketching as you read across a dense text.

Volume of reading can quickly drop as students inch their way through tricky parts of a text, so across today's lesson you will want to emphasize that the strategy you are teaching should be used only when students encounter difficulty. If students are reading along in the text, making sense of the author's points—the main ideas and supporting details—they should keep reading on, with a strong reading pace. That is, today's strategy is one that should be selectively used, as needed, with small technical parts.

"Teach students to expect hard parts to come up in their reading, and then, rather than skipping over those parts when they encounter them, to read them extra closely."

At this point in the unit, there are many options for your use of the learning progression. As you confer and lead small groups, you'll probably want to refer to various strands that are relevant to your students' work and needs as nonfiction readers.

Don't Skip the Hard Stuff

CONNECTION

◆ COACHING

Share an anecdote about struggling to set up something complicated, and use it to illustrate that the difficulty came from trying to tackle dense, technical text.

"Readers, last night I was struggling to set up my DVD player so I could watch the new DVD I just got of 'Modern Family.' I found a manual for the DVD player and turned to a page that had a lot of complicated instructions and a diagram, too, and I started trying to figure out the names and the purposes for each of the wires and the buttons. Pretty soon my brain felt like . . ." I gestured to show that the manual had fried my brain.

You can easily change this minor example if this does not seem authentic to you. That is, use an example of a time when you faced a challenge as a nonfiction reader.

Role-playing the part of a frustrated reader, I continued. "I thought, 'This is too much for me. I'm just *no good* at DVDs.' I tried calling everyone I knew who could help but no one was around so I started thinking, 'Oh well, I don't really want to watch "Modern Family" that badly anyhow.'

"Suddenly, I had an epiphany. I realized that my problem with the DVD player wasn't a DVD problem—it was a reading problem. More specifically, it was a *nonfiction* reading problem.

"Here I was trying to tackle this dense, technical text, full of all kinds of phrases like 'This unit is NTSC compatible' and 'a DTS decoder' and 'natural wave forms.' I could pronounce the words, but just saying them didn't help me figure out what those complicated parts meant.

"And," I leaned in close. "I think I'm not the only one who's felt this way. I've been noticing that as you're researching, you've been paying a lot of attention to the stories in your texts—about the aftereffects of the tsunami and how it shaped people's lives—and that very few of you are researching the safety and prevention of your topic, the hard technical parts. I'm thinking it's because those technical parts feel so tricky to handle."

❖ **Name the teaching point.**

"Today I want to teach you that when researchers encounter complex, technical parts of their text, they tackle them head-on. They read (and sometimes reread) everything on the page closely, pausing after a chunk to think about what it's teaching. Then, they talk or write to develop their ideas."

TEACHING

Demonstrate for readers how you tackle hard, technical parts of a text by reading and pausing often to say what the text is teaching.

"Yesterday, the drought group was trying to figure out what happens when droughts aren't occurring, how people and animals and land get the water they need before a drought. They were reading *Everything Weather*, and they got to this part on the water cycle, and they were saying, 'Boy, is this turning my brain to jelly!' I asked them if we could tackle it together today. What do you say?" The kids seemed game.

"Alright, that's the spirit!" I placed pages 18–19 under the document camera. "One way we can do this is by pausing after reading a chunk of the text and thinking, 'What is this part teaching?' Then, we can say back the parts we understand in our own words." I began reading.

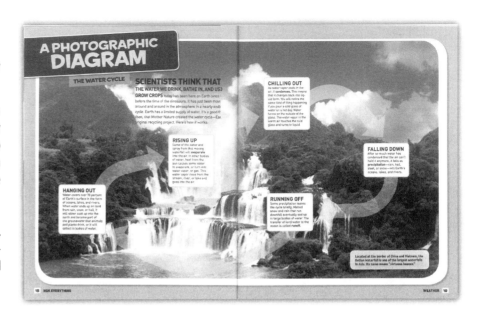

A Photographic Diagram: The Water Cycle

Scientists think that the water we drink, bathe in, and use to grow crops today has been here on Earth since long before the time of the dinosaurs. It has just been moving around and around in the atmosphere in a nearly endless cycle. Earth has a limited supply of water. It's a good thing, then, that Mother Nature created the water cycle—Earth's original recycling project. Here's how it works:

"Phew, I think my brain's already starting to turn to jelly. Let me pause and say back in my own words, 'What is this part teaching?' Well . . . I think it's teaching that all the water we have has been here for a long time, before the dinosaurs." I looked back at the text, studying it closely, and gave students time to think alongside me. "Oh, and it's also teaching that the water moves in some kind of cycle. I don't know what kind, but I see that word *endless*, and I remember from looking in words that you could look at parts of words. The word *less* is there, which means without. So it must be a cycle without an end, like maybe it goes on forever."

You'll want to slow your demonstration down at this point because this is your chance to emphasize the work one has to do as a reader to tackle difficulty.

"Ok, now that we're clear on what that part is teaching, let's read on, thinking, 'What is this next part teaching?' Ready?" I read on in the text.

Hanging Out

Water covers over 70 percent of Earth's surface in the form of oceans, lakes, and rivers. When water ends up on land from rain, snow, or hail, it will either soak up into the earth and become part of the groundwater that animals and plants drink, or it will collect in bodies of water.

Rising Up

Some of the water and spray from this moving waterfall will evaporate into the air. In other bodies of water, heat from the sun causes some water to evaporate, or turn into water vapor, or gas. This water vapor rises from the stream, river, or lake and goes into the air.

"Alright, the author's getting into some really technical parts here. Let's stop, and think, 'What is this part teaching?' Explain to your partner what it's teaching." I knelt down and listened to Izzy and Malik as they shared.

"I think the 'Hanging Out' part makes sense. It sounds like the water falls from the sky—see where it says *rain, snow, or hail*, and then it soaks into the ground, or goes into the lakes and oceans and rivers," Izzy started.

"Yeah, but that 'Rising Up' part doesn't make sense to me. What does 'this moving waterfall' mean anyway?" Malik replied.

Model how you use writing to better understand what a hard chunk of text is teaching.

"Sometimes, even when you pause to think, 'What is this part teaching?' you can still be unsure. In situations like that, it helps to reread and then write to understand what the text is teaching. Let me show you what I mean."

I reread the section titled "Hanging Out," and then I paused, picking up my marker and sketching in my reader's notebook as I talked. "Let me try making a sketch of this and see if it helps me to understand it more. So, this first part teaches about how water falls from the sky as rain, snow, and hail. And it falls into the ground and into water like lakes and oceans." (See Figure 12–1.)

"And then, this second part, it sounds like it's talking about how the sun makes the water hot enough that it turns into vapor, and it leaves the earth and goes back into the sky." I projected my revised notebook page for students to see (see Figure 12–2).

Debrief. Name the process you just went through in a transferable way.

"Readers, we just worked through this hard, technical part to help the drought team, by reading a chunk and then thinking, 'What is this part teaching?' Sometimes, we stopped and talked to tackle the hard part, and other times, we wrote and sketched to understand what it was teaching."

ACTIVE ENGAGEMENT

Channel readers to read another part of a technical text, and then pause, talking and writing to determine what that part of the text is teaching.

"Readers, I'm going to read aloud the next chunk of text. When your brain starts feeling like jelly, hold up your hand in a 'stop' motion, so I know it's time for us to stop and think, 'What is this part teaching?' Ready?" I started reading.

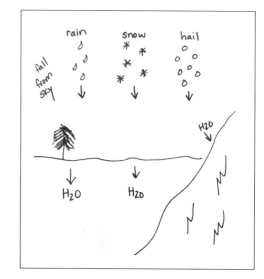

FIG. 12–1

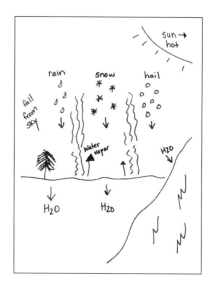

FIG. 12–2

126

Chilling Out

As water vapor cools in the air, it condenses. This means that it changes back into liquid form. You will noticed the same kind of thing happening if you pour a cold glass of water on a hot day. Water forms on the outside of the glass. The water vapor in the warm air touches the cold glass and turns to liquid.

Hands popped up all across the rug. "I agree, readers, this part is tough. Listen while I read it again, let your eyes linger on the text, and get ready to explain to your partner what this part is teaching." I reread the chunk. "Turn and talk: what is this part teaching?" I knelt down to coach partnerships.

After listening in for a minute, I handed my marker and reader's notebook to Fatima and Rafael. "Will you add to our notes so they capture what this part is teaching?" They eagerly got started, and I asked them to project the page when they were finished (see Figure 12–3).

Offer a tip: when reading difficult texts, readers study text features as closely as they study the text, working to determine what the features are teaching.

A minute later, I paused the students and offered a tip. "You can study text features the same way you're studying the text in this tough, technical text. You can read a text feature closely, asking, 'What is this part teaching?' Will you try that right now with this diagram of the water cycle?" I projected the diagram on pages 18 and 19.

I listened in while Leah and Alyssa talked. "I see this is a diagram, and it's not totally drawn. There's a photograph of waterfalls, a pool, clouds," Alyssa said.

"You're describing what you see," I said. "Make sure you're thinking, 'What is this part teaching?'" I left the girls to work.

LINK

Debrief what kids did so that they might try it with other texts on other days, and urge them to tackle the hard parts today and every day they read.

"Readers, this is some serious work here. As we said earlier in this unit, learners embrace challenges. Readers like you see challenges as an opportunity to grow. So today, as you read and research texts with even greater complexity, whenever you feel you're comprehending what you are reading, learning main ideas and details from the text, read on with a strong reading pace. And whenever you feel you're coming to a part that might turn your brain to jelly, pause and think, 'What is this part teaching?' You might need to reread, and you might need to write and talk to figure out what the hard part is teaching. I imagine I'll see a lot of notebooks open and Post-its tabbing pages where you didn't skip the hard parts, but rather, where you tackled them. And I bet sometimes I'll hear you whispering for a minute with a partner to work through one of these tricky parts." I gestured to our anchor chart, specifically to the section on tackling the hard parts.

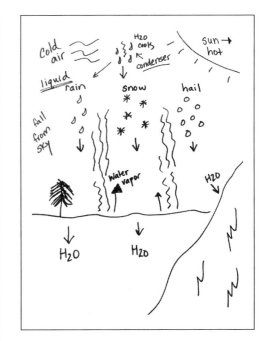

FIG. 12–3

This link is meant to help students understand that knowing when and how to use strategies is crucial. That is, readers need to know strategies, but also how to be strategic.

To Read Nonfiction Well . . .

- Make a connection to your text
- Preview the whole text and predict how it might go
  - Use prior knowledge of the topic
  - Scan the text features
- Figure out the text's structure and use it to determine importance:
  - Problem/solution
  - Compare/contrast
  - Cause/effect
  - Chronological
- Tackle the hard parts of nonfiction reading:
  First, notice:
  - Misplaced, misleading, or poetic headings
  - Fact overload
  - Confusing beginnings that don't directly introduce the topic of the text
  - Long detours with extra information that can pull you away from the main idea
    Then take action:
    - Read and reread
    - Ask, "What is this part teaching?"
- Notice if a text is hybrid and figure out which lens to read through, and when
  - Narrative lens
  - Expository lens
- Figure out the meaning of unknown words:
  - Look *in* the word
  - Look *around* the word

"Inside your topic bins I've placed a few extra maps, graphs, and charts that you may want to read as well. Take a minute to plan with your research team, then off you go."

Tackling Complex Texts through Small-Group Work

TODAY AS KIDS GO OFF to continue their research, you'll likely notice a bit of excitement as children look at the maps, charts, and graphs you've placed in their bins. Be on the lookout for readers who seem daunted by information with such complexity. Then, too, notice whether the additional layer of complexity has led to some students reading at a snail's pace, and if that's the case, help these readers to balance times when they read and reread slowly and analytically with times when they read nonfiction much in the same way they tend to read fiction more quickly.

Above all, notice whether kids are really wrapping their minds around the complicated aspects of their topics. If you can, set them up to explain the way their topic works to others and to you. Rafael, for example, said to me and his research team, "I'm reading about how hurricanes form. I learned that the atmosphere . . . without it, we wouldn't be living. We'd be floating up into space. Which I thought was pretty cool. Jason and I were just saying how it would be really fun to have a day without atmosphere, where you just float around!" He grinned conspiratorially at Jason, who seemed quite taken by the idea.

Jason jumped onto Rafael's idea, saying, "That would be awesome! Only we'd get stuck on the ceiling if we were inside. But oh, the school would float up too!"

I knew this imaginative pair would be off and running with this theme, so I steered the conversation for a moment to other members of the research team. "So Fatima, you were reading about hurricanes too? What can you add to what Jason and Rafael learned?"

"Umm . . . Well, the atmosphere comes in contact with ocean waters which makes the air warm. But without the atmosphere we wouldn't be living on the planet, and the atmosphere is very important for us." She stopped as if finished, so I gestured to suggest she continue. "The atmosphere is sort of like when the cold air pushes down . . ." Fatima's voice trailed off for a second as she paused and glanced down at her notes. "When cold air presses down on the hot air, the hot air goes up, so if we

didn't have the atmosphere the hot air would push down on us, and we would go up. So we would die because we wouldn't have any oxygen to breathe, and the pressure would be too much. Even the barometer would say so." She added, "I also thought that was so cool because you just take the atmosphere for granted! You can't see it, so you don't think about it."

(continues)

MID-WORKSHOP TEACHING **Using a Learning Progression to Self-Assess Cross Text(s) Synthesis**

"Readers, I am seeing many of you tackling the hard parts of your nonfiction texts with gusto! As you tackled the hard parts in your reading, one thing you can be thinking about is how the new information you're coming across fits with what you already know and how it changes your thinking. Tomorrow, of course, you'll celebrate the end of this bend by teaching another research team about your subtopic. To get ready for that, it will be important to make sure you're connecting your new learning to all that you've previously learned. Right now, will you take a moment to assess yourself against this learning progression? You might study your recent writing about reading, or you might reflect on recent conversations with your research team. What are the ways in which you are representing and applying what you're learning? In other words, in what ways are you able to show what you know?" Give students a few minutes to read across the learning progression strand and self-assess their recent practice while you coach in.

"Move beyond noticing what you're already doing well! Think about what you can do next as a nonfiction reader, based on our progression, set a goal, and go for it!"

Jason hadn't seemed to really hear Fatima's complex and somewhat convoluted exposition, or if he had, he understood it better than I did, so he pressed on to a new aspect of the topic. "Well, I'm also wondering if without the atmosphere, would we have hurricanes or tsunamis or twisters? I mean, with no atmosphere to trap it, everything would just float out into space."

Listening to him, I knew he was talking about gravity, and I saw the word in his notebook. I did not want to take him off course by making an especially big deal over the need to use technical vocabulary, but I also didn't want to leave the teaching moment behind. I tapped the word *gravity* in his notebook, and he got the hint, restating his idea to include that word.

At this point, I jumped in. "Wow. My head is spinning over all you are saying. I thought you would be talking about big storms—hurricanes and tornadoes and stuff, but you have tackled the science behind all that, the hardest and most complex topics of all. Atmosphere, air pressure, gravity, barometers—these are gigantically complex words and concepts, especially in relation to how this all affects extreme weather like hurricanes. You must be proud of yourselves as a team for going for the hard stuff."

Then, shifting to the teaching component of this small-group work, I said, "I want to give you a tip. When you get to complex topics such as these, you need to shift how you read and talk. The words in your books may not be hard, but really understanding the ideas will be hard. You need to think to yourself, 'Whoa! This is hard!' and then do the extra work necessary to truly understand these complicated ideas. It is like when a car goes up a really steep hill, the motor needs to shift into low gear because it is traveling steep terrain. When you are working on dense concepts like you've been tackling, your talking and thinking needs to shift into a different gear."

Finally, I added, "Will you take the next few minutes to see if you can think of some reading strategies you could use to make sure that everyone in your research team totally grasps the concepts you are talking about? You might decide to make diagrams and put them at the center of your conversation or to read a section of text super slowly—perhaps with one person reading a bit aloud and then everyone talking and thinking really hard about that passage. You might decide to ask each other tons of questions or to try using your teaching voice and finger and gestures not only to teach, but to understand. After you figure out what you can do to understand this complex stuff, get started, and I'll come back to see if I can help."

Before I moved on to work with another group, I recorded notes on the conference I'd just conducted. I was aware that I'd celebrated how the youngsters were tackling the hard science of their topic and extolled the group members to "shift into a different gear" when handling such complex topics but, that I really hadn't done a lot yet to help them know what that might entail. I made a few, quick notes about the work I could do with them in the future.

Informational Reading Learning Progression		
	Grade 3	Grade 4
	INTERPRETIVE READING	
Cross Text(s) Synthesis	When I read two texts (or parts of a text) that teach about the same subtopic, I can find the information on a subtopic from both texts (or parts of one text) and put that information together.	As I read two or more texts (or parts of a long text) on a topic, I can collect and merge information and ideas from both texts (or parts of a long text) in a way that makes a new organization for the combined information. If there are ways to categorize the information on the subtopic, I sort information from both texts into a category.

Presentation Preparation

Alert readers that they will soon be teaching other research teams what they have learned, and to do so, teams need to prepare.

"Readers, tomorrow we will be wrapping up the work of this bend of the unit. Specifically, we will be pausing to teach one another what we have learned in our research teams before we compare everything we've learned about one topic across this bend to another topic in the next bend. I'll tell you more about it soon, but for now, your teams need to get ready to present your kind of weather or natural disaster to other groups.

"Will you and your group think about how your presentations might go? And be sure to think about what information you will still need to gather, what reading you might need to do tonight, to get ready. I've charted a few things to think about when teams prepare a presentation." I gestured to a chart that I had created earlier.

"I am going to give you several minutes to discuss and make plans with your team."

When Preparing for a Group Presentation, Think About...

• **What will we present?**

• **What information do we still need to gather to be ready?**

• **How will we present our information?**

• **What materials will we need to present?**

• **What will be the order of our presentation?** (1st) (2nd) (3rd)

FINAL PREPARATIONS

Researchers, your presentation on your topic is tomorrow! Today in school, your research team made a plan for what you might teach and what information you would still need to gather in order to do that teaching. To get ready tonight, you might do a bit more research to fill in any gaps, using any books, articles, websites, or videos you can find on your topic. Synthesize this new learning with your previous learning, thinking about how it adds to and changes what you already know.

As you read this evening, continue practicing your efforts to tackle the hard stuff in your nonfiction books. For instance, you might continue slowing down when you reach a hard, technical part, breaking it into parts and thinking, "What is this part teaching?" Or, you might work to form full definitions of the tricky words and concepts in your books, reading more books, going online, or talking to family members to learn more.

Celebration

Teaching One Another

ear Teachers,

This session is the culmination of all you have taught and all your students have learned over the last few weeks. Of course, you have been focused on teaching nonfiction reading skills and strategies, but you have also been helping your students to work in research teams to become experts on their various topics, and for your students this has been exciting and important work. So, we suggest that you take this day as an opportunity for your research teams to gather together and plan a quick course that they will teach to their classmates about their chosen topics.

The opportunity to teach one another offers students one more chance to reflect on their research, to synthesize the information learned across a variety of sources, to embed technical vocabulary in their teaching, and to practice their presentation skills—all within the authentic context of teaching one another.

As you prepare for this session, you will want to carefully consider the timing and logistics of the day's work. We suggest that you begin with a lesson devoted to helping students to plan their teaching, then provide students time to work in their research teams to prepare, and then to finally come together in groups to teach one another. Therefore, you may choose to devote approximately twenty minutes to each of these endeavors and alert students to the time they will have to prepare and teach one another.

You will also need to consider the logistics for your class in terms of the numbers of students in each group and their configurations. One way to do this might be to set kids up to conduct a teaching carousel. You might set up different research teams to make concentric circles. For instance, the drought team could make a circle around the flood team. Members of each team would find a partner to teach for several minutes, and then one of the teams would rotate in one direction. For example, the drought team could rotate one person to their left, and then each partnership teaches their subtopic to a new individual of another team. If you have an odd number of groupings, a pair of readers from one group could go together.

MINILESSON

For your connection, you might begin by reminding students of the ways they have taught one another; this could also be used as a means to monitor their own learning. You could say that this session takes that work even further by providing a time to really pull all of their learning together, as a way to show off and share all they have learned in their research teams.

For review, you could remind students of the ways they've taught one another throughout the unit and in previous years. It would make sense to bring the chart used in the Session 3 Share, and taken from the third-grade unit *Reading to Learn*, into this session as a tool for students.

You might also want to remind students that when you read a great story, a great chapter book, you don't keep it to yourself. Instead, you recommend the book to your friends and family, hoping they will read it and love it as much as you have. Similarly, when you become an expert on a topic, you don't keep your knowledge to yourself. Instead you share your knowledge by teaching others. For your teaching point, you could say, "Today I want to teach you that experts live in the world differently. They don't keep their expert knowledge to themselves. Instead, they share this knowledge by teaching the people in their communities."

You'll probably want to use a quick demonstration and then guided practice as your teaching methods for this minilesson, focusing on the causes of droughts, since this is the subtopic you've used in earlier sessions, and the one that students know well. By referring to the "To Teach Well" chart from earlier sessions as well as the demonstration notes you've taken on the causes of droughts, you can think aloud briefly about the author's points—the main ideas and supporting details, as well as the gestures, charts, and diagrams you might use to teach others.

After looking over your notes, you might say, "Well, it seems to me that I should have a chart that shows that there are some common human causes of droughts as well as natural causes of droughts. I could use that chart to teach about the differences between the various causes of droughts." As you plan out your teaching, refer to the "When Preparing for a Group Presentation, Think About . . ." chart you began with students in the previous session, revealing new questions on the chart as you make your plan.

Once you've done a brief demonstration, you can guide the students to take a few minutes to practice this work with their initial subtopics. You'll probably want to nudge them to revisit their plan from the previous session, and to first think about the main ideas and supporting details they plan to teach. Next, you can prompt them to consider how they will teach and the tools they will use to teach well. As students work to prepare their teaching, you can prompt them to rehearse so they'll be sure to use their explaining voice as well as any other relevant points on the chart.

For your link, you will want to set students up to go off to continue their preparations. You'll want them to make quick plans with their team members and to rehearse so that their teaching can be its very best. You'll need to remind them to move quickly because they will only have about fifteen minutes to put their presentations together.

To teach well . . .

- Know the main ideas and supporting details
- Use an explaining voice
- Use gestures
- Use a teaching finger to point out charts, illustrations, and diagrams to help explain

It's worth the time to actually rehearse a presentation. When you teach your students to rehearse you may need to show them that rehearsal is not a summary of the plan. Instead, rehearsal is a practice round in which students actually give their presentation.

CONFERRING AND SMALL-GROUP WORK

During your conferring today, you will probably need to support students in really doing their best teaching. For some, this will mean using their voices to take on a teaching tone and teach well, while for others it may mean a return to main ideas and supporting details. In addition, you may need to help teams remember to make use of their existing work. In some pilot classrooms there were students who approached this teaching task as an entirely new endeavor. Instead, you'll want to guide students to make use of their notes and key vocabulary words and concepts when they are preparing their teaching—this should feel like the natural culmination of the work for this bend of the unit.

Mid-Workshop Teaching

For your mid-workshop teaching, you may want to teach students to think about ways to engage *their* students. "The best teachers don't just deliver information, they also engage their students," you can say. "So let's make a quick list of ways we can engage our students. Take a minute to think about a time when you have been really interested in your learning. What did your teacher do?" After giving students a few minutes to come up with some ideas, you could add their ideas to your "To Teach Well . . ." chart.

To Teach Well . . .

- Know the main ideas and supporting details
- Use an explaining voice
- Use gestures
- Use a teaching finger to reference charts, illustrations, diagrams
- **Engage your students**
  - ask questions
  - make comparisons
  - tell mini stories
  - be dramatic

Then, you can encourage your students to embed some of these engaging practices into their rehearsal for their teaching, before helping them to transition into the "teaching one another" part of the session.

As mentioned earlier, you will need to organize your research teams in ways that make sense for you and your students. Once your teams have prepared their teaching, you could direct them to create "jigsaw" groups so that members from each group are now represented in a new group and then prompt students to teach one another. In some of the pilot classrooms, teachers paired students so that they had a teaching partner in the new group configurations. This was particularly important for students who were learning English or who were in need of a little extra support while teaching.

As students work in these new groups teaching one another, you'll want to move from group to group offering compliments that can serve as coaching for all of the students. You'll also probably want to recap

When Preparing for a Group Presentation, Think About...

- What will we present?

- What information do we still need to gather to be ready?

- How will we present our information?

- What materials will we need to present?

- What will be the order of our presentation?

many of these compliments for the whole class before charging them with teaching someone at home tonight.

At the end of the session, you might gather students together to rally them around the work of the final bend. You might say, "Readers, tomorrow, we move into the final stage of our work in this unit. Not only will you draw upon everything you know from these previous two bends, but you'll do it by studying *another* extreme weather or natural disaster topic." At this point you might tell children which topic each research team will begin studying, that the hurricane group will be studying tornadoes, and vice versa, that droughts and floods will swap topics, and that earthquakes and tsunamis will swap, too. Depending on the time available and your preference you might instead choose to reveal this news tomorrow.

Homework

If you do choose to tell kids which new topic their team will be studying, you might encourage teams to do a little research at home, on the Internet, or at the library, culling information that might go with their new topic of study. Otherwise, you might ask readers to spend a final day reading on their first research topic and to spend a few minutes teaching someone what they learned from this focus study.

Sincerely,
Emily and Mike

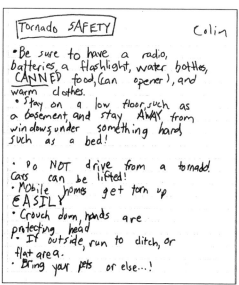

FIG. 13–1 These notes show different ways students prepared information for their presentations.

Session 14

Reading and Thinking across Two Topics

Comparing and Contrasting

IN THIS SESSION, you'll teach students that researchers often move from studying one example of something to studying a second example, thinking about ways the second example is similar to and different from what they already know.

GETTING READY

✔ Assign research teams to new spots in the meeting area so they are sitting near the students who previously studied their topic. You may want to place papers in the meeting area specifying the new seating arrangements (see Connection).

✔ Keep the research teams from Bend II intact, and give each team a new topic to study. We suggest that the tsunami team study earthquakes, the earthquake team study tsunamis, the hurricane team study tornadoes, the tornado team study hurricanes, the drought team study floods, and the flood team study droughts (see Connection).

✔ Prior to the session, prepare a student who was a member of the flood research team in Bend II to engage in conversation with you about the topics you are passing along to each other (see Teaching).

✔ Be sure students have their reader's notebooks on the rug to jot notes (see Teaching).

✔ Prepare a chart titled "Researching a Second Example." This will become your anchor chart for the bend (see Active Engagement). ✲

✔ Place a book with a compare-and-contrast text structure in each research team's topic bin. On the page that reveals the compare-and-contrast structure, place a purple Post-it. You will channel kids to these pages in the text (see Mid-Workshop Teaching).

✔ Create a chart titled "Phrases We Can Use When Comparing and Contrasting Information," and fill it with compare-and-contrast sentence starters (see Mid-Workshop Teaching). ✲

THIS SESSION launches students into the third bend, the homestretch in this important unit of study. In this bend, you'll ask students to research a second topic under the larger themes of extreme weather and other natural disasters, and to conduct this second investigation with more independence. Children will continue to work with their same research team so that the new investigation can stand on the shoulders of the previous one. The topics studied in this bend will be the same as those studied earlier, with two research teams exchanging topics and assisting each other. We recommend that the researchers who studied hurricanes now study tornadoes, those who studied earthquakes study tsunami, and those who studied drought study floods—and vice versa.

To teach these culminating sessions, it is important to fix one's eyes on the ultimate goal, asking, "Before the unit is over, what do I hope to have taught readers? During this final week of the unit, what is the most powerful contribution I can make to kids' lives as nonfiction readers and as people?"

This entire unit has been designed to help students read in a way that allows them to learn about the world. It's impossible to emphasize enough the importance of this. The world's knowledge is expanding at a breathtaking pace: in the four years from 1999 to 2002 alone, the amount of new information produced in the world approximately equaled the amount produced in the entire previous history of the world (Varian and Lyman, 2003). To manage their own learning life, children need to learn to be job-captains of this. They need the metacognitive skills to apply the strategies they have learned throughout this unit to a mind-bogglingly diverse array of texts, including maps, photographs, videos, charts, collections of data, digital texts, and the like. They need, also, to understand that studying one topic will lead them inevitably to studying another topic. The boundaries between topics aren't clear, and a good deal of learning involves synthesizing and analyzing, comparing and contrasting.

As your students go from studying one topic to studying another, they'll read differently because of what they already learned. They'll investigate the second topic, asking, "How is this the same as what I already know? How does this add to or change what I know?"

That is, a research team that has already studied hurricanes and now shifts to a study of tornadoes will not simply learn about the causes of tornadoes; instead they will learn about the causes of tornadoes *in relation to hurricanes.*

"The boundaries between topics aren't clear, and a good deal of learning involves synthesizing and analyzing, comparing and contrasting."

This, then, becomes a bend not only focused on conducting independent research, but also on comparing and contrasting. Students will compare and contrast subtopics as well as topics. Are the tools used to measure the strength of hurricanes the same as those used to measure tornadoes? Do people write about prevention of hurricanes in ways that are similar to how they describe prevention of tornadoes?

There is a reason why the skills of compare and contrast are highlighted in global standards. First of all, twenty-first-century literacy will center around learning from online resources. Eighty-seven percent of teens are online and they are online for an average of two to three hours a day, five days a week (Rosen, *My, My Space, and I*). This means that the challenge is not to read a single text but to negotiate a spider web of linked texts. In the twenty-first century, research by definition involves constructing knowledge from a mosaic of texts, and that means it involves comparing and contrasting. What does one text say that another doesn't? How is one subtopic like and unlike another? The researcher needs to be analytic and to move between chunks of information.

In this homestretch of the unit, you will remove scaffolds, release constraints, and invite learners to pursue their own important purposes. Part of this will likely involve use of the Informational Reading Learning Progression. This tool will be useful to you and your students across this last bend of the unit. Today's session involves particular work with comparing and contrasting, and mains idea(s) and supporting details.

Reading and Thinking across Two Topics
Comparing and Contrasting

CONNECTION

Revise the seating chart so research teams that will trade focus topics sit alongside each other. Channel those teams to talk about the topics they are passing along to each other.

"Researchers, when you come to the meeting area today, you'll see I have revised your seating chart somewhat." I again had papers positioned on the carpet of the meeting area with names written on them. The papers kept the research teams from earlier in the unit intact, but simply positioned some of the teams differently. The children didn't, at the time, know why.

Once students had settled into their new rug spots, I began. "During our last reading workshop, you learned about each other's topics. And I know that as you learned about another form of extreme weather, you sometimes thought, 'Hey, that's the same as . . .'

"Today each research team will get a chance to deepen that work. You'll begin a crash course in a second form of extreme weather or related natural disaster. I'm going to suggest you study topics that are somewhat related to each other, because the connections will be especially explosive. Tsunami and earthquake research teams will switch topics. Hurricane and tornado teams, you will swap topics. And the drought researchers will study floods, while the flood researchers study droughts."

"You are sitting close to the team with which you'll exchange topics—talk for a few minutes with the team that will study your topic next. Help that team get interested in the topic you've been studying for the last two weeks. Turn and talk."

❖ **Name the teaching point.**

"Today I want to teach you that researchers often shift from studying one example of something to studying a second example of that same thing. It is powerful to learn about the second example through the lens of thinking, 'How is this similar to what I already know? How is this different?'"

Children whose teachers taught Units of Study for Teaching Reading units during third grade participated in third-grade research projects on animals. During that project, each small research team studied one animal during Bend I, and then a second animal during Bend II, and they then did compare-and-contrast work across those animals. The upcoming bend will follow a similar plan, and you could mention this to your students if they did study within a Units of Study curriculum during third grade.

TEACHING

Demonstrate how you plan to study a second topic, comparing it to the first. Channel the class to engage in written conversations about what they notice you doing.

"I'm going to meet with one member of the flood research team. As we talk about how to go forward with our flood and drought research, will you jot notes about ways you think you can use the next few days to do some powerful work as well? In a few minutes, you'll get a chance to discuss your notes with your team."

I asked Madison, one of the members of the flood research team during Bend II, to come to the front of the meeting area. "Madison, we're swapping topics, so first let's give each other some pointers. Let's look at our list of subtopics and tell each other which were rich ones to study," I said, "and if a subtopic was important to both drought and floods, that will *definitely* be worth comparing and contrasting!" We looked together at the list of subtopics, and talked about which ones had especially yielded for us.

~~Drought~~

Extreme Weather and Natural Disasters

- Causes
- How they are measured
- Prevention and safety
- Important events
- Effects
- Firsthand experiences

We also talked about other subtopics we had ended up adding to our initial list. The drought team had added "Where droughts happen" and the flood team had added "Famous floods."

Demonstrate that you inquire about rich subtopics to pursue in the new topic and imagine pursuing them as comparative studies. Also ask for a guided tour of resources.

I issued a reminder to the class. "Keep jotting notes with your team about what Madison and I are doing that you and your team can also try."

I turned back to Madison. "So you said that there is a lot of good stuff to learn about the 'causes of floods.' From the class research on droughts, I know that 'causes of droughts' was a good topic as well, so I'm thinking that now, those of us switching to a study of floods should learn about causes and then do some comparative research between the causes for floods and for drought."

It's always nice to involve your students in the teaching of a minilesson. You will send the message that everyone in the classroom can serve as a teacher.

Keep this conversation extremely brief and to the point. You may need to prep the child you bring to the front of the meeting area.

Madison nodded. "I was thinking something sort of the same for my team. I know we are mostly studying drought now, and I think one of the subtopics we should look at will be effects of drought. That subtopic was important for both droughts and floods, so probably it'll be a good thing to compare."

"Later, we could probably think about other topics that are important, whether one is studying droughts or floods," I said, "but the other thing I want your help with are resources. Your bin is going to be our bin now, so can you talk about which texts you think we should start with, especially if we really want to know the causes of floods and of droughts." Madison dug through the bin and pulled out several texts on floods and started touring me through them.

ACTIVE ENGAGEMENT

Channel observing students to talk with their research teams about whether they imagine following a similar action plan, and about other things they imagine they'll want to do.

I paused at that point and said to the groups, "Right now will you talk about the action plan you saw us shaping? What steps did you see Madison and me take? Are you going to proceed in similar ways? Turn and talk."

The children talked as I listened in. After a bit I said, "From what you are saying, it seems like these are some steps that Madison and I have taken . . ."

As you listen to students' conversations, be sure to take quick notes so that you can recall their ideas when you share with the class.

Researching a Second Example

- **Don't just start reading: Talk. Plan.**
- **Decide on subtopics to investigate first, doing so in a comparative study.**

"What other ideas do you have for how your research team can proceed? Think together with your team and develop an action plan."

As children talked, I said, "When thinking about how to proceed, make sure you draw on all that you have learned earlier in this unit." I drew students' attention to our "To Research Well . . ." anchor chart from the previous bend. I gestured to some of the charts we'd been using from Bends I and II, including "To Research Well . . ."

Before long, we had added more points to our chart.

If you always tell your kids, "Sit here, read this, and read it in such and such a way . . . When you are finished, do this . . ." then how will your teaching help kids with the big work of authoring reading lives that matter? In this bend of the unit, you encourage students to make a lot of choices about how they will proceed, letting them author their procedures for research, so that you can coach them in the work that matters most.

Researching a Second Example

- Don't just start reading: Talk. Plan.
- Decide on subtopics to investigate first, doing so in a comparative study.
- **Decide who will do what, when, how.**
- **Preview texts, thinking, "How is this structured? How will I read it?"**
- **As you read, think, "These are similar because . . ." and "These are different because . . ."**

LINK

Channel kids to talk with their sister research team—the one with whom they are exchanging topics—to identify subtopics that yielded and are promising for a comparative study.

"I can tell you are eager to get started, so right now, will the two groups that are swapping topics have the conversation that you have been planning? Why don't you start just like Madison and I did, and tell each other which subtopics proved important to your research? See if you can find some subtopics in which you think comparative thinking will really pay off. Turn and talk."

As the groups talked, I listened in and coached, saying things like, "Don't forget to also talk about whether there were other subtopics that emerged as essential." After a moment, I said, "So tell the other group the subtopics you think your team might investigate first. Try the idea out and get some feedback."

After a bit, I voiced over to the whole class saying, "Once your research team begins to get some sense of a couple of subtopics to pursue, be sure you get a guided tour of the resource bin. Learn which sources will be most helpful."

Again, I listened in to the conversation, coaching into it. Leah was holding up *Nature's Extremes* for the new tsunami group to see. "This book is really hard," she said, "so maybe read it after you read some of the other ones, but I think that when you read about tsunamis you'll be like, 'Wait, this is practically about earthquakes!' Tsunamis are really connected to earthquakes." She held up a large visual that highlighted the various earthquakes around the world and the tsunamis they caused. "It's really hard to understand everything that causes them. So probably two people should study the science of tsunamis and what causes them together. All of the stuff you know about earthquakes will help you a

If the conversation that ensues feels like an important one and yet you are worried about timing, you needn't get restless over whether the minilesson is going too long. You aren't blabbing away for excessive lengths of time, which is the thing to avoid—this is actually work time. If it is productive, let it go on a bit.

lot." Chloe and Leo decided they would tackle the complex science behind the causes of tsunamis. "Here, start with this book," said Leah. "It's a lot, lot easier."

Once I felt sure that each group had a starting place, I called them back together. I took note of the groups that seemed less sure of their focus so that I could visit them first and help them get off to a strong start. "Researchers, you should have your marching orders. Get started! Find a place to work where you'll be sitting near each other. You might also choose to sit near the group that used to study your topic in case you have questions."

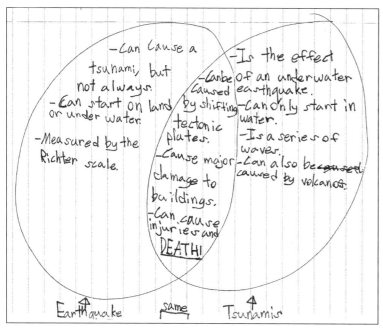

FIG. 14–2   As your students work today, they will begin to compare and contrast the information they are learning. Some of them may use diagrams like this to take notes.

Getting Research Groups Underway
Launching the New Work

WE HAVE OFTEN likened a reading workshop teacher to the circus man who gets plates spinning at the ends of sticks, and then moves quickly among those spinning plates, using a light touch to keep them spinning. That circus man will be busy on any given day, but on the day when he needs to set the plates in motion, he will be especially busy. That's your job today. It is made all the more challenging by the fact that you will want your students to feel as if they're making the decisions, launching the plates on their own . . . This, of course, slows things down.

For the first part of today's workshop, you'll be working with small groups, then later, with individuals. Either way, it will help to keep the image of that circus man in mind. Imagine yourself getting to each of your research teams once within just that first ten minutes of the workshop when they are talking in the meeting area. To do that, you absolutely can't settle down with one group and make yourself too comfortable!

Some teachers find that it helps to kneel uncomfortably alongside one tableful of kids, or to crouch awkwardly alongside a group, because the sheer discomfort keeps them from staying too long with one group! That solution is beyond the call of duty, but the point remains—if you're going to keep the plates spinning, you need to move quickly from one small group to another.

Coach, then move on. Coach, then move on.

In general, it helps to listen to the members of a group for a moment, then to coach into what the group is doing so as to get them started in a direction that feels productive. Then, move on to another group, hoping to circle back to that original group before the research teams disperse or during the share at the end of the workshop. If the groups are working in corners of the meeting area, you can think of yourself like the dials on the face of the clock, turning from one small group to the next, the next, the next, circling back to each group more than once.

Once students begin to read, you will probably want to help them compare and contrast while they are reading. You may convene a few students who could especially use help with this. They may come from different research teams, so you'd need to work with one team's topic to illustrate a way of progressing.

You will probably start by hearing about a subtopic that at least one of the teams represented in the small group had decided to focus on—say, the effects of tornadoes (and hurricanes) and then locate and begin to read a relevant section from one of the easiest texts in their bin. You might say, "Let's put this book where all of you can see it, and let's read it in unison, like we do during shared reading. Let's stop often to talk about what we are learning and thinking." Then after the group reads a chunk, and recalls it in a boxes-and-bullets fashion, you can nudge the one member of the group who has studied hurricanes previously to think, "How is that the same as what I already know about hurricanes? How is that different?" Emphasize that it is helpful to extract a sort of outline of the new text, popping out the author's main points—the main ideas and supporting details—so you can then return to that boxes-and-bullets outline, thinking, "Okay, let me take this first big idea. Is this the same for hurricanes? What about this first supportive point?"

That work might take ten minutes. Stop to recall the steps and then perhaps provide guided practice to the kids who need to do similar work with different topics.

Frankly, it's a bit of a euphemism to describe the work you do today as conferring. It is more like fast-paced coaching. Your focus will be on moving really quickly among the small groups, getting one going and then bringing another in to see the work that you helped the first group to launch.

(continues)

You may see some students studying the second topic as if it was an entirely distinct bit of research, one having no relation to the first subtopic. That is a decision a researcher could make, but you might gather these kids together and tell them, "Earlier you learned that when you go from reading one source on a topic to another, you read, thinking, 'How does this fit with what I already know? What's new and different? What's similar?' Let's try thinking that way together, about tsunamis and earthquakes."

"Can I interrupt? Would you and your research teammates find the book in your bin into which I put a purple Post-it with a star on it, and turn to that page." I gave students just a moment to find the right page, then continued, "That passage marked with a starred Post-it has a compare-and-contrast structure, and I thought that because you are doing comparative research, you and your team might read this over, and notice the sorts of sentences that support comparison work. What sorts of sentences do you see authors using to compare and contrast two topics? Record some of those."

I gave the teams just a few minutes to do that. I made my way to each group quickly, ensuring that each research team had found at least one sentence to share out. I gave students a chance to share their findings with the class and then revealed a chart with the sentence templates that I had prepared prior to today's session, based on the sentence templates I knew they'd find in their books.

"Researchers, you won't find many places where *the authors* have been comparing your current topic with an earlier one, but just because the authors haven't been laying out similarities and differences in an obvious way, doesn't mean *you* can't still think about them as you read.

"Let's say one text talks about the waves during a particular hurricane, and another text talks about the same thing in relation to a tornado. Those two authors may not be making comparisons, but you can make them. Part of being a researcher is seeing things that others have missed!

"As you continue reading and taking notes, see if it works for you to be using some of the sentence frames on our chart to think about comparisons between your two topics. Get back to work."

Phrases We Can Use When Comparing and Contrasting Information...

ALIKE   DIFFERENT

• ____ and ____ are alike because...

• ____ and ____ have differences, too. One difference is...

• Both ____ and ____ (what?)

• For... not unlike ... (what?)

• It is interesting to note that ____ and ____ are different in this way. Whereas... on the other hand...

Holding onto the Author's Points
Main Ideas and Supporting Details

Channel students to use what they know about note-taking to set up a system for keeping track of the information they are learning.

"Readers, eyes up here. When you made plans for what you would read first, how many of you made the wise decision to start by reading the easier texts that overview your topic?" I gave a thumbs up to signal that I'd like them to let me know with this gesture, and most signaled that yes, that was what they'd done. "Wise decision."

"Can I ask you something else? Do you remember that earlier in our nonfiction work, as we read, we used text structure to preview a text and decide how to read it, then collected the author's points, main ideas (I pointed to the palm of my hand), and the supporting details (I gestured to my fingers)? You all are going to be developing expertise on your new topics, comparing and contrasting the information you learn with what you already know, so you will probably want to return to that work from the beginning of our unit.

"You can decide whether you will be taking notes on the author's points in your reading notebook, or on Post-its. Either way, you probably will want to outline the main ideas (I showed my palm) and some of the supports (I touched one finger, then another to illustrate bullet points). You may, however, invent some other system for getting your arms around your topic. You are definitely the authors of your own learning lives right now, and my job is to observe and admire the way that you organize your learning. Right now, will you take a moment to decide on a system you'll use for keeping track of the new information? Remember, you needn't get every little detail down—just the big ideas and concepts." I gave the students a few moments to make decisions and begin to tackle this work. I watched as Leo set up a few pages of blank boxes and bullets in his notebook, and as Chloe made a quick tracing of her hand on a notebook page and wrote "Causes of Tsunamis" at the top.

Though students were still busy, I asked them to pause. "Readers, we have just a few minutes left to read for the author's points. You and your group need to decide what to do with these last minutes. You may want to return to the subtopics you read about today and jot some main ideas and specific details on your flowchart or in your reading notebooks.

"Then again, one of you may want to teach the others in your group about the author's points you've read. If you do that, be sure you organize your lessons into main ideas and supporting details, and remember to use gestures, expression, and expert vocabulary to teach well. I'll circulate to admire the learning work you are doing together."

In workshop teaching it is important to return to skills and strategies you have taught before in order to help students recall what they have learned and practiced. This share aims at supporting students' transfer of skill work from one day to another.

It's helpful to give students choices as they research and collaborate so that they learn how to make decisions. If, instead, we give precise directions for every tiny step students take, they will always wait for our instructions and will learn to be dependent instead of independent.

BRINGING WHAT YOU KNOW TO A NEW RESEARCH TOPIC

Readers,

Today you started to research a new topic, a second type of extreme weather or natural disaster. Tonight, continue your research. As you read on about your topic, whether you choose to continue reading an easier text that overviews your topic or jump into a new text, bring everything you know from researching your first example with you. Use the "Researching a Second Example" chart we started in class today to get ideas for your research.

ANCHOR CHART

Researching a Second Example

- Don't just start reading: Talk. Plan.
- Decide on subtopics to investigate first, doing so in a comparative study.
- Decide who will do what, when, how.
- Preview texts, thinking, "How is this structured? How will I read it?"
- As you read, think, "These are similar because . . ." and "These are different because . . ."

As you read tonight, add to your notes on your topic. Continue reading for the author's points. You might take notes in your reader's notebook or on Post-it notes, or you might develop your own way to write about the main ideas and supporting details you learn.

Session 15

Seeking Out Patterns and Relationships

T ODAY YOU'LL BEGIN by telling kids the purpose for the day's work. In his book *To Sell Is Human*, Daniel Pink points out that much of what we do in our daily lives is simple marketing. Doctors sell diagnoses to patients. Consultants sell advice. Teachers sell the habits, skills, and mindsets of a love of literacy and achievement. Today, you'll recruit kids' passion to tackle the complex work ahead.

To do this, ask kids to think of people they know who are preoccupied with something. Try it yourself. Perhaps you know someone who is obsessed with fitness. Her interest may have begun with a fairly defined focus—say losing weight for a daughter's wedding—but then her field of interest broadened to include nutrition and apps that help track caloric intake; as well as exercise and resting heart rates. More importantly, she began to think across those fields of knowledge. What is the best form of exercise for a whole body workout? How do athletes eat before and after workouts? Finally, she probably began to think about a bigger field of knowledge, such as the relationship between mental health and physical health, or the role of economics in health and nutrition.

This unit invites readers to experience stages of learning so that in these final sessions, they do the kind of thinking that is characteristic of experts. You'll invite students to think from one focused field of knowledge to another, broader field. You'll invite students to see patterns in the details, to grow hunches, and to think more conceptually. In the previous session you launched the work by showing kids that readers can think across two extreme weather events and natural disasters—floods and droughts. Today, you'll extend this work by showing children how they can extend the reading-across-a-topic work that they've done often in the previous two bends of the unit. The research teams studying specific weather events such as hurricanes or tornadoes might begin studying extreme weather in general, or in climate change. Research teams studying specific earth events such as earthquakes or tsunamis might broaden their field of knowledge by looking at natural disasters in general. You'll teach students that as their focus becomes broader, it will pay to think more about patterns and relationships.

IN THIS SESSION, you'll teach students that one way to deepen expertise on a topic is to move from studying specific topics to thinking about patterns and relationships across the bigger field of knowledge.

GETTING READY

✔ Ask each team to bring their bin of research materials with them to the meeting area (see Teaching and Active Engagement).

✔ Be prepared to read aloud and project "What Is a Tornado?" from *Everything Weather* and "Tsunami" from *Hurricane & Tornado* by Jack Challoner, or substitute two passages you studied with the class on your subtopics (see Teaching).

✔ Prepare to read aloud and project excerpts from two additional texts on your subtopics for students to study. Here we recommend "Fast-Moving Water" from page 9 of *Cobblestone* (March 2012) and "Katrina Strikes" from page 14 of *Cobblestone* (March 2012). These articles are available in the online resources (see Active Engagement).

✔ Make an enlarged copy of the notebook entry you scrawl on your clipboard after today's Reading Workshop ends (see Teaching).

✔ Keep your "Phrases We Can Use When Comparing and Contrasting Information" ready for reference (see Active Engagement).

✔ Be prepared to add "Look across books at similar subsections to think about patterns and relationships" to the "Researching a Second Example" anchor chart (see Link).

Seeking Out Patterns and Relationships

CONNECTION

Recruit students' commitment by explaining that experts go from learning about focused topics to learning about a field of study.

"Researchers, you're in the final bend of the unit, the final stretch of your research, and I want to talk to you about expertise. What I want you to know is that thinking changes once a person develops expertise.

"Right now—think of someone you know—or once knew—who is *obsessed* with a topic." I gave a second of silence. "Maybe you are thinking of someone who is obsessed with dinosaurs, or horses, or soccer. The person who is obsessed with a topic has expert knowledge—that person doesn't just think about a particular subset of the topic," and I made my hands into the lens of a microscope and peered through my hands at a little topic. "No, the expert ends up learning about the whole world of that topic.

"The expert obsessed with dinosaurs might start out being interested in the *T. Rex*, and soon he is interested in all dinosaurs, and then in all the ancient creatures. He wants to know what happened to them and why they are extinct, and so he becomes interested in paleontological digs and geological periods, too. You see how an expert's focus keeps getting bigger and bigger as his field of interest grows?

"It's more than that, too. The expert doesn't just see distinct facts. The expert also sees patterns and develops ideas that are bigger than that one topic. For instance, when an expert studies the different kinds of dinosaurs, he or she begins to see that each dinosaur relied on a different kind of environment to survive. Some needed access to animals and meat to eat. Other dinosaurs needed access to huge amounts of leaves and greens. When those things disappeared, so did that species of dinosaur. The expert can see a bigger pattern: animals become extinct when the food, weather, space, and other factors they need to survive start to disappear.

❖ Name the teaching point.

"Today I want to teach you that to develop expertise on a topic, nonfiction readers go from learning about specific related topics (such as tornadoes or floods) to learning about their bigger field of knowledge (extreme weather). As a researcher's focus gets bigger, the researcher thinks more about patterns and relationships."

When you begin a minilesson by drawing on kids' own experiences, you immediately establish a connection between the children and the content you are about to teach. Like all connections, you'll want to keep this brief so that you can get to the heart of the minilesson as quickly as possible.

150

TEACHING

Tell students that researchers develop expertise by looking across the subtopics of related topics. Ask teams to lay out a book for each topic they've studied and look across the tables of contents.

"So what does this mean for our last bend in this road of study? Let's think together about how we go from learning about particular topics—droughts, tornadoes, and hurricanes—to becoming an expert about extreme weather in general. Hmm . . ."

"Here's the thing, researchers. Listen up because this is important and sophisticated work for kids your age. Expert knowledge is the knowledge that a person *makes*, on his or her own, by putting together specific knowledge on one topic, and another topic, and another topic. Experts come up with their own discoveries and ideas and hunches as they think between related topics they know well. Experts grow their own ideas and synthesize what they are learning across topics.

"So research team members, lay out two books on the weather-related topics you know. If you look in your research team bin, you'll see that you have some of the texts from each topic you studied, both the one you're already an expert on, and the one you've just started learning about. Once you have these books in front of you, open each to its Table of Contents, if it has one."

Demonstrate how you read across two books about tornadoes and tsunamis to look for patterns.

"So researchers, what do we do next? Remember, to become experts . . ." and I referenced a written version of the day's teaching point:

> Researchers go from learning about specific topics (such as hurricanes or floods) to learning about their bigger field of knowledge (weather). As a researcher's focus gets bigger, the researcher thinks more about patterns and relationships.

"It seems like one place to begin is to try noticing patterns about weather in general that come up when looking across whatever subtopics we have studied. Are you game?"

"Now, this is going to be tricky," I cautioned, "because our topics may not exactly line up. But let's grab two passages that seem to do similar jobs in two of the books, and read them, looking for patterns. These are both overviews," I said, and I displayed an enlarged copy of "What Is a Tornado?" from *Everything Weather* and "Tsunami" from *Hurricane & Tornado*. I read:

> Tornadoes, also known as twisters, are funnels of rapidly rotating air that are created during a thunderstorm. With wind speeds up to 200 mph (482 kph), tornadoes have the power to pick up and destroy everything in their path.

You might notice that we've chosen to model here with a combination of topics that don't match the paired topics students are studying. The purpose is to leave to students the work of comparing and contrasting across their own paired topics.

If your students studied unit 2, Reading to Learn: Grasping Main Ideas and Text Structures, in third grade, you may explicitly reference the similar work that students did when they went from comparing and contrasting the animals they studied to studying topics such as warm- and cold-bloodedness across animals, or adaptations across animals.

Often mistakenly called tidal waves, tsunamis are triggered by earthquakes beneath the seabed and can devastate areas, such as here on Okushiri Island, Japan.

"Remember we are looking for patterns, and for things we can say, or ask, about weather in general. We're thinking about hunches that we can develop. You are probably being reminded of some things you already know about weather. And you might have some new questions.

"Study the thinking I do because soon you'll have a chance to do something similar," I said and started to scrawl thoughts onto my clipboard, saying them aloud as I wrote. After I'd written a line or two, I just mimed continuing to write and "wrote in the air" so as to save time.

> A pattern I see between tornadoes and tsunamis is that both are super powerful—they both destroy whatever is in their path. They flatten things. They have similar effects.
>
> When I think about patterns in their causes . . . there is a pattern because they both begin, or are triggered, by a different weather event—tsunamis from earthquakes, and tornadoes from thunderstorms.
>
> One bad thing gets another bad thing going. Dominoes.
>
> Do most examples of extreme weather get caused by or triggered by another weather event?

You'll probably want to write on paper, tucked onto a clipboard rather than on a large sheet of chart paper because you can go way faster that way. Also, if it helps, you can actually have written these thoughts onto the page on your clipboard (secretly) prior to now, and can use that written record to remind you of the thoughts you want to say aloud. Later it might be helpful to produce an enlarged copy of whatever you write.

ACTIVE ENGAGEMENT

Read aloud two new excerpts on the related topics, asking kids to think about similarities and differences, and to look for patterns in the information.

"You game to try what you just watched me do? Let's read across other related subsections on two different weather topics. Think about what you can learn about weather in general, and think about ways these topics are similar and different. Try to see patterns across the information, and to think intensely." I displayed an enlarged copy of two more excerpts, which I read aloud.

> *Flash floods are America's deadliest weather hazard, says the National Weather Service. . . . Flash floods happen when prolonged heavy rain can't drain quickly enough—typically, within six hours of a rainstorm. Without warning, sudden surges of water weaken or wash away bridges, dams, and roads. They uproot trees and destroy homes and other buildings. The average annual damage in the United States from flash floods is more than two billion dollars*

> *In terms of wind speed, Hurricane Katrina reached 120 miles per hour at landfall of August 29 in Louisiana, earning a high Category Three classification. Hurricane Katrina could easily have surpassed Galveston's death toll had it not been for the massive evacuation that took place on the Gulf coast. The evacuation, which saved so many lives, was made possible by modern weather forecasting and constant alerts to the public. Meteorologists were able to track Katrina as it formed in the Bahamas, cut a path through Florida, and then zeroed in on Louisiana.*

"Turn and talk."

As children talked, I moved among them. "Readers, if it helps, use some of our compare-and-contrast sentence stems," I said, gesturing to the chart that contained compare-and-contrast prompts.

I voiced over. "Looking across weather events is paying off. Be sure when you do that you compare apples to apples, not apples to bananas. If you are interested in the way that droughts occur slowly over time, then take that concept—weather events that occur slowly over time—and think, 'Which of the other kinds of weather are similar to droughts in that they occur slowly, over time?'"

I reconvened the class, and for a few moments we shared the most dramatic of their ideas.

> ### Phrases We Can Use When Comparing and Contrasting Information...
>
> (ALIKE) (DIFFERENT)
>
> • ____ and ____ are alike because...
>
> • ____ and ____ have differences, too. One difference is...
>
> • Both ____ and ____ (what?)
>
> • For... not unlike ... (what?)
>
> • It is interesting to note that ____ and ____ are different in this way. Whereas... on the other hand...

As you read these yourself, you will want to try your hand at the work you have asked kids to do. What do you see in the way of similarities and differences? Do you notice that both kinds of weather events cause damage by water, though the timing is very different? Flash floods happen in an instant, while hurricanes form and strengthen over time before landfall. You probably notice that technology and the ability to predict and track hurricanes has made an impact on their effects—they are less deadly because meteorologists are able to warn people about them and evacuate the area.

Be sure to voice this while there is still time for kids to do this work, reading across the passages, and talking about what they see. You are setting kids up to consolidate information in ways that are really interesting. Tsunamis and floods do damage with water, while tornadoes do damage with wind, and hurricanes combine the two. We have a longer time frame to warn people and react to hurricanes, but we can't predict when thunderstorms and rainstorms will lead to tornadoes and flash floods, or when tsunamis and earthquakes will strike. Droughts, on the other hand, occur slowly over time.

LINK

Channel readers to talk in their research teams, assigning themselves jobs, planning work for the day, and anticipating the team conversation they will have later on.

"So readers, we could talk for a very long time about the other insights you are gleaning from reading across just these two subsections, but I think it is time for you to do this work with your research team. So I'm going to give you exactly four minutes—no more—to decide on the reading work you and your team will be doing today. Who will do what? Your team will meet at the end of today's workshop, so plan on what people will bring to that research team meeting. Start talking!" I added the day's work to our anchor chart, and then I moved around the rug to support teams as they planned their work for the day.

As you listen in and coach, one of the questions to ask is whether it is best for the research team to have a divide-and-conquer strategy, with each team member taking on a different subtopic and preparing to teach what that person learns to the others—or will it be better for them to overlap the assignments so there are more opportunities for conversation? We'd generally opt for the latter, especially for readers needing some support. It could be some team members work alone, some in pairs, to tackle a topic. Don't discourage a plan to alternate between reading and talking, as the thinking burden in today's work is very high.

ANCHOR CHART

Researching a Second Example

- Don't just start reading: Talk. Plan.
- Decide on subtopics to investigate first, doing so in a comparative study.
- Decide who will do what, when, how.
- Preview texts, thinking, "How is this structured? How will I read it?"
- As you read, think, "These are similar because . . ." and "These are different because . . ."
- **Look across books at similar subsections to think about patterns and relationships.**

Look across books at similar subsections – Think about ...

Patterns   Relationships

Balance On-Going Work with New Thinking

THROUGHOUT TODAY'S WORKSHOP you will probably want to refer to the Informational Reading Learning Progression. The "Analyzing Author's Craft" strand may be especially helpful as you confer and the "Questioning" strand will be useful during the mid-workshop teaching. You may choose to spend some of your time today meeting with research teams, or you may pull students across different research teams who need support with particular skills. If students struggle with their note-taking or you find that it is dominating their time, help them organize their thinking in more expeditious ways.

Support students as they develop skills in note-taking.

You'll find that some students are doing very little note-taking, though this may or may not correspond to the amount of talking and thinking about their topic they are doing. Alternately, students may be taking notes prolifically, but in ways that keep them bound to small, less sophisticated ideas. That is, at this juncture, students should be organizing their notes by big ideas or large questions that are guiding their inquiries.

MID-WORKSHOP TEACHING   Readers Question to Push Their Thinking Deeper

"Readers, can I stop you for a minute? I've noticed many of you with two books open, reading across sections about different types of extreme weather and doing the sophisticated compare-and-contrast work that we practiced together today. But I want to remind you that as you're reading, you can take a few moments to push your thinking by asking yourself some questions. As readers research the similarities and differences of the things they are studying, they ask, 'Why?' 'Are others the same? What explains this?' These questions lead to more thinking, more talking . . . and to more reading!"

If they seem to be jotting every note there is to be taken about the effects of tornadoes or the causes of mudslides, you might wonder whether they have taken the last few days of teaching to heart. If this is the case, you might revisit some of the ways that researchers make their ideas bigger, such as connecting information to what they already know and writing to explain things to themselves and others. You might also revisit earlier conferring sections in which we talked about talk and writing prompts students can use to deepen their thinking.

Other students might be focusing on their new subject and skipping the compare-and-contrast work of the bend. In this case, suggest that students begin by focusing on one subtopic at a time, first focusing their attention solely on similarities by reading between two texts, and looking for ways in which their types of extreme weather are similar. Teach them to note and record similarities, using the phrases you introduced in the previous session.

Once students feel as though they have captured all of the similarities, they can read between those same two texts, this time looking for ways in which their types of extreme weather are different. Then, they can tackle the next subtopic in the same way.

Help students consider the author's intentions.

Some of your students may be ready to make comparisons that require analysis of the content choices made by authors. I recognized this as a need when I pulled up to listen in to the research team that read about tornadoes in Bend II and was studying hurricanes in Bend III. As Jack flipped through some of the books his team had already read, he noticed that on one hand, his books about tornadoes often had a section about people who study tornadoes, but on the other hand, his books about hurricanes hardly had anything on the people studying hurricanes. I decided to capitalize on this opportunity, helping Jack to think more deeply about the choices the author made, channeling him to think about why the author would devote so much text to one subtopic and not another.

(continues)

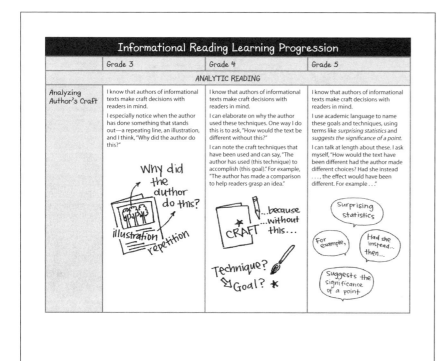

Informational Reading Learning Progression

	Grade 3	Grade 4	Grade 5
	ANALYTIC READING		
Analyzing Author's Craft	I know that authors of informational texts make craft decisions with readers in mind. I especially notice when the author has done something that stands out—a repeating line, an illustration, and I think, "Why did the author do this?"	I know that authors of informational texts make craft decisions with readers in mind. I can elaborate on why the author used these techniques. One way I do this is to ask, "How would the text be different without this?" I can note the craft techniques that have been used and can say, "The author has used (this technique) to accomplish (this goal)." For example, "The author has made a comparison to help readers grasp an idea."	I know that authors of informational texts make craft decisions with readers in mind. I use academic language to name these goals and techniques, using terms like *surprising statistics* and *suggests the significance of a point*. I can talk at length about these. I ask myself, "How would the text have been different had the author made different choices? Had she instead . . . , the effect would have been different. For example . . ."

"Why do you think your authors would do this? Why would they write about people who study one form of extreme weather—tornadoes—but hardly anything about people who study another form of extreme weather—hurricanes?" I asked. Jack thought for a moment, and then looked up at me in an appeal for help. My ideas about this were quickly forming, but I remembered this was my chance to help Jack to construct his own ideas, not to give him mine. Instead I said, "Let's take a look at a place in the text where this was true. Studying that might give us some ideas."

Jack flipped through his bin and pulled out a copy of *Everything Weather*. "It happened here," he said, opening to the section titled "Storm Chasers" on page 40. "See how almost everything is about chasing the tornado. There's the Team Twistex vehicle that studies tornadoes and there's that crazy picture of the person dropping the video camera and then running that shows a tornado coming right at him." I knew it would pay off to linger on this page, so I said, "What about people who studied hurricanes? Did the author mention them at all?" Jack scanned the page and then said, "Barely. She named hurricanes as one thing storm chasers chase, and there's this teeny tiny picture of a Bill Olney studying a hurricane, but that's it."

"I wonder why the author did that?" I thought aloud. I wanted Jack to construct some tentative theories. I knew his ideas about the author's intent needn't be *right* (after all, unless he could interview the author, he couldn't know for sure what she meant to convey). Nevertheless, I knew studying an author's choices would open up a whole new field of options for him as a researcher. "Start with 'Maybe it's because . . .' or 'It could be because . . .' and make an educated guess about why Kathy would have done this."

"Maybe she did it because there are more people who study tornadoes, so she wanted to say more about them?" Jack said, still a little hesitant.

"Or 'Perhaps it's because . . .'?" I prompted, pushing Jack to consider multiple ideas.

"Or perhaps . . . perhaps . . . she wanted to blow our minds. Like it says on the cover, 'Facts, photos, and fun that will blow your mind.' That picture of the hurricane researcher in the plane isn't going to blow anyone's mind. It doesn't look scary at all. He's just sitting back, and it seems like the computers are doing all the work. But that picture of the tornado hunter dropping the camera and then running makes me super nervous. So maybe she did it to surprise us and scare us," Jack said.

I wanted to name for Jack what he had done. "This is powerful work, Jack. You're noticing a choice the author made and considering multiple reasons why the author made that choice. We can't know for sure, but we can push ourselves to consider multiple options. Keep noticing and questioning the author's choices as you read on."

Promoting Substantive and Effective Conversations in Research Teams

Launch research teams into discussions, and coach in response to what you hear.

I asked for the children's attention and said, "I'm not going to say anything because I don't want to take up even a second of your work time today. Get into your research teams right away, and get to work together."

As kids talked, I moved among them, coaching into their conversations and occasionally making voiceovers to the whole class. "Researchers, I'm noticing some of you are talking about different types of extreme weather and natural disasters without using the technical vocabulary. Can you put your word bank—the list of words that you have been compiling since the first bend of our unit—front and center in this conversation, and try to remember that a mark of an expert is that you use technical vocabulary? Try to name the specific equipment or measurement scales that meteorologists use," I reminded the class.

A few moments later, I voiced over, "Researchers, you guys are on fire with ideas, but can I ask you to pause and think about your talk, and whether you are using your very best conversation skills? Think for a moment about the qualities of a really good conversation . . ." I gave them a minute of silence. "Will you talk not about your types of extreme weather, but about your conversation for just a minute?" As children talked, I celebrated that they recalled that good conversations take a single idea and stay with that idea for as long as possible, and that in a good conversation there are follow-up questions and kids use phrases such as, "I agree with you because . . ." and "Where do you see that?"

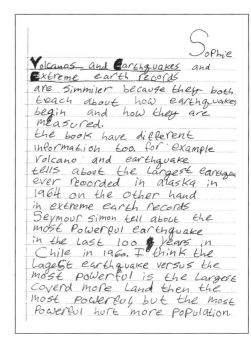

FIG. 15–1   Sophie's writing represents her comparing and contrasting work as she moved between two texts.

READING TO DETERMINE THE AUTHOR'S MAIN POINTS

Readers, today, you started to become more of an expert, not just on one type of extreme weather or natural disaster, but on extreme weather and natural disasters as a broader topic. To do that, you had to think across several different types of weather or disaster events, and you started asking complex questions and making comparisons across topics.

Tonight, continue with your research on your new topic. Read on in texts on your topic, pausing to think about the author's main points—the main ideas and supporting details you learn as you read, and add your new learning to your notes. Make sure your notes are clearly organized and structured so you can share your learning with your research team. And, as you read, keep the questions you have about your topic and the comparisons you've already noticed in mind, and jot down *your* ideas about what you are learning.

Session 16

New Topics Lead to New Investigations

MUCH OF YOUR TEACHING within the third bend of this unit is focused on helping students synthesize information across texts. From the first lessons, you taught students to compare and contrast across topics, supporting them as they entered their second topic differently based on their experiences researching their first topic. Then, you coached students to consider how the new information they were learning fit with or changed what they already knew. By now, your students are noticing patterns and relationships across texts, pushing themselves to grow deep ideas through their synthesis work. Today, you will show students how to take this work further, demonstrating how reading across several texts can spark deep questions that lead to in-depth inquiries.

Look at ways you can use your read-aloud time to extend this work. Up to this point, you may have been reading through sections of text and talking about authors' main points in isolation. Start looking at ways to incorporate cross-text work into your read-aloud, so students have regular, supported opportunities to synthesize information. You will want to orchestrate opportunities for students to synthesize information across subtopics within one text as well as across related topics. The Informational Reading Learning Progression includes a specific strand on "Cross-Text(s) Synthesis," and studying this strand closely will help you plan read-alouds based on where your students' synthesis work currently falls.

To begin this work, you might read aloud a part in *Everything Weather*, ask students to turn and talk to recall parts where that same subtopic was addressed in *Hurricane & Tornado*, and then reread a part from *Hurricane & Tornado* that students identify, coaching students to consider how the information in the two parts of the text fits together. Push students to extend their thinking by noticing patterns and relationships, as well as by letting their rereading spark new research questions. In addition to the "Cross Text(s) Synthesis" strand, you'll probably want to make use of the "Growing Ideas" and "Questioning the Text" strands.

We are sure you will find powerful ways to extend this work. One teacher we work with asked students to bring a text they were studying in their research team to the rug, and to open to a page they knew inside and out. Holding their familiar texts, she read

IN THIS SESSION, you'll teach students that as researchers read across topics, the new information they learn ignites new inquiries, and then they read on to investigate their questions.

GETTING READY

✔ Prepare to share a video with students of a man rubbing two sticks together (Google search term "Fire making with sticks Andrew Newton"). A link is available on the online resources (see Connection).

✔ Find a passage from the demonstration text to read from as a way to spark questions about your topic. We chose "Wild Weather Zones" from pages 28–29 in *Everything Weather* by Kathy Furgang (see Teaching).

✔ Students should bring their reader's notebooks and a pencil with them to the meeting area (see Teaching and Link).

✔ Have your reader's notebook ready to record your research questions (see Teaching).

✔ Select a second passage from a demonstration text to refer to as a way to spark additional ideas for research. We chose the "Deadly Droughts" section from page 47 of *Hurricane & Tornado* (see Teaching).

✔ Ask students to bring their research bins with them to the rug (see Active Engagement).

✔ Be ready to add a new bullet to the "Researching a Second Example" anchor chart (see Link).

✔ Have ready to reference the charts "Ways to Push Our Thinking" and "Techniques for Writing to Grow Ideas" (see Conferring and Small-Group Work).

✔ Have sections of "What Do You Do with an Idea?" by Kobi Yamada ready to read aloud (see Share).

✔ Chart paper and markers (see Share)

aloud parts from *Everything Weather*, asking students to consider how the information she was reading fit with the parts they were holding. Another teacher asked students to bring their reader's notebooks with them to the read-aloud, and after reading each section of *Everything Weather*, she gave research teams time to talk about how the information she shared fit with their current topic. This work is called for in world-class standards, which ask students to "integrate information from two texts on the same topic in order to write or speak about the subject knowledgeably."

"Today you will show students how reading across several texts can spark deep questions that lead to in-depth inquiries."

The questions students develop today will become a key part of the research they do moving forward. As you preview the upcoming lessons, you will notice that the questions students develop today anchor the reading and research they do across the remainder of the bend. By the end of today's lesson, you'll ask students to read through the research questions they've developed and to identify a few possible questions that could guide their inquiries. Today's work, then, sets students up to develop their own agendas, agendas that may run counter to the texts they are reading, and to read across texts with those agendas in mind.

New Topics Lead to New Investigations

CONNECTION

Ask students to share discoveries on their topics. Share a video of a man rubbing two sticks together to ignite a flame, and ask students to think about how it relates to their work.

"Readers, earlier in this unit, I saw you thinking across *texts*; now you've begun thinking across *topics*. Some pretty exciting stuff happened when you compared subtopics across hurricanes and tornados, floods and droughts, and so forth. Turn to someone sitting near you—someone from another research team, if that is easy—and share some of the early discoveries you are making."

The room filled with talk until I said, "Alright, researchers, look back up here. We are going to watch a short video clip. It may at first seem irrelevant—but it is not."

I cued up the video "Fire making with sticks," by Andrew Newton (https://www.youtube.com/watch?v=ZYcBiEX9p6w). The children watched as a man rubbed two sticks together—sawing them back and forth—until eventually he had a pile of kindling smoking, then in flames.

Ask the kids to figure out how the video relates to their work. After they talk, use the video to accentuate that the point of the comparative work is to spark ideas.

When the clip ended, I called, with urgency, "So how does that relate to what you are doing? Turn and talk!"

Some of the children had no trouble seeing the metaphor. "He rubbed the sticks together, sort of like how we are rubbing what we're learning about tornadoes and hurricanes together, and just like he made sparks and then fire, we are making sparks, our ideas! It's the same!"

"Eyes back here," I said, nodding. "As you all were saying, that man rubbed two sticks together and created sparks . . . and they ignited into an impressive flame. Yesterday and today, you are rubbing two topics together—and the goal is not a two-column chart of similarities and differences. The goal is more exciting and important. The goal is for this research to spark ideas that ignite, ideas that matter."

◆ COACHING

If showing a video is extremely difficult for you to pull off in a minilesson, you can simply say to the kids, "Last night I watched . . ." and then describe the clip. That will decrease the entertainment and that is not inconsequential, but it is okay. Either way, do watch it, and do allow kids the fun of thinking, "How does that relate to what we are doing?"

Name the teaching point.

"Today I want to teach you that when you move from one subtopic to another, it is like taking two sticks and rubbing them together. When you take your two topics and research further, it 'sparks' new questions. As you move from topic to topic, you can think, 'What questions does this spark for me?'"

TEACHING

Demonstrate by reading and thinking aloud about the class topic, showing students that you take a part of the text and study it, knowing you can generate questions from almost any text.

"Let's take a subtopic we have been studying as a class—the causes of droughts and floods—and see if by thinking across both droughts and floods, we can spark some ideas, some questions about the topics." I turned to *Everything Weather* and said, "I'm just gonna look at interesting parts and see if there is anything in them about the causes."

I turned to the "Wild Weather Zones" section (pages 28–29) and looked at a map of the world, turning the book around so that students could study the map with me. "We could roam through lots of pages, looking for an idea to hit us over the head, but usually I find that to get an idea, I can take almost anything, and if I really study it, expecting to grow an insight, I will. I say to myself, 'This one bit of text will generate a question or an idea that I can go with . . .' and it usually does. So let's really look at this map, keeping the causes of drought and floods (or just those topics, in general) foremost in our minds."

I ran my pencil over the map, and thought out loud. Then my pencil paused on Australia between the part of the map that showed drought and the part that showed floods. "Hmm, . . . You know what's weird? This is a map of Australia here," and I pointed to the blue parts of the map that indicated areas where monsoons often cause dangerous flooding. "They have flooding." Then my pencil moved to sections of the map that showed drought. "And over here, still in Australia, they have a huge area that's affected by droughts! And this part, right in the middle of Australia, is prone to *both* droughts and floods!"

Demonstrate that if you have paused to think after reading a text and you feel the spark of an idea, however small, it is important to nurture that little spark, helping it ignite an idea. Rally students to write alongside you.

"That's making me think about some bigger ideas about the real problem of droughts and floods, not just Australia, but anywhere, isn't it for you? So much is going through my mind right this second—it's like I can feel those sparks in my mind. Are you feeling it, too? I'm thinking we need to develop our ideas, right? Pick up your pen, and let's jot about whatever it is we're thinking."

Be sure to pause here to let the information sink in with your students. As much as this is your demonstration, you want to engage your students by setting them up to think alongside with you.

The room was filled with the scratch of pens. I jotted, eyes glued to my own page, as I recalled reading about political battles in the U.S. over whether water is a resource that is locally owned or not, and about the battles between the rights of farmers, of environmentalists, the tourism business.

Highlight a few research questions students generated.

After a bit, I called kids' back, and asked for their thinking. Taylor said, "I was thinking about how interesting it is that two places right next to each other can have such *different* weather. And, from our social studies work last year, I wondered if maybe it has to do with the mountains and the sea, and with where clouds go up and go down."

I nodded. "Taylor—if droughts and floods were your topic, you could stop comparing and contrasting them and start researching that topic, the idea that landforms may have some impact on extreme weather. You could ask yourself, 'How does the location of places that flood and have droughts relate to the physical geography?' You could read about that, but also you could study tons of maps and get your own theories going! Your spark would have ignited a whole research project!

"What were some of the other ideas you guys wrote about?"

Madison explained that she wondered why people live in places that aren't near water. "Do they have no choice? Maybe they are born there and have nowhere else to go?" I nodded and pointed out that because this actually is her research team's topic, she could go with that idea and research the relationship between population density, droughts, and floods. I added, "One thing I have read about is this—with global warming, there are places in the world that are flooding a lot—flood regions. When people build there anyway—maybe they want the ocean view—and then the flood comes, should the nation pay for them to rebuild there again?"

Demonstrate how you identify research questions from a careful study of the text.

I continued on. "But I am still thinking about the idea the map gave me. The way there are areas of flooding right beside areas of drought . . . I mean, whoa!" I grabbed for "Deadly Droughts" on page 47 of *Hurricane & Tornado* and held it up to show students the picture of an African child, emaciated because of the lack of food due to drought in his country. "I keep thinking of this little boy. The part of Africa where he lives doesn't have enough water . . . but now I am realizing that other parts of Africa don't have drought at all." I drew my finger across the whole central region of Africa.

"One question I am coming to is this: 'Aren't there ways for people to share water?' That also makes me wonder who all that water belongs to, because that will impact how people share it. So I'm thinking another question could be, 'Who owns water?'" I jotted these questions quickly in my reader's notebook.

The truth is that it is not the easiest thing in the world to generate interesting questions from kids' books about floods and drought. We deliberately took those topics because they are less exciting, on the surface, than the others. It has benefited us enormously to read adult books on water, because these books have helped us to know some of the truly fascinating aspects of this topic. One certainly relates to the question of who owns water.

This lesson is less about teaching children to ask questions—they ask them all the time!—and more about inspiring them to let topics spark lines of inquiry in their minds. For that reason, as mentioned above, I wear my excitement on my sleeve.

Debrief by recapping the way you allowed your two topics to spark new questions.

"Do you see the way that by rubbing two topics against each other and by pausing to think, to expect ideas to come, and then nurturing those ideas, making them get bigger, you can end up with a whole research project? And we might stay with that research project, or continue reading and researching for a bit to develop more ideas, waiting to decide on a direction to pursue with depth."

ACTIVE ENGAGEMENT

Give students an opportunity to come up with questions on their own research topics.

"Now it's your turn to give this a try. Quickly get yourself organized with a partner and choose a subtopic to focus on, then do a little reading across a few texts on your topic and let the sparks fly!"

I moved from partnership to partnership, helping them to get organized and providing some coaching.

"Tsunamis seem impossible to prepare for, right?" Izzy asked Malik as they looked up from their text.

"Yes, it's not really possible to prepare for an earthquake either, but people can do drills to prepare for what to do when it happens, like a fire drill. I don't think there are any tsunami drills, are there?" Malik replied.

"Hmm, . . . not that I've read about. But you can have special buildings that stay strong during earthquakes. I read about how countries where they get earthquakes a lot build things in special ways, places like Japan and California." Izzy looked at the map in her book of tsunami-prone areas. "Why don't places where they get a lot of tsunamis, like Thailand," she suggested, "build special kinds of homes and buildings?"

Malik shrugged his shoulders as if to confirm her question. He glanced over at the book Izzy was holding. "The houses in Thailand look kind of old and like the owners don't have a lot of money. Maybe they didn't have enough money to make anything special."

Next, I listened to Rafael and Jason discuss their emerging questions about tornadoes.

"According to this text, the deadliest tornado was in 1925, when 689 people died," said Rafael. "When I think about the stories we read about in our hurricane research, I'm wondering why hurricanes are so much worse than tornadoes?"

"Maybe we know when tornadoes are coming better than hurricanes," added Jason. Listening, I pointed out that they absolutely had found a topic they could pursue: early warning systems for both hurricanes and tornados . . . perhaps for all natural disasters.

Depending on the needs of your class you may need to break this active engagement into smaller steps. You may choose to give students a minute to prepare and then call for a two- to three-minute reading time, followed by another minute or two for discussions.

LINK

Reconvene the class, recap the work of today's lesson, and set students up to continue their research independently.

"Researchers, you've come up with some very interesting questions. Let's not lose track of them." I asked students to open their notebooks and jot down the questions that felt most important to them. As they did that, I added a bullet to our anchor chart:

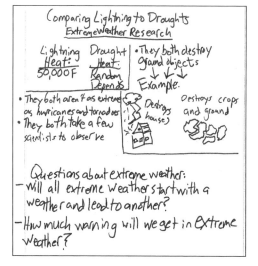

FIG. 16–1   This student added his initial questions to his existing notes.

ANCHOR CHART

Researching a Second Example

- Don't just start reading: Talk. Plan.
- Decide on subtopics to investigate first, doing so in a comparative study.
- Decide who will do what, when, how.
- Preview texts, thinking, "How is this structured? How will I read it?"
- As you read, think, "These are similar because . . ." and "These are different because . . ."
- Look across books at similar subsections to think about patterns and relationships.
- **Let your research spark questions and ideas.**
- **Nurture those sparks into research projects.**

Let your research spark questions and ideas.

Nurture those sparks into research projects.

Help Students to Elaborate as They Compare and Contrast

SOME STUDENTS WILL START OFF comparing topics on a very superficial level. For instance, a student might start by saying: "Hurricanes and tsunamis both do damage because of the water." Recognize that this is a start and then step in to help them think about these two topics on a deeper level, seeing the larger similarities and differences between their two weather events. One way to do this is by returning to the use of thought prompts, introduced in Bend II. We often underestimate the importance of oral rehearsal of ideas, so you might start off by saying: "Let's take your idea and see if we can grow it into something bigger and better." Ask the student to repeat his or her idea about hurricanes and tsunamis and then introduce one prompt after another.

I tried this work with Jasmine, who in her notebook had initially written, *Floods and droughts both do damage because of the water*. "How about we use some of these prompts to help develop that idea to say more?" I said. I asked Jasmine which she'd like to try, and after a moment she was ready to share her thinking.

"Well, *this is giving me the idea that* too much water is a huge problem, but so is too little water, so *this makes me think* that balancing the amount of water is what is really important."

Jasmine was getting the hang of it, so I linked my conference. "Remember that you can go on and continue elaborating. Try saying a few more of these prompts in your head or to your partner, Angel. And then you might write long your ideas across these two natural disasters. Think of these ways to push your thinking every time you are comparing and contrasting topics."

Teach researchers to react to information by writing about it.

You'll also want to be on the lookout for students who are asking questions, but not using these questions to propel them into new areas of research. When you see students who are moving in this direction—passively generating questions without actively pursuing answers—you can pull them together to say, "Today I want to remind you that we don't just ask questions. We try to answer them, too. To do this, we can't just collect questions, we need to nurture them into research projects. And the best tool for thinking is the pen."

Ways to Push Your Thinking

- The important thing about this is...

- I'm realizing...

- This is giving me the idea that...

- This connects to...

- The thought I have about this is...

- What surprises me about this is...

- This makes me think...

MID-WORKSHOP TEACHING **Nurturing Sparks of an Idea**

"Readers, can I have your eyes and your attention for a minute? You've jotted lots of ideas and questions, and that is great. But remember in the video that once the man saw a spark in the kindling, he nurtured it, he fanned it and blew on it until it turned into a full-fledged fire. Had we just kept reading more stuff after we sparked the idea about the relative location of droughts and floods, that idea would be the tiniest thing imaginable. You have to develop your tiny ideas into something bigger. You need to notice that you have an idea, and then pause to think, to write, and to find other texts (or other parts of the one text) that go with the idea."

I gestured to Anthony, who was seated near me. "For example, Anthony has been reading about tornadoes, and he has a whole list of questions here." I displayed them on the document camera. "But he didn't keep reading on and gathering more. No! He just did something smart. He reread his questions and thought, 'Which is worth pursuing?'"

> Over water, what creates a waterspout instead of a hurricane?
>
> Why are there five categories for both hurricanes and tornadoes?
>
> Why don't we name tornadoes like we name hurricanes?
>
> Is what makes a tropical storm turn into a hurricane the same as what makes a thunderstorm turn into a tornado?
>
> How can tornadoes form over both land and water, but hurricanes can only form over water?

"First, he crossed out the ones that weren't that important. Then he looked for questions that would help him grow some big ideas. He got going on the last one—how hurricanes and tornadoes form, and he is going to research that more.

"Will each of you make sure that you have not only taken the time to generate some ideas and questions, but have ranked them so that you can spend time nurturing your strongest spark of an idea? Right now, talk to someone who can help you do that."

You'll want to explain to students that this work is not easy. "All of this takes much more than just collecting information and listing questions in your notebook. It also takes sitting with all we have collected, all we have learned, and doing that stuff that only humans can do. When we research and generate questions, we also react—we laugh, we are amazed, we realize something new, we begin to care. The best way I know how to do that is to sit with my pen in hand, looking over all I have collected, and to let that stuff get to me, just as I might let a story get to me. And then, I write. Look at *whatever* you have collected, *whatever* you have learned. Look at all your data on droughts and floods, or hurricanes or tornadoes, or earthquakes or tsunamis, and be scared, be amazed, realize something new, begin to care about a cause." You can guide your students to write little patches of thought. You will probably want to draw upon the techniques for writing to grow ideas that you may have taught your students in writing workshop. "Remember," you can say, "you've learned a lot about ways to grow ideas in writing workshop and you can use these same techniques to react to the information and questions you have about your research topics."

Techniques for Writing to Grow Ideas

- Write a thought. Try to use precise words to capture that thought. Often it takes a sentence or two to capture a thought, not just a few words.
- Sometimes it helps to write, "In other words . . ." and to try saying the same thought differently, reaching for the precisely true words. Then you can say, "That is . . ." And try again to say the thought.
- Once you've recorded a thought, it helps to think more about that thought. Usually an idea comes to the tip of your pen if you keep your pen moving.
- Pause to reread. If a line seems especially important, true or new, copy that line onto the top of a clean white sheet of paper and write to grow that idea, using all the ideas described above.

With this group of students, you'll want to be sure that you also help them to consider the balance between writing and reading. That is, while writing is a great tool for thinking and reacting to learning, a great tool for using questions to propel our research forward, we also need to be sure that students are, above all, reading during reading workshop.

(continues)

When helping students find researchable topics, you'll find that asking them to focus not just on effects but causes will be incredibly helpful. For instance, rather than noting that droughts and floods seem to wipe out huge numbers of people because they happen in such populated areas (like Madison began to notice earlier in the lesson), channel her to instead investigate the cause of this population density. If these places are so horrible to live in, why live there at all? Is it an issue of preference? Money? The same questions can apply to preparedness and the connection between death tolls in countries with the infrastructure to support serious weather events versus places that do not. Rather than letting Izzy and Malik harp on issues of death tolls in tsunamis and earthquakes, I guided them to focus on the issue of preparedness—something that will yield far more in the way of research—and you'll likely have many readers who will benefit from similar work.

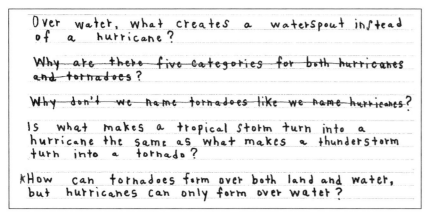

FIG. 16–2 Anthony narrowed his research focus by determining significance.

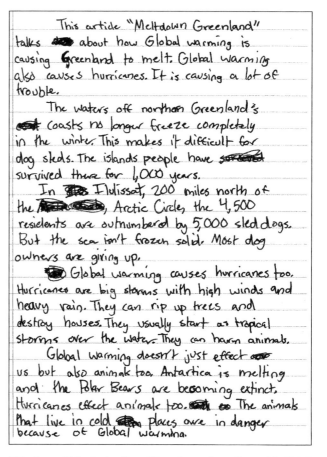

FIG. 16–3 This student's writing shows her attempt to think across texts and topics and to grow ideas based on the information she is learning.

Asking Bigger Questions

Reconvene the class and provide another example of the way ideas develop.

"Readers, let's get together for a few minutes." As children settled in the meeting area, I said, "Before we talk, will you review your notes and put your finger on a question you have asked about your subject? If you haven't asked one, do so now—quickly."

Once most kids had located a question, I said, "Earlier we talked about taking your observations and ideas and rubbing your two topics together until sparks ignite. This reminded me of a story I just love, a story that classrooms all around New York City went crazy for. It's about a boy, and he's got this idea just following him around. At first, he doesn't know what to do with it. He tries to walk away from it, act like it's not his, but it just follows him. People even make fun of him for his idea. But listen to what he does, because I think we could try these same things."

I flipped halfway through "What Do You Do with an Idea?" and started reading aloud.

> *I decided to protect it, to care for it. I fed it good food. I worked with it, I played with it. But most of all, I gave it my attention.*
>
> *My idea grew and grew.*
>
> *And so did my love for it.*
>
> *I built it a new house, one with an open roof where it could look up at the stars—a place where it could be safe to dream.*
>
> *I liked being with my idea. It made me feel more alive, like I could do anything. It encouraged me to think big . . . and then, to think bigger.*
>
> *It shared its secrets with me. It showed me how to walk on my hands. "Because," it said, "it is good to have the ability to see things differently."*
>
> *I couldn't imagine my life without it.*

Explain to children that they, too, can make something larger of their ideas. Coach in as readers nurture their ideas through questioning and writing.

"Questions are just questions if you don't allow them to become something bigger . . . something grander. Each of you has tiny bits of questions and ideas in front of you. But if you take those tiny bits and you work with them, feed them, play with them, like the boy in the book, you can make something more out of them. Right now, take the question that is under your thumb and do like the boy did. Pay attention to it. Nurture it by asking related questions or writing a bit about it. You might try starting with something like, 'Could it be that . . .?' and see if that leads to larger ideas."

As kids worked, I observed, fascinated. I watched as Izzy, Malik, Leo, and Chloe spread three books in front of them, scooting back from the rug area to make more room. As I glanced over, I saw that they were making an intricate timeline of the warning systems in place for tsunami and earthquake preparedness, with tsunamis in green and earthquakes in blue. Izzy saw me watching and explained what they were doing. "Right now we are getting all of the information we can about how people know a tsunami or an earthquake is coming. Then we are going to look at these different places and see if some places have better warnings than others." I spoke to the group a bit, asking what their predictions for their findings were and we decided that places that are poorer would most likely have less warning time and probably even more deaths because of this.

Highlight the work of one group as a way to lift the level of the work of all groups. Emphasize asking questions that apply to broader issues, people, or places.

I voiced over to the whole group. "Boys and girls, Izzy and her group are doing two things that are very impressive and might help you make your ideas even bigger. First, they are asking how their questions apply to more than one group of people. Rather than simply studying the warning system for tsunamis and earthquakes in Japan, they are comparing those systems to ones like it in California, Indonesia, and other places. This will make their ideas about warning systems *much* bigger.

"Listen to this second thing they are doing. It knocked the socks off of me! Leo, Chloe, Izzy, and Malik aren't just pursuing a research question, they are making predictions (or in science terms, hypotheses) about the results. But their hypotheses aren't just random guesses. They are guesses that are related to social issues. For instance, they are thinking about how what they find about early warning systems connects to poverty, how it connects to issues of fairness in the world, even how it connects to who does and doesn't have power. Isn't that brilliant? As you continue to nurture your ideas, see if you can try these two things." I turned to a sheet of chart paper and quickly jotted a list.

1. Think about how your ideas apply to more than one person or place.

2. Think about how your ideas apply to social issues (poverty, race, power, fairness, and more).

You might be afraid that your students will struggle to come up with ideas. And they might. Be sure to give them time to think and to stay positive so that they can rise to the challenge.

Even if only a handful of students come up with ideas, the examples you share now will be supports for this on-going work.

Channel students to reread their questions, and select a question that will drive their upcoming research.

Soon I asked children to reread what they'd written and to star a question (or a few related questions) or an idea from our share meeting or from earlier in the day, that represented a direction they wanted to go in for all or part of their upcoming research. I asked those that hadn't selected a direction for their research to gather with their research team and to see if some of them wanted to inquire in a similar direction—or not. I also suggested they begin, quickly, to consider whether the resources we had in the classroom could be helpful to them or not.

 ## PURSUING A SPECIFIC RESEARCH DIRECTION

Readers, today you generated lots of questions and ideas about your weather topics—and for many of you, your research direction might be changing. Instead of comparing hurricanes and tornadoes, you may be focusing more and more on how to make sure that people get information from early warning systems for those and other kinds of natural disasters. You may be focusing on a particular part of the world that can teach lessons to the rest of the world. You may be trying to understand the arguments for and against some laws or some policies.

You can only pursue the research direction that is interesting you if you can find resources for that topic that are ones you can read or learn from. So tonight, if you have access to the Internet, will you search for materials that you can learn from? Search also in the books you have on hand about weather to see if there are sections that may relate to your new research direction.

Once you've found your sources, read purposefully and take notes on what you learn in your notebook. You might not be able to find a clear answer—there's still a lot about these natural disasters that we don't understand—but use what you learn tonight to try to grow your best ideas instead. Become accustomed to thinking about the possible relationship between a map or a paragraph and your question. The books may not always come right out and address your topic—you may have to do your own thinking.

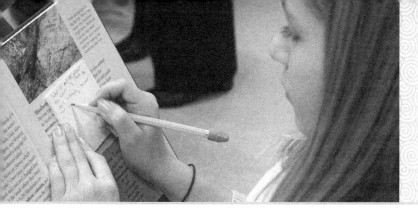

Readers Come to Texts with Their Own Agenda

IN THIS SESSION, you'll teach students that researchers develop their own agendas related to their topics, and they bring these agendas with them as they read. Sometimes, these agendas run counter to how texts are organized or the author's purpose, so researchers must reorganize the information they are learning to fit with their agenda.

GETTING READY

✔ Students should bring their questions from the previous session, the texts they found related to this question/these questions for homework, as well as any other texts on their topics (see Connection).

✔ Enlarge pages 18 and 19 from *Everything Weather* (see Teaching).

✔ Have the "Researching a Second Example" anchor chart nearby to reference (see Link)

✔ Have the "Common Nonfiction Text Structures" chart nearby to reference (see Teaching).

✔ Prepare a one-day chart titled "Our Research Questions" (see Connection).

✔ Add to your "Researching a Second Example" chart (see Link).

TODAY'S WORK will help kids see their role in the larger act of reading and researching. On some level, the act of reading and researching has three parts: the author's role and her agenda, the text's role as a vehicle for an author's agenda, and the reader's role and her agenda. Sometimes these agendas align. A reader seeks to understand the cause-and-effect relationships that transform the cocoa bean into a chocolate bar, and he finds the perfect partner in *No Monkeys, No Chocolate*. However, sometimes these agendas do not align. Perhaps a researcher is eager to learn about storms in relation to one another, and she picks up *Everything Weather* to address her query. She finds sections that teach about storms in isolation but no sections that teach about storms in comparison to one another. Today's teaching will help kids understand what to do when their agenda does not perfectly align with a text and importantly, will also help them see that their agenda matters.

With the states' recent focus on world-class standards, the role of the author and the text has taken a prominent role, as well it should. All readers should be able to read and interpret a text for what it is and what it says. All readers should examine an author's purpose, perspective, and background and how those elements might influence an author's credibility or believability. Nearly all other sessions in this unit of study have been devoted to the task of analyzing what the text says or what the author wrote and why.

Today's session will continue the work of reading a text closely, but this time, you'll teach readers to think about a third aspect of reading, which is that readers should think about their own agenda as it compares to what an author's text says. Part of this thinking extends from Louise Rosenblatt's work with the reader-response theory. Rosenblatt writes, "The special meanings, and, more particularly, the submerged associations that these words and images have for the individual reader will largely determine what the work communicates to *him*. The reader brings to the work personality traits, memories of past events, present needs and preoccupations, a particular mood of the moment, and a particular physical condition. These and many other elements in a never-to-be-duplicated combination determine his interfusion with the particular contribution of the text" (*Literature as Exploration*, 1995, 30). This means that while a research club might read a common text, written by an author with one agenda, each reader, coming with his or her own research question and set of prior experiences, will take something different from the text.

"Readers should think about their own agenda as it compares to what an author's text says."

You'll help kids do this work by asking them to read again through the lens of structure. In Bend I, you taught kids that when a reader determines a text's structure, her brain then knows the mind work that is required to read it well. Today, however, you'll be teaching kids that sometimes when you encounter a text's structure, your brain might be running *counter* to the agenda presented by the author. You will teach researchers that when this happens, it can help to reorganize the information into a new structure, one that complements their own agenda.

Readers Come to Texts with Their Own Agenda

CONNECTION

◆ COACHING

Ask students to record a research question they selected and to post it publicly, and then quickly gather with their texts for the minilesson.

While students were still at their tables, I said, "Researchers, will you jot down the research question you're planning on pursuing, likely the one you found more resources for last night? Write it on a Post-it note, add your name, and then attach it to this piece of chart paper as you make your way to the rug with all your texts on your topic." I tapped a one-day chart titled "Our Research Questions," and gave students a minute to gather.

Use a metaphor to explain what it means to come to something with your own agenda. Ask students to imagine how two people might see a game of baseball, if each had their own agenda.

"Readers, I want you to imagine something with me for a moment. Let's imagine that a few nights ago there was a Little League baseball game. And now let's imagine that one person at that game went to *really* watch it. That person paid attention to things like who was getting runs, the strikes and ball count, what team was up to bat, bases stolen, who was winning, who was losing . . . In other words, that person basically watched the game and took it in in the way it is usually intended to be watched.

"But let's imagine there was another person who went to the game that night and this person was very interested in . . . say . . . how coaches coach kids' teams. Do you think this person paid attention to the exact same things that the first person paid attention to?" The students slowly shook their heads. "No, probably not, right? This person probably paid attention to things like how often coaches went out to talk to players, when they made pitching changes, what kind of things the coaches told the kids in between innings, stuff like that. And do you see how because this second person had a very different agenda, what that person took in from the game—the way this person sort of 'read' the game—would be very different from how the first person did?"

The metaphor here serves as a way to illustrate your point—that people can see events in different ways depending on the framework with which they choose to view the event. It's important to convey to students that people can not only choose the lens with which they read the world, but they can also understand that other people might read the same world with a different lens.

Emphasize that the different agendas while viewing a baseball game is a metaphor for how readers can read texts differently based on their agendas.

"Readers, I am asking you to imagine these two people at the same baseball game seeing it so differently because the same way two people can view a baseball game differently based on coming to the game with different agendas, readers can read texts differently, based on their particular agendas—their purpose for reading."

❖ **Name the teaching point.**

"Today I want to teach you that readers can come to texts with their own agendas. At times readers' agendas may match how the text is organized and intended to be read, but sometimes readers' agendas run counter to how texts are organized. In those times, readers organize the information they learn in the way that best fits with their own agenda."

The term agenda may be new to your students, or this may be a new use of the term, so you'll want to be sure to clarify this before moving on, if necessary.

TEACHING

Explain more about what you mean by how a reader's agenda might be counter to how texts are organized by offering an example.

"Let me give you an example to show you what I mean when I say that a reader's agenda could be counter to how the text is organized. Let's say that I pick up an article about causes and effects of hurricanes. But I'm reading it because I'm trying to figure out which is a more terrible natural disaster—earthquakes or hurricanes. So, even though the text is organized in a cause-and-effect structure," and I gestured toward the "Common Nonfiction Text Structures" chart from Bend I, "and pretty much set up for me to organize information according to causes and effects of hurricanes, I'm going to be reading it and organizing information in my own mind in a compare-and-contrast structure—comparing and contrasting hurricanes and earthquakes as I read. Do you see that?"

Common Nonfiction Text Structures

Structure	Transition words
Chronological	first, then, next, after that, finally, before, after
Problem/solution	a problem is, a solution is, if . . . then . . . , so that
Cause and effect	because, since, reasons, then, therefore, so, in order
Compare/contrast	different, same, alike, similar, although, but, yet, or

Let readers know that their own personal inquiry project research foci may very likely lead them to approach texts with a different agenda.

"As you all now have your own research focus that you are interested in learning more about, it is very likely that when you approach texts with this new agenda, you may be approaching them in a way that is different than how they were set up to present information."

Involve readers in thinking along as you model how your research focus might lead you to approach the class read-aloud with a particular agenda and how you might read it differently.

"Readers, I want you to think along with me and let's consider together how my research focus might lead me to approach this part of *Everything Weather*, the photographic diagram of the water cycle, with a different agenda. You'll remember that we read this a few days ago when we were pushing ourselves to not skip the hard parts. Well, today, we have a different agenda. We're going to read this thinking about the research question, 'Who owns water?'" I projected the image for students to study alongside me.

"Hmm, . . . Let's see, when I look at this page, I see the diagram and the text explaining the water cycle, but I also see this huge waterfall, with trees and mountains all around it. I don't see houses or buildings—things that are clearly property owned by someone—I see land. Of course, people own land, but this looks more like a national park or forest preserve, land that might be owned by a big group of people or a nation. It's interesting, because I know it's important to understand the water cycle—that's the point of this section really, but when I read with my research question, 'Who owns water?' in mind, it changes the way I approach my reading, and the way I think about the text and the topic.

"Let's read a bit of text with the research question in mind and see how that changes the way we take in the information we are reading." I read aloud from the text.

> *Scientists think that the water we drink, bathe in, and use to grow crops today has been here on earth since long before the time of the dinosaurs. It has just been moving around and around in the atmosphere in a nearly endless cycle.*

I looked around at the students to be sure they were as amazed as I was before thinking aloud, "This is fascinating when I think about the question, 'Who owns water?' If the water has been here since before the dinosaurs, moving through an endless cycle, how can *anyone* claim to own water? I know this section is aiming to teach readers about the water cycle, but when I read it with my own research agenda, my own question, it helps me to think about and develop some ideas about my research question."

Debrief. Name how reading with your research question in mind led you to approach the text differently.

"Do you see how my agenda, my research question, led me to read this text slightly differently than it had been set up to present information? When Kathy Furgang wrote this section, her purpose was to teach her readers about the water cycle. To explain how water never really goes away, how the water we use today is really the same water that was in circulation when dinosaurs roamed the earth. But when I approached this section of text through the lens of my research question, wondering 'Who owns water?' my learning was totally different!"

It's nice to return to familiar texts so that your students can see the new work you are teaching.

Teachers who piloted this unit found that their students were right there with them as they read this section of text, but if your class is not seeing the impact of the research question on the reading of this text, you'll probably want to take the time to reread the snippet of text and give students the opportunity to make meaning.

ACTIVE ENGAGEMENT

Charge students with studying one of their texts, considering how their research focus might lead them to approach that text with a counteragenda.

"Readers, now I want you to give this a try. I asked you to come to the meeting area with some of your texts. Instead of turning to the ones you found last night that you think will help you to answer your question, I want you to turn to a text that you did not necessarily expect to help you with your question. Just like I did, ask yourself, "What's my research question?" and then read that text through the lens of your question, with that agenda in mind. Start looking through your text now." Students bent their heads over their books.

After a bit of time, I said, "Turn and talk with your partner about how your research question changed the way you approach your text." I knelt down as students talked, listening in to partnerships and coaching them to lift the level of their work.

If students find this work challenging, you might coach them to begin by naming what the text and/or author aimed to do and them comparing that to their research question.

Listen in and coach. After a bit, convene students and share out some of what you heard or ask a few students to share.

"Readers, listen to this. Colin said that he is reading a book about hurricanes and where they occur. The book seems to set up to almost draw maps and diagrams in his mind as he reads, but he said that he is also reading through the lens of his research question, asking, 'What makes certain areas more dangerous?' So as he reads he will be organizing information sort of by boxes and bullets, listing out some characteristics of the areas that are more prone to hurricanes. And Leah is focused on the research question, 'Which strategies work best for protecting people from earthquakes?' She said she is reading a book about building storm earthquake-safe housing and structures and as she reads, she'll be thinking about which kinds of buildings can keep people safe from earthquakes in particular. Leah said that she'll also be thinking about whether storm-safe buildings are the best ways to keep people safe, or whether there are precautions that can be made to keep people who live in earthquake-affected areas safe. So cool, right?

"Let me just share one more. Taylor is focusing on the research question, 'How can we prevent extreme drought?' She is reading a book all about the history of droughts and climate change and is especially focused on looking for parts about why certain parts of the world are in danger of drought, and how to protect them. She's sort of organizing what she learns by problem, solution.

Point out that all of these ways of approaching the text will help readers discover what they want to learn about—their own agenda.

"Readers, the point is that each of these research questions creates an agenda that will let the reader discover what he or she really wants to learn more about. Even though the reader won't necessarily take in information from the text in the way the text was set up to present it, the reader is still learning something—taking in information that matches his or her own agenda."

LINK

Send students off to continue to read and research, reminding them to let their research focus guide their reading.

"So readers, you have all determined a research question, and that question should now guide your reading. You want to learn as much about your research focus as you can and organize the information in your mind and on paper in the ways that will best help you. At times, you may decide you want to read a text and let that text's structure help you figure out the author's points—the main ideas and most important information to hold onto—but at other times, you may decide to sort of read against that text's structure as you come to the text with your own agenda. That will change the way you read and think about the text *and* your topic. Learn as much as you can today, readers! Go!" As students transitioned to independent work time, I added today's focus to our anchor chart.

ANCHOR CHART

Researching a Second Example

- Don't just start reading: Talk. Plan.
- Decide on subtopics to investigate first, doing so in a comparative study.
- Decide who will do what, when, how.
- Preview texts, thinking, "How is this structured? How will I read it?"
- As you read, think, "These are similar because . . ." and "These are different because . . ."
- Look across books at similar subsections to think about patterns and relationships.
- Let your research spark questions and ideas.
- Nurture those sparks into research projects.
- **Decide whether to read with your agenda or the text's agenda in mind.**

Decide to read with your agenda OR the text's agenda.

Supporting Students as They Continue to Read for a Text's Main Ideas While Reading with Their Own Agenda

A S STUDENTS START TO READ with their own agendas in mind, they may revert back to picking up isolated facts and details. "Oh, this relates to my research focus," they might say, "and so does this." You will want to support students in considering ideas instead of just collecting facts. If you see one student who seems to be listing assorted facts, assume there are likely others, and net a quick group.

You might show students how as you gather facts—the National Weather Service was founded in 1870; engineers use weather data to design buildings that will survive storms—that you pull back to look at patterns and connections as well. Even with just these two facts, you might say that one idea you have is that weather data is helpful to many different professions, or even that newer construction must be better equipped to deal with weather-related challenges. Then push students to look over their lists of facts, this time asking themselves what patterns they notice. What facts seem to go together? What bigger groups might be made?

Use the Informational Reading Learning Progression to confer.

As this unit draws to a close, you might approach your conferences carrying with you all the strands of the Informational Reading Learning Progression you've taught into so far. We recommend that in addition to carrying the fourth-grade sections of the learning progression, you also carry a few grade levels above and below so you can accurately assess where students are and determine their next steps. When you pull up next to a student to confer, use the research phase of your conference to quickly assess where a student's work currently falls on the learning progression. You might notice that while students are demonstrating part of the work of a level, they have omitted the other work, and you could choose to support them in doing all the work of a level. Or, you might find students are mastering the work of one level and are ready to be introduced to the work of a new level.

For example, you introduced students to the "Cross Text(s) Synthesis" and "Analyzing Parts of a Text in Relation to the Whole" strand of the progression as part of Session 5. When you initially introduced the strand, you shared grades 3 and 4 from

(continues)

MID-WORKSHOP TEACHING   Writing to Capture Thinking

"Readers, let me pause you briefly. Many of you are organizing the information you're learning to match your plan. I also want to be clear about what the expectations are for you and all fourth-graders when developing powerful research questions and then reading with your own questions in mind." I handed out copies of the "Growing Ideas" and "Questioning the Text" threads of the learning progression.

"Take a moment to look this over with someone next to you. Will you notice what's expected of third- and fourth-graders when it comes to growing ideas and questioning the text? What are fourth-graders expected to do that third-graders aren't asked to do yet?" Give students a few minutes to read and mark up the progression, and then ask them to talk in partnerships about what they noticed.

"After you talk, will you look back at the writing you've already done today? Now that you know what's expected of fourth-graders, you might need to revise your jottings to be sure they grow ideas, raise questions, and references the information you are learning. Later you will have conversations about these ideas with your research team."

the progression. Since synthesizing has been a huge emphasis of the work in Bend III, it's likely you have a few students who are ready to move toward fifth-grade level work with this strand. Look to the next level of the progression to get ideas for how to push these students.

As you do this research, as with any time you confer, it's likely you'll notice more needs than you are able to address during one conference. If this is the case, jot down these needs as *next steps* in your conferring notes. Then, you can address these needs during future conferences or group students with similar needs together for small-group work.

Hurricanes
In the Eye of the National Hurricane Center

safety

· Satellites used to watch storms develop M
· Storm clusters ⟶ hurricanes
· National Hurricane Center predicts storms to protect people.
· track weather and give alerts
· fly planes into storms to figure out location and M strength
· drop tools into the storm to get info M
· radars give info M
· all the info goes in a computer and creates a M model

M = measuring

FIG. 17–1   Notice the way Anthony coded his hurricane notes, by marking items related to safety and measurement.

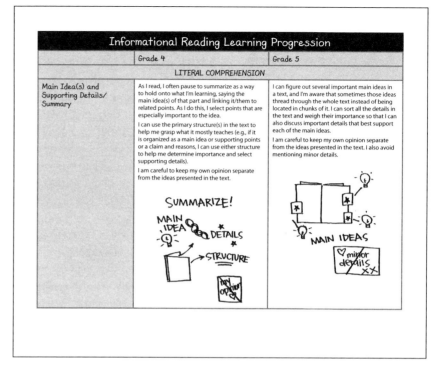

Research Team Conversations

Explain to the class that all the reading they do can change their thinking, if they let it. Set students up to reflect on ways their thinking about their research topics has evolved.

"Readers, I want to fill you in on one thing that is true about any kind of reading, narrative or informational, and it is this: when you read, you become a different person. We began this unit talking about reading in a different way, making a commitment to learning from our texts, reading and responding in a 'Reading to Become Smarter' way. Not only can we let nonfiction reading change our attitudes and mindsets toward reading, but we can also let nonfiction reading change our *thinking*. When we read nonfiction, we *think* differently, too.

"Think about your research topic. Think about everything you have learned so far. What about your thinking has changed? What new ideas do you have that you didn't have before? Take a moment to look over your notes, and as you do, I want you to think: '*I used to think . . . but now I realize . . .*'" I fell quiet as children shuffled their papers and reread sections of their notes. I gave them a couple of minutes to reflect independently.

"Turn and share with your research team. How has your thinking about your research topic developed and changed?" The classroom erupted into conversation. I listened, in awe.

I reconvened the class and asked several students to share their thinking. Malik began.

"I mean, I used to think that tsunamis were just big waves, like the Big Kahuna for surfers. But now I realize that they are actually caused by tectonic plates moving, and they are really really dangerous," he said.

Izzy was next. "Yeah, and tsunamis are sometimes like three big natural disasters put together. They are caused by earthquakes, they make big tsunami waves, and then they can also cause floods. It makes me think that tsunamis are the most dangerous natural disaster of them all."

"Researchers," I continued, "I hope you are all as impressed with your thinking and ideas as I am. Not only have you made a commitment to learn from your texts, it seems you've made a commitment to think *beyond* your texts. You've gone from studying one topic (one kind of extreme weather) to generating ideas about that topic, to comparing two related topics, and now to generating ideas, lines of thinking, and expertise about a bigger field of knowledge. Bravo! I cannot wait to see where you go next."

Revision of thought is tricky work. You've likely seen students hold steadfast to their ideas when challenged, or read on past conflicting evidence without giving it a second thought because it doesn't fit with their idea. Celebrate the revisions your students name out here, no matter how small. You are helping them develop a revision mindset, so they are more likely to remain open to new information moving forward. This is no small feat!

RESEARCHING WITH MULTIPLE AGENDAS

Researchers, tonight, as you research, continue holding your own agenda in mind as you read. Your research question should be front and center as you tackle your new text. That is, if you are reading about droughts, your agenda might be, "Who has power over water?" If you are reading about earthquakes, your agenda might be, "Where are the most potentially dangerous places to live?"

One thing to consider though, is just like your ideas about your topic evolved as you gathered more information, so too could your research question. As you read tonight, you may find that your initial question along with your new learning may lead you to an additional research question or idea; try holding an additional agenda or question in mind as you tackle your reading. If you are studying tsunamis, perhaps one question you are holding is, "What part of the tsunami causes the most destruction?" And another could be, "How does poverty influence tsunami damage?" Read with both these agendas in mind, adding the new information you learn to your growing collection of notes on your topic.

Session 18

Evaluating Sources

WITHIN A WEEK, your children will present their thoughts and opinions about their topic to wider audiences, and so today gives you a chance to teach them about some of the ways to make sure that what they have learned will be ready to be brought into the public eye. This session is in a sense helping kids construct a bibliography for their upcoming presentations. You are, in a way, teaching them to get their footnotes together. However, the real work of the session is not so much in teaching them how to organize a footnote or a bibliographic entry, as it is teaching them how to double-check the credibility and reliability of their sources.

You may ask, "Isn't it better to check the reliability of sources before one does research, rather than at the end?" Of course you are right (and some of our pilot classrooms did teach this lesson in Bend II, which is an option for you, too). But in this particular teaching sequence, there were other critical lessons to teach early, and the larger point is that kids need to know how to do this work moving forward.

You may also ask, "Fourth-graders evaluating sources? Isn't that a bit complicated?" Frankly, these are questions we asked, too. Now that so many kids are on the Internet, however, we have found that asking fourth-graders to evaluate sources isn't so very out of the norm. Luckily, the TCRWP has also developed an ongoing collaboration with the Colonial Williamsburg Foundation in which we've dug into the study of American history. As part of this collaboration, we've learned more about the use of primary and secondary sources and ways to use these as an integral part of our history instruction.

When students study primary sources from any given time period, it is always important to delve into the source and evaluate its credibility and trustworthiness—this is central to the work historians do and, of course, central to the work of researchers of all ages.

Almost forty years ago, in what is now a classic book, *The Process of Education*, Jerome Bruner (1976) wrote, "The foundations of any subject may be taught to anybody in some form . . . there is nothing more central to a discipline than its way of thinking. There is nothing more important in its teaching than to provide the child with the earliest opportunity to learn that way of thinking—the forms of connection, the attitudes, hopes, jokes,

IN THIS SESSION, you'll teach students that researchers become experts by evaluating the credibility and trustworthiness of sources.

GETTING READY

✔ Ask students to bring their reader's notebooks with notes from the previous day's homework with them to the meeting area (see Connection).

✔ Have your own reader's notebook with a full page of notes (see Connection).

✔ Prepare a chart titled "Questions Researchers Ask about Their Sources" (see Teaching and Mid-Workshop Teaching).

✔ Make sure you have page 64 of *Everything Weather* by Kathy Furgang and the author/photographer information from the book ready to share (see Teaching and Mid-Workshop Teaching).

✔ Ask students to bring their research bins with them to the meeting area (see Active Engagement).

✔ Bring "Researching a Second Example" anchor chart (see Link).

✔ Be ready to show the U.S. Drought Monitor website (http://droughtmonitor .unl.edu/; search term "US drought monitor"). A link to this website is available on the online resources (see Share).

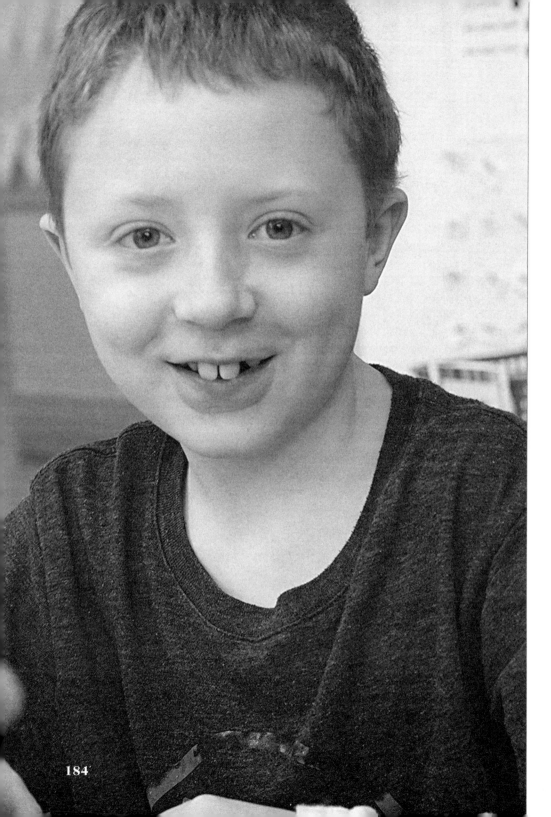

and frustrations that go with it. In a word, the best introduction to a subject is the subject itself. At the very first breath, the young learner should, we think, be given the chance to solve problems, to conjecture, to quarrel as these are done at the heart of the discipline."

Today, following Bruner's theory that the essentials of any discipline can be taught to students in the earliest years—we break the work of evaluating sources into small parts that still address the major work of evaluation, while providing students with questions that will guide their inquiry and practice with texts that are, and are not, credible and trustworthy.

This session helps students to consider their sources by identifying authors and/or contributors, by considering the publication process, the timeliness of the material, and potential bias of the source. Evaluating sources is tied to the Internet research students conduct and this is highlighted in the session so that students will become more savvy researchers, learning to ask critical questions. Will students be evaluation experts at the end of this session? Probably not, but they will have an awareness of some of the most important work researchers grapple with—the credibility and trustworthiness of their sources. This will set them up for the research they will do this year in fourth grade, but also next year as they learn to evaluate not only sources, but also arguments, as well as in the years beyond.

Note also that part of evaluating resources may be to determine the difference between facts and opinions. We have included teaching on this topic in the Conferring and Small-Group Section as well as the Mid-Workshop Teaching, but teachers who have a keen eye toward high-stakes testing may choose to highlight this angle even more as you tailor your plans to suit your students' needs. In addition, you may want to make use of the "Analyzing Perspective" strand of the learning profession today.

Evaluating Sources

CONNECTION

Suggest students share the work they did last night reading with multiple agendas in mind.

I waited until the students were gathered in the meeting area with their reader's notebooks. "Last night, you read with your agenda in mind, but you also pushed yourself to read with other agendas, holding additional ideas and research questions in mind as you read. Right now, will you open up your notebook to the work you did last night, and take a moment to share some of it?" I gave the students a minute to talk, and then I drew the class back together.

Share a story about a time you jotted notes on a topic without considering the authors behind each text.

"Researchers, I tried this work last night, too. I read with our research question, 'Who owns water?' in mind, and I pushed myself to come up with another agenda to read for: 'Why do people continue to live near areas that flood?' Let me tell you a little story about what happened to me last night, and will you see if maybe, just maybe, this is true for you too?"

I launched into my story. "I was at my house reading, pen in hand, notebook open, book next to me, and as I read I just kept seeing things that fit with my agenda, so I was furiously jotting. Anyone else have that happen?" Heads nodded. I turned my reader's notebook toward students so they could see my page full of notes.

"Well, here's the thing. As I was jotting furiously, and thinking all about my agendas, I realized I was only thinking about the information the books were teaching. I wasn't thinking at all about the fact that authors, real live people, had written my books. I was just writing down everything I read like it was perfectly good information. The more I thought about it, the more I started to worry that maybe some of my sources were not very trustworthy. Did anyone else experience that, anyone else read without thinking about who did the writing, or where it came from, or when?" I shot my hand up in the air, and hands quickly flew up around the rug. "Yeah, I thought that might be the case."

❖ **Name the teaching point.**

"Today I want to teach you that researchers become experts by evaluating the credibility and trustworthiness of their sources."

What you do in today's session you'll do over and over throughout your teaching: model the type of behavior you have seen and want to see in your students. That is, you will most certainly see students writing down everything they read as if it were perfectly credible. You may even have a skeptic or two in your classroom who doubts the credibility of the sources she reads. But even if you don't yet have a student who is thinking critically about the agenda and identity of the author, in today's Connection, you're planting the seed of the types of thinking you'd like to see throughout the session and throughout the remainder of the unit.

TEACHING

Explain the concept and purpose for today's teaching point.

"I know, those are some big words to begin with—let me explain a bit about credibility and trustworthiness. Often when people talk about credibility they are referring to believability—does the information presented seem believable? If I came into the classroom one morning and said, 'Everyone, come quickly, aliens have landed in the school yard!' You would probably say, 'That's not credible—that's not believable.' When researchers look at sources of information, they are concerned with how credible the source and the information are because they don't want to be led to believe something that is not true. Similarly, researchers are concerned with trustworthiness—about how reliable the source or information is because, again they don't want to be led to believe something that is not true.

"I see many of you nodding your heads; I can tell that you agree that this is important. Of course just like we don't want to be led to believe something that isn't true, we wouldn't want to teach one another information that wasn't accurate either. So the question becomes, 'How do we know if our sources are credible and trustworthy?'

"Luckily, we're not the first researchers to grapple with these important questions—this is an issue all researchers face, so it will be helpful for us to know and use some of the questions researchers ask about sources."

Direct students' attention to the chart that will support their evaluation of sources.

"I've made a chart of some of the main questions that will help us to consider the credibility and trustworthiness of our sources. Take a moment to read these questions, and then we'll get started putting them to use." I revealed a chart that featured a series of questions and gave the students a moment to read it.

Questions Researchers Ask about Their Sources

- Who wrote this? What makes this person qualified to write this text?
- How was the material published? Who reviewed the material?
- When was this published? Is this information still relevant?

Demonstrate the evaluation of one source, thinking aloud as you move through each of the bullet points on the class chart.

"Let's put these questions to work and evaluate the credibility and trustworthiness of our sources—sounds very grown-up, right?" I made fun of the fancy words a bit, putting on my best professor voice to add a little humor to the lesson, before turning to *Everything Weather* and studying the cover.

"Okay, well, first question, *'Who wrote this? What makes this person qualified to write this text?'* Let's see, Kathy Furgang and National Geographic Explorer Tim Samaras . . . Well, that tells us something, right? National Geographic sounds important and I know this organization has been around for a while. I remember reading National Geographic magazine when I was a kid. So it's pretty old. Let's see what else we can find out." I turned to the inside of the book,

Questions Researchers Ask About Their Sources

- Who wrote this? What makes this person qualified to write this text?
- How was the material published? Who reviewed the material?
- When was it published? Is this information still relevant?
- Is there an obvious opinion in the text?

There are more questions we could ask to support the evaluation of sources, but if you put too much in front of students they won't be able to attend to the initial work at hand. We chose to parse out various aspects of evaluation across this session.

thumbing through the pages, "There is usually more information about the authors in the books, on the back cover or the back page. Here it is, on the last page."

I turned to the back of the book, to the author biographies and continued, "It says here that Kathy lives in Albany, New York, and has experienced blizzards and ice storms. It also says she has been a writer for fourteen years and is the author of dozens of science books and textbooks—hmm, . . . she seems pretty qualified to write this book," I commented, looking up at the students to see their reactions.

"Let's look at what else is back here." I scanned the back matter. "Wow! Check out this long list of all the people involved in writing the book!" I turned the book toward the class so they could see the long list of contributors. "The fact that so many people were involved, so many people reviewed the material and they are all listed here on the back page of the book, and that this book was published by the National Geographic Society—all of this makes me feel as though this source is pretty credible. We can trust how the book was published and reviewed." I pointed to the second bullet on the chart. "But let's keep going and check on a few other points.

"One question to go. *'When was this published? Is this information still relevant?'* I can find out when it was published by looking at the copyright," I said as I scanned the page. "2012, well that was fairly recent, so it seems credible, like the information is still pretty accurate—maybe there have been recent developments since scientists are often learning more, but it seems that much of this information is still relevant."

Summarize your evaluation of the source.

"Okay, well, I'm feeling pretty relieved—I think this source is fairly credible, fairly trustworthy, which is really good news for us since we've been using it for the last two weeks or so, right?" I joked a bit with the students as I wrapped up this demonstration. "I think we have been learning from a credible and trustworthy source."

ACTIVE ENGAGEMENT

Set students up to evaluate sources in partnerships.

"Okay, now you are going to take some time to evaluate your own sources. In your partnerships choose a source to evaluate; you are going to work together to answer these questions." I watched as the students selected materials in their partnerships and directed some to choose articles while others chose trade books. "Researchers, look across a variety of sources in your research teams—if one partnership is evaluating a book, another partnership should evaluate an article or material from a website. Try to mix it up so you are looking at different types of sources."

It is likely that trade books will be easier for students to evaluate than articles because they tend to include biographies of the authors involved, as well as back matter that may include bibliographies, additional suggested resources, author's notes or source notes. This wealth of information tends to be more accessible for students in trade books, whereas pieces of it are often absent in the articles students hold. Because of this, you might choose to channel students who need additional support to work with trade books, but you'll want both so that students recognize this difference.

Coach students as they work in partnerships, celebrating successes and supporting struggles.

As students dug into their materials, I moved from partnership to partnership helping them to navigate their texts and these questions. As I moved from group to group, I voiced over some of the things I heard students thinking about as they worked to evaluate their sources.

"This is so interesting. Leo and Chloe have been reading a Melissa Stewart book, and the author thanks a professor from American University who reviewed the material in the book. They're thinking that this boosts the credibility, the trustworthiness of this source. Be sure you really pay attention to the publishing information—if you don't read carefully, you may miss it. Similarly, Jason and Jordan just found that in the back of one of their books, the writers actually included a section that has the heading, 'How This Book Was Researched.' Look out for this kind of information because it can help you to evaluate the trustworthiness of your sources."

After giving the partnerships another minute, I pulled up alongside Angel and Jasmine who were studying an article they had retrieved from the Internet. "We can't find the author—we just have the information about droughts," Angel pleaded. While Angel and Jasmine were worried, I had expected this issue to surface.

"Researchers, can I stop you for a moment?" I waited for the students' attention and then continued. "Angel and Jasmine have come across a problem that all of you will face at some point—they can't find the name of the authors of the material they printed from a website. So, for now this means they have questions about the credibility, the trustworthiness of this source. But since they have been keeping track of their resources and where the information comes from, they can return to the website and search for the author's information. Usually you can look for an 'About Us' section on a website to find out more about the people who contribute to the site. So this just means that Angel and Jasmine need to do a little more research to find out if this source is credible, if it is trustworthy. Take another minute to evaluate your sources in your partnerships with this new information in mind."

LINK

Bring the class back together to set them up for continued research.

"Researchers, you will want to add the evaluation of sources to the list of things you do as nonfiction readers and researchers. Moving forward, you will always want to evaluate how credible and how trustworthy sources are, no matter what you are reading. This information will help you determine to what extent you can believe what you are reading."

When providing examples for students you'll also want to be sure to name the transferable work for all students. Be sure that you are attentive to the needs of everyone—for those who are having success, as well as those who might be struggling, as I did with Angel and Jasmine.

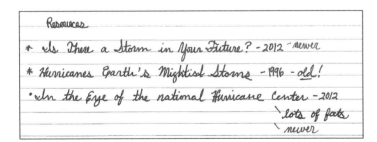

FIG. 18–1   These notes show the way one student evaluated his sources.

Support Readers Who May Struggle in Determining Facts versus Opinions; Further Evaluation Skills

AS CHILDREN READ ARTICLES from various sources, keep an eye out for those who struggle to discern the difference between fact and opinion. In articles especially, people are often quoted as sources, and these sources sometimes provide opinions. You want to be on the lookout for students who hold those opinions as facts, allowing it to sway their thinking one way or another, or giving an opinion more credit than it's due.

When I joined Jasmine in a conference, she was reading an article about the 2014 floods along the upper Mississippi. I began the research phase by asking her how her reading work was going, and what she was learning. She replied, plain and simple, "This is not a good place to live."

"What makes you say that?" I asked. Jasmine pointed to a person quoted in the article, a distraught business owner whose store had flooded. I complimented Jasmine on her use of citing primary sources in an article and then shifted into teaching mode.

"You know that information texts are ones that teach us facts and information, things that are true about the world. What I want to teach you right now, though, is that sometimes information texts also contain opinions. You recall that opinions are beliefs a person holds; they can't be proven true or false. For instance, I might say, 'Ray's has the best pizza in New York City.' That is an opinion, because it is something that I believe, it's the way I feel, but other people might not necessarily agree with me, and I can't really *prove* that Ray's is the best pizza in the city. So that statement is an opinion, not a fact. Whenever you are reading an information text and you come across a quote, or even just a bit of text that seems sort of like the author's feelings on the topic, ask yourself, 'Is this a fact—something that is always true in the world, or is this an opinion—something that one person could feel or believe, but about which another person might feel differently?'" I asked Jasmine to take a look at her notes and determine which of her jottings might be facts and which might be opinions.

"I think that maybe this part about it's not a good idea to live next to the river, that might be an opinion," she said.

"Why do you say that?" I asked.

"Well, it's just one person's feelings. There's another person in the article who talks about how wonderful it is to live near the Mississippi because the water and trees are beautiful. I think that's another opinion, because it's what someone else believes." After helping Jasmine determine whether the quotes in her article contained facts or opinions, I showed her the strategy of making a T-chart where she could note facts and opinions, and show the text evidence that supported her findings.

Further students' understanding of credibility and trustworthiness.

Some of your students will be ready to think more about credibility and trustworthiness by attending to the citations in the texts they are reading. Readers will probably face fewer citations in trade books than they will find in articles. You may choose to bring students from various research teams together and ask them to each bring their own articles to the small group, or you may provide one article for students to study together. You'll want to teach students to ask, "What sources are cited? Are these sources credible?" Part of this work will involve helping students to first identify the citations in a text, and then to determine some background information about the source. In an article about Hurricane Sandy—in which information from the National Weather Service is cited, students will need to first know what the NWS is or will need to figure out, from the context of the article, that the NWS is a government agency that forecasts the weather for public safety. Then they will need to evaluate the credibility and trustworthiness of this organization in terms of the topic at hand. After evaluating one citation, you'll want to be sure that students have opportunities to evaluate other sources in other texts.

"Researchers, I want to alert you to another thing you'll want to consider when you are evaluating sources. For a moment, I'd like you to think about opinion writing.

"You know that in opinion writing you're sharing your point of view on your topic. You want the reader to feel the same way you do about your topic, and you come right out and make a bold thesis statement about it, right? Well, information writers have a point of view about their topics, too. But sometimes the writer's point of view might be a bit harder to find. As researchers we need to be on the lookout for the goals that authors bring to texts. Looking for the author's point of view is another way to evaluate sources.

"We can do this kind of work in *Everything Weather*." I opened the book and read aloud from the copyright page (page 64) to the class. "In the section about the National Geographic society it says, 'The Society works to inspire people to care about the planet.' This is a particular point of view; the Society has a goal and by writing books like this one they hope to achieve their goal. Now, you might be thinking, 'Well, that's good they write books to get people to care about the planet—that's not a bad thing,' and you'd be right. However, this is important: authors bring a point of view to the text, and that isn't necessarily bad, it's just another thing to pay attention to when you evaluate sources. I'm going to add this to our chart. As I do, talk to your teams about the point of view your author brings to your sources."

Questions Researchers Ask About Their Sources

- Who wrote this? What makes this person qualified to write this text?

- How was the material published? Who reviewed the material?

- When was it published? Is this information still relevant?

- Is there an obvious opinion in the text?

Help students consider a different lens for source evaluation: helpfulness.

If you have students reading from websites, watch out for the way readers can become "lost" in the results of their Internet searches, as well as "lost" while reading from individual websites, scrolling through pages that don't particularly advance their research. You could support these students by helping them with their search options and the use of transition words. You might also help them by teaching them to evaluate the results of a search. Instead of simply clicking on the first site that pops up (the most popular), you can teach students to scroll through their results to quickly rank them according to which seem to be the most helpful. Of course, students will still need to read the information found on the individual sites to evaluate their helpfulness, but you will be teaching them to screen their results, which will help them become more efficient researchers.

Evaluating the Agenda of Online Resources

Demonstrate for readers how you might evaluate online resources, and highlight what to look for if they do their own research online.

"Researchers, many of you are researching your topics online. Some of you do this at home, others in the library, and still others of you have used our classroom computers to do your research. Not only is it important that you pay attention to the authors and contributors of a paper text, but it is equally important that you pay attention to those of a website. You can often find this information on the 'About Us' or 'Contact Us' section of a site." On the Smart Board, I displayed the U.S. Drought Monitor website (http://droughtmonitor.unl.edu/) and clicked on the "Contact Us" link at the bottom of the homepage. It opened to a page of general contact information as well as a list of contributing authors' names.

"Tell me what you see? What do you notice on this page? Turn and talk to your team." I leaned in and listened to what kids said, coaching as needed to lift the level of individual work.

"There is an address to write to and phone numbers to call. If people give you their contact information, it could be they are more trustworthy," Leah said.

"And there are a lot of names in the author section. They all look like they work for important places like in the government or something," Alyssa said. I called the class back together.

"Another tip I have for you when it comes to evaluating sources is this: pay attention to the site's domain name. Different domains mean different things. If the site has a '.com' domain, that means it is a place for commerce, for money-making, and business. If it has a '.org' or '.gov' or '.edu' domain, that means the site has some public funds because it is a government agency or a public university. You'll notice that the U.S. Drought Monitor has a '.edu' domain.

"It's not that '.com' domains are bad—many of them are quite good and useful, but you will always want to keep in mind the potential bias of a source. In the case of '.com' websites, they might be influenced by their advertisers—people who pay them money to put advertisements on their sites, or the site might have been made to advance particular ideas or sell particular products. It's important to know as much as possible about your sources when you are conducting research and teaching others—this is one of the ways you truly become an expert."

Sometimes when asked to name what they notice, students summarize. "It's the 'Contact Us' page," the students might say. If so, be ready to push them to name precise details.

If you have time, you could share a few more websites with the class. Now that you've taught them a few points about evaluating online resources, you could ask them to direct you as you navigate the site or to rank the sites in terms of credibility.

RANKING THE TRUSTWORTHINESS OF SOURCES

Researchers, next week, you will be sharing the information you've learned with an audience. To get ready for our celebration, you'll need to learn as much as you can about your topic, from sources that are credible and trustworthy. One way to do this is to take the sources you've been using, and rank them. You spent time today evaluating those resources, and now you might decide:

- Which resources are most trustworthy? Least trustworthy? Why?

- Which resources have the strongest opinions? Which resources have fewer or less obvious opinions?

Take these thoughts into consideration as you consider which information you have learned is most important to share with others. Be sure to continue reading and researching with your agendas in mind.

Reading Closely, Thinking Deeply

IN THIS SESSION, you'll teach students that nonfiction readers think about the decisions nonfiction writers make—the ways those authors seem to want readers to think or feel about a topic.

GETTING READY

✔ Choose two texts on the same topic that are crafted to evoke different feelings. Here, we use "Deadly Droughts" from page 47 of *Hurricane & Tornado* and "Drought Rearranges Kingdoms" from page 18 of *Calliope: Exploring World History* (March 2012 issue). The Calliope article is available in the online resources (see Teaching). 👆

✔ Make a three-column chart, and label the columns as follows: The author uses . . . (techniques); In order to . . . (goal); This affects me as a reader because . . . (see Active Engagement).

✔ Mark two texts from each club's bins with Post-it notes to draw their attention to pages where studying techniques and goals will pay off (see Link).

✔ Ask students to bring their research bins to the meeting area (see Link).

✔ "Phrases We Can Use When Comparing and Contrasting Information" chart, from Session 14, copied onto bookmarks or index cards (see Conferring and Small-Group Work) 👆

✔ Print on two different shades of colored paper and cut out the goal cards that can be found in the online resources. Prioritize which cards you introduce based on your students' familiarity with the goals (see Mid-Workshop Teaching). 👆

A S YOUR STUDENTS move between different texts on their new topic, they'll be reading these texts differently, not just because they approach this topic with knowledge about a parallel topic, but also because they approach this topic with more knowledge of the genre of nonfiction. They'll be old hands at reading books, articles, and websites, and at watching videos related to weather and other topics. Today, you note this expertise and point out that one of the side effects of expertise is that they'll bring a new sort of awareness to their reading.

You'll explain to them that as they continue to pick up books, this time about a second topic related to extreme weather events, they're apt to find themselves thinking: "Yep . . . I've read a book like this before," and then be able to describe how they expect the book to go, saying, "In a book about droughts and floods, the first picture usually shows caked, dry earth, stretching for miles side by side with a landscape covered in water up to the treetops. Then, the book will probably switch to the human face of the disasters—perhaps showing small children floating by half-submerged houses in makeshift boats."

Of course, until you point out that they'll be approaching the next round of texts with this sort of awareness, chances are very good they'll do nothing of the sort. It is within reach for them, however, to notice that several sources on the same topic each approach that topic using different craft techniques. Thinking about the different craft techniques that writers have used can be useful to your students if you are inviting them to write their own information books, as this nourishes their awareness of options for their own writing. It can also lead students to ask that all-important question: why? Why might one author use full-page landscape pictures to capture a kind of extreme weather event while another author tends to insert little clipped photos into small spaces within a text? Those choices create an entirely different tone. What are the messages the two different authors are trying to highlight, and how do their decisions contribute to those messages?

Today you will help students consider these questions and more. You will teach them that analytical readers ask, "What does this author want me to think or feel about this topic?" and that they then think about the ways in which the author accomplished that task. The ways, or techniques, however, will be less important for today's lesson. You will focus more time on those tomorrow. Today, help children to read nonfiction with the same emotional energy and empathy that they do fiction, and to understand that nonfiction is a *person's* truth, not necessarily *the* truth.

"Help children to read nonfiction with the same emotional energy and empathy that they do fiction, and to understand that nonfiction is a person's truth, not necessarily the truth."

During your mid-workshop teaching, you will introduce students to one tool that will help them name what the author wants them to think or feel about a topic: the goal cards.

While the illustrations are supportive, it's likely that giving your students the entire sheet of goal cards at once would be overwhelming. For that reason, we recommend that prior to today's lesson, you spend time studying the cards to determine which goals your students will already know well. Then, you might choose to introduce just four or five goal cards to your students today. You can save the rest to introduce in future minilessons and read-alouds, or use them to extend the work students do within your small groups and conferences. We also suggest that you copy the goal and technique cards on different shades of colored paper so that students can easily distinguish between the two sets.

Students cannot become critical consumers of texts—and few things could be more important than this—until they are aware that texts are made on purpose, as a result of decisions that people make, and the craft decisions made by an author affect the message that the text conveys. Readers and viewers need to become accustomed to thinking, "What craft decisions did this author make? How else could the author have made this text? Why might the author have made this decision—how does it forward a particular spin on a topic?"

Reading Closely, Thinking Deeply

CONNECTION

Explain to students that as they become experts on various kinds of weather events, they also become experts on a far more important topic—nonfiction texts.

"Readers, I think you know that this unit isn't just about becoming weather experts. You are studying weather so that you can achieve a much larger goal—and that goal is to become profoundly stronger as nonfiction readers."

"As I watch you, I see that this is already happening. You'll pick up a book on tornadoes and say, 'Yep . . . I know how this one will go. This looks like a hybrid text, one of those books that starts with a narrative, the story of a person or two that were devastated by a tornado. Then it will shift to expository, telling a bit about how tornadoes form . . .' and so on." The students nodded in agreement.

"In a nonfiction study like ours, it is important to study the topic we are learning about, but it is just as important to study the texts themselves . . . to think about how they were made and why they were made that way."

⚜ **Name the teaching point.**

"Today I want to teach you that nonfiction readers think about the decisions nonfiction writers make—the ways those authors seem to want us to think or feel about a topic. This is especially important when reading several texts about the same, or similar, topics."

TEACHING

Remind students that texts should affect them and that studying those influences can give them precious clues as to the intent of the author.

"Readers, when we read stories, it is natural for us to talk about the way they affect us. In read-aloud, for instance, we talked about the ways we empathized with Rob in *The Tiger Rising*—the way his sadness seeped into everything around him, including us.

◆ COACHING

It is important to remember—and to remind students—that units are almost always about larger goals than they seem to be. (While you are pretending that students know this, it is unlikely to have even crossed their minds!) While learning about weather is a fun thing to do, the work of this unit is much larger and far more challenging. Tony Wagner, author of Cre-ating Innovators, rarely gives a speech without reminding us that knowledge and facts are a dime-a-dozen, a click away on Google. Knowing what to do with information, how to get it, how to analyze and think about it . . . that is the ultimate goal of education.

When doing this work with students, we find that it is most successful to begin with the influences that a text has on them rather than with a close analysis of sentence-level techniques. In this way we tap into the students' feelings as readers.

"But in nonfiction, we don't always stop to ask, 'What am I feeling right now? What effect is this text having on me? Am I frustrated? Sad? Mad? Nervous? And more important, what did the author *do* to make me feel that way?'"

Show students two texts on the same topic, recruiting them to study the different feelings they convey.

"Let's start off by looking at two different texts on droughts. Before we jump into a close study of what the authors have done, let's let these texts wash over us and affect us." I put two texts about droughts up on the white board, knowing that each would convey different feelings. The section "Deadly Droughts" (page 47) in *Hurricane & Tornado* had several photographs scattered about the page with captions detailing the ways droughts affect everything from wildlife, to agriculture, to human life. The article "Drought Rearranges Kingdoms" from the magazine *Calliope: Exploring World History* (page 18), on the other hand, was a two-page spread—both of the same landscape—one ravaged by drought and the other not.

"Turn and talk to your research team. What do these two texts make you think and feel? How are those thoughts and feelings about the texts similar? Different?"

I listened in as students talked, giving coaching tips as I went. "It's often helpful to look at the *way* things are written, the font," I said to Leo's group. "That can have a big effect on the way we feel about a topic."

I moved to the next partnership and observed. "Why did the author put in a picture of a dead animal? It looks like a horse. It's gross!" said Angel, turning away from the *Hurricane & Tornado* text. "I think it's sad. I like horses," said Jasmine.

Getting them back on track, I chimed in. "Wise question, you two: out of all the thousands of pictures an author could have chosen, why did she choose these?"

Highlight a few student observations, or call on students to share what they observed.

Once students had developed some ideas, I pulled them back together for a quick share. Taylor began, "We noticed that both pages are dark," she began. I gestured for her to add on. "Like on the drought page," and she pointed to the first page of the *Calliope* article, "there are all of these dark clouds and the ground is gray and all broken. There isn't any grass or trees or anything."

"Yeah, it looks like a scary movie," added Jordan. "I wouldn't want to go there. But then on the other side the author shows us what it would look like without a drought. It's a lot better."

"What about this other article?" I nudged. "Does this author seem to be focusing on the bad effects of drought on grass and plants?"

Jack threw his arm up for a chance to speak. "I think 'Deadly Droughts' isn't as scary at first, because it isn't all dark and dusty, but when you look closer, it is really bad."

"What do you mean by that?" I prompted him to say more.

To begin, we make reference to the first reading unit of the year, likening nonfiction topics to characters in books and suggesting that we should react to and study them in similar ways.

The structure of this lesson deviates a bit in the beginning, and yet is one in which we've found a lot of success. You'll begin by asking the students to join you in comparing and contrasting the effect the images from two texts have on them. This will help them to see that despite writing about the same topic (in this case, droughts), texts can convey different messages. Then, you will revert back to your classic model/active engagement structure: first modeling how you study the craft moves the author made in a text and then giving students an opportunity to do the same.

After studying these two texts myself, I know that one of the main differences is that the Calliope article focuses on the effects of drought on the world—trees, earth, and so on. The DK Readers section makes an effort to show various ways droughts affect the world, including people and animals. Therefore, my question about whether the other article focuses on grass and plants is very purposeful.

"The author of 'Deadly Droughts' shows pictures of people and animals all over the page. This little boy" (he climbed up onto his knees to point at a picture) "is covered with flies and he looks like he's starving. I predict that's probably because of drought. And the animal up there died because he didn't have enough water. So even though when you first look at it, it doesn't look as bad as the other book, once you look more closely, it is about really sad things."

"Ah, interesting! So one author shows us how devastating droughts are by making them feel big and powerful and how they affect the whole world, turning it to brown. And the other author gives us specific examples of the many ways droughts affect communities—including animals and people."

ACTIVE ENGAGEMENT

Explain to students that while they may have thought they were simply looking at pictures, they were actually doing high-level analytical work.

"Readers, while it seems like we've simply been comparing and contrasting pictures, we've actually been doing very high-level analytical work. What I mean by this is that we've been setting ourselves up to consider not just *what* authors do, but *why* they do it."

I unveiled the following chart:

This author uses . . . (technique)	In order to . . . (goal)	This affects me as a reader because . . .

Rally students to discuss authors' goals and techniques. Construct a chart with students that details what they noticed.

"Let's jot a few of the things we noticed about each article we studied earlier. Turn and talk to your research teammates and decide on one or two big moves one of the authors made. What did he do? What do you think he was trying to achieve? How did it affect you as a reader?"

As the students turned and talked, I tried to fill in a few common observations on the chart, then added to it after calling students back.

Jason began by pointing out that the author of the *Hurricane & Tornado* article included an image of a starving boy and a dead animal.

"Hmm, . . ." I asked Jason and the others. "Should we put that on the chart? Do you think lots of authors include pictures of dead animals and starving children? Or do you think there's a way that we can make it more general . . . something that many authors do to get our attention? Turn and talk."

You'll notice that I make a point of renaming what students notice in the language of "goals" and "techniques." I know that hearing this higher-level language will help students to internalize it for themselves, and that I will teach into it further both today and tomorrow when they receive the "Goal and Technique" cards for informational writers.

When we came back together, Jason and others were ready to revise what he noticed.

"Maybe we could say that authors included 'Shocking or sad pictures,'" said Alyssa. Jason added on, "Yeah, that's what we thought too. And they do it so that they show us how bad things are and make readers feel sad."

Nodding my head, I added their observations to the chart. After a few more minutes of discussion we had a chart that looked like this:

This author uses . . . (technique)	In order to . . . (goal)	This affects me as a reader because . . .
Shocking or sad photographs	make the reader feel emotional and realize that the topic is really serious	it makes me sad or full of shock or want to take action
Dark colors	to show that something is scary or serious	it is scary
Bold, strong words	to show that something is important and why; to get the reader's attention	it makes me pay attention to that word and sentence
Different font sizes	to show what is most important	it makes me pay attention to the parts that the writer wants me to

While your students won't say exactly what's on this chart, you can use the information and ideas here to guide their conversations as you hear students approximate. We're also sure that your students will surprise you with their particular insights, so be ready to create a chart that reflects your students' thinking.

LINK

Remind students that letting a text affect them is one way readers understand the larger message a writer is trying to convey about a topic.

"Great work today, readers. When we really pull in and study the decisions that nonfiction writers make, we often find that those writers are trying to make us think or feel a certain way about a topic. Studying the ways they do this can especially pay off!

"Right now, will you and your research teammates pull out your books? You'll see that two of them have Post-its hanging out of them. These are pages I marked for you, where I know this work will especially pay off. As you go off today, let's start our reading time in research teams. Look at your two pictures side by side, the way we did in the mini-lesson, and see if you can develop theories about what the author did, how he did it, and why. Take a minute to make yourself a three-column chart, like the one we used today, in your own notebook."

When all students had created their charts and located their premarked book, I sent them off.

This link asks students to begin the workshop by practicing the work of today's minilesson. We think this is a good idea today because it would be too easy for students to leave the whole-group lesson and ignore this somewhat challenging work.

Supporting Students as They Compare and Contrast across Texts

YOUR STUDENTS are likely to be in very different places when it comes to their ability to read like writers. Some will take immediately to the work you did in the beginning of today's minilesson, noting places where authors do *something* to affect readers and vocalizing the influences that various texts have on them. For others, it will not come as easily.

Help students to put language around newfound ideas.

Once students become accustomed to identifying goals, you will want to help them rehearse sharing these ideas with their research teams (or writing about them in their reading notebooks). In both cases, you'll want to emphasize the importance of stating an idea and then backing it up with evidence. For a single idea about one text, you might teach students that instead of saying "there is a comparison," they can instead try phrases like:

- "The author makes us feel _____. One place (s)he does this is when _____. This makes _____."

- "I think the author is using _____ to make the reader think/feel _____."

When comparing the goals of one author with another, students can revisit the prompts for comparing and contrasting you taught them earlier in the unit, this time using them to discuss craft.

For many students, having these prompts on little bookmarks or index cards is especially helpful, because they can put them on their desks while reading and note-taking, and refer to them while having a conversation with their research team.

Using tools to help students deepen their analysis of craft and structure.

As you confer today, you might choose to carry the "Analyzing Author's Craft" strand of the Informational Reading Learning Progression, spanning several grade levels, with you. This strand of the progression details several ways students can approach work with craft and structure, beginning with helping students notice and name the techniques their authors use, to analyzing those techniques, and considering why authors might have used them. Looking across the expectations for several grade levels will likely be useful as you determine what students are currently doing when they analyze craft and structure and as you consider their next steps.

As you talk with a reader, you might begin by noticing the kinds of goals they are discussing. One reader might notice that the diagram showing how tornadoes form teaches him some important information about how tornadoes begin and grow. Using the progression, you might compliment the reader on what he is noticing, saying,

---

Phrases We Can Use When Comparing and Contrasting Information...

ALIKE   DIFFERENT

- ____ and ____ are alike because...

- ____ and ____ have differences, too. One difference is...

- Both ____ and ____ (what?)

- For... not unlike ... (what?)

- It is interesting to note that ____ and ____ are different in this way. Whereas... on the other hand...

"Readers, I've put a baggie and some little blue cards on each of your desks. 'What in the world are these?' you might be wondering. Well . . . you are about to find out! Don't flip them over just yet, though.

"Today, you've paid special attention to analyzing the moves that informational writers make. Specifically, you asked yourself the question, 'What do I think the author wants me to think or feel about this topic?' What the author wants you to think or feel can also be called a *goal*. It is the goal of that writer. And we've learned that not all authors have the same goals. One author might want you to see how extraordinary tornadoes are, while another might want you to see how powerfully destructive they are. Another author might want you to understand how to protect yourself from them. No matter what the author's goal, it is sure to turn up in his or her writing!

"You have been coming up with your own ways of describing authors' goals, and that is fine, great even, but I wanted to let you in on a little secret: readers and writers have already developed some terms and ways of describing the goals you are noticing." I asked each child to turn each of his or her cards over, reading the goal and looking at the picture.

"One of the first goals we identified was after seeing the picture of the dead animal in our drought book. We wrote," and I turned to our chart, "that the author probably did this to make the reader feel emotional and realize that the topic is really serious. Take a look at your goal cards. Are there other goals the author might have had or new ways of saying the same thing?"

Soon, as a class, we had decided that the animal picture could "Build a Mood," "Suggest the significance of a point (or idea)" (in this case, that droughts are deadly), or "Hook the Reader."

"With the person sitting next to you, see if you can match up some of the cards with the goals you've already noticed."

"You are really looking at illustrations closely, and you're noticing that sometimes illustrations teach you information that's not in the text." Then, looking to the work of the next grade level, you might say, "Can I give you a tip? When you notice what an author is doing, it helps to think about what else the author could have done. You might even ask, 'How would the text have been different without this part?' Then, you can come up with a few possible answers."

We also recommend you add copies of the goals and techniques cards to your conferring toolkit. As students notice and name additional goals, you might have additional goal cards ready to add to their baggies.

Readers Reflect and Set New Goals

Rally students to use an anchor chart to reflect on their recent reading work, and channel them to set powerful goals for their work moving forward.

"Readers, find a place to stop in your research." After students looked up I continued, "Today you have been thinking a lot about the choices authors made as writers. This has been interesting work that has helped us to see more and think more about our texts and our topics. This is certainly work you will want to continue.

"But the thing I want to draw your attention to is that it's not just the authors of our texts who make decisions. Every day you make decisions about the reading work you are doing. Today, I want you to take a few minutes to look back over the charts that we have used throughout this unit as a way to question and reflect on your reading decisions." I gestured to the three anchor charts, "To Read Nonfiction Well," "To Research Well," and "Researching a Second Example."

"I'm sure you all know what's coming next, right?" I smiled at the class and continued. "When we reflect on our choices it gives us an opportunity to revise those choices or to set new goals for ourselves. Take a moment to talk with the people in your team about your choices and your goals for tonight's reading. Remember, there are only a few days left in our unit, so let's make these powerful goals!" Once students had a chance to discuss their goals I prompted them to record these goals in the form of a self-assignment in their reader's notebooks.

UTILIZING RESOURCES TO WORK TOWARD GOALS

Readers, in the last few weeks you have become experts on weather-related topics, but you've also become expert nonfiction readers. Today in reading workshop, you had a chance to reflect on your reading work and to set goals. Tonight as you continue to read and research at home, refer to your self-assignment and be sure that you are working toward your goals.

Remember that you have a variety of tools to use as resources—your research notebooks, your copies of the class charts, and your recollection of our class work. When you come to school tomorrow, you should be ready to talk about your work and your progress.

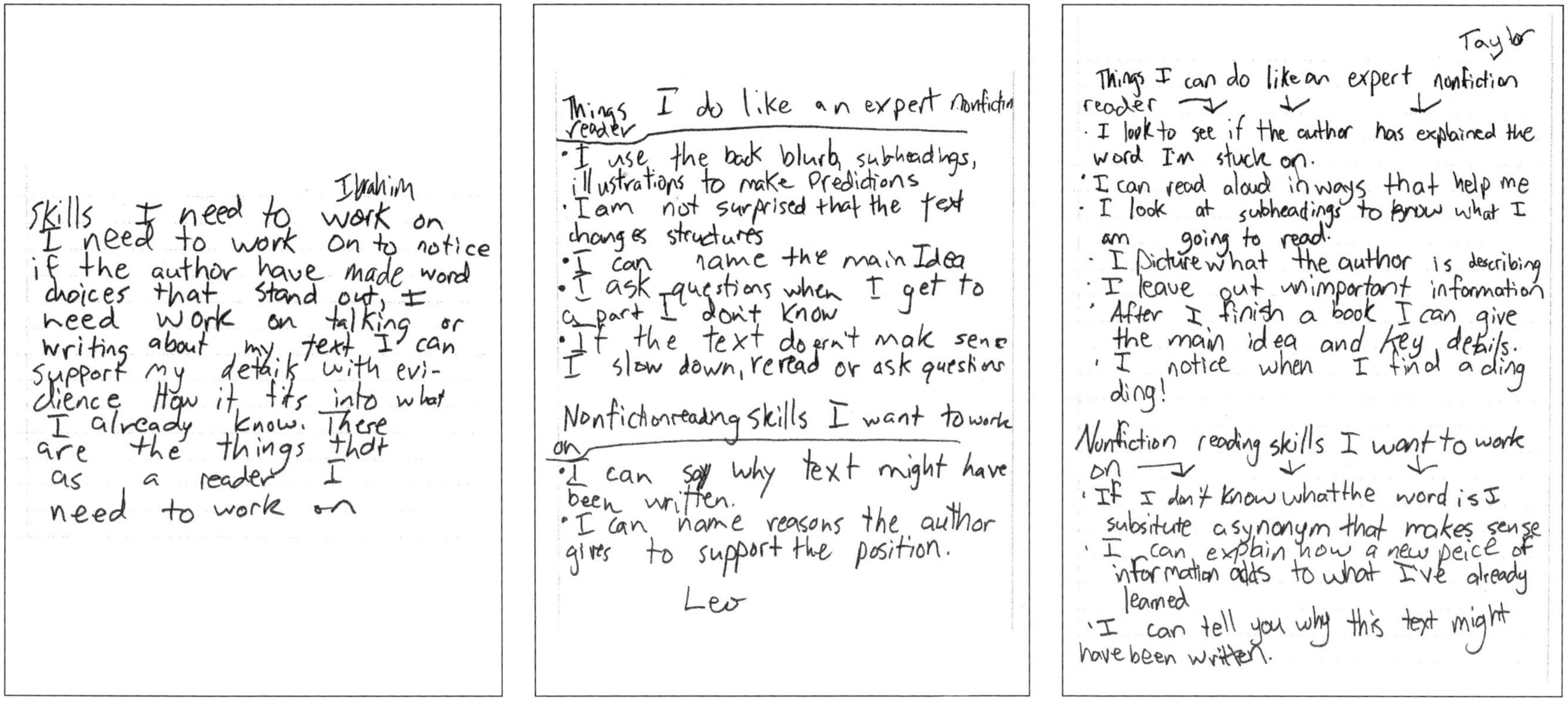

Skills I need to work on   Ibrahim
I need to work on to notice
if the author have made word
choices that stand out, I
need work on talking or
writing about my text I can
support my details with evi-
dience How it fits into what
I already know. These
are the things that
as a reader I
need to work on

Things I do like an expert nonfiction reader
• I use the back blurb, subheadings, illustrations to make Predictions
• I am not surprised that the text changes structures
• I can name the main Idea
• I ask questions when I get to a part I don't know
• If the text doesn't mak sens I slow down, reread or ask questions

Nonfiction reading skills I want to work on
• I can say why text might have been written.
• I can name reasons the author gives to support the position.
                    Leo

Taylor
Things I can do like an expert nonfiction reader → ↓ ↓ ↓
• I look to see if the author has explained the word I'm stuck on.
• I can read aloud in ways that help me
• I look at subheadings to know what I am going to read.
• I picture what the author is describing
• I leave out unimportant information
• After I finish a book I can give the main idea and key details.
• I notice when I find a ding ding!

Nonfiction reading skills I want to work on → ↓ ↓ ↓
• If I don't know what the word is I subsitute a synonym that makes sense
• I can explain how a new peice of information adds to what I've already learned
• I can tell you why this text might have been written.

FIG. 19–1   These students wrote about their progress and goals as nonfiction readers. Notice the variety of goals presented.

Analyzing Craft

Studying How Nonfiction Authors Achieve Their Goals

ear Teachers,

We are placing this day in your able hands, sure that you will each find your own creative ways to introduce the second half of the goal and technique cards—the "Writers of Informational Texts Use Techniques Such As . . ." sheet. As with the goal cards, you'll want to prepare for today's session by cutting apart the technique cards. Two words of advice: first, trust us when we recommend that you copy "Goals" on one color paper and "Techniques" on the other. Otherwise it will be a matter of seconds before one finds its way into the other's pile. Second, don't overload students with these cards. Pick the goals and techniques that you have taught, those your students know well, and save the others for future lessons, small-group work, and conferring. As with the writing checklists from the Units of Study in Argument, Information, and Narrative Writing, these tools are not meant for teaching, just reminding and identifying. If a student doesn't know what parallelism is, they'll be hard-pressed to identify an author's use of it and will be all the more likely to feel overwhelmed by the cards. So, even if you begin with three or four cards, you are taking a stride toward helping your students to recognize not just an author's intent, but the way in which he or she accomplishes it.

MINILESSON

In the previous session, students became accustomed to studying the major goals that authors have (often referred to as author's purpose). Today you will teach them that when we see an author trying to accomplish something, we can ask *how* they do this. In other words, they can study the techniques an author uses to achieve goals. You might remind them that as writers themselves, they have a wealth of techniques for achieving goals. For instance, when they want to build tension in a n rrative story, they slow down the action, add inner thinking and descriptive thinking, and more.

Then, name your teaching point. You might say, "Today, I want to teach you that readers study texts to find out what techniques or craft moves an author uses to achieve his or her goals."

We recommend you bring back the text from the previous session since the children are already familiar with it. You might explain that while they noticed a lot, they didn't necessarily have the words to express everything they saw. Technique cards can give them the words, the vocabulary, to name what they notice an author doing.

Ask each research team to lay a set of technique cards before them. Lay your cards out much the same way the students do. If you are able to make an enlarged set of cards, we recommend you do so, because they will be easier for students to see. You might choose to read over the cards once, giving the students a quick preview. (You'll notice that we left parallelism off of our list below because that is something we were sure the students hadn't learned yet. You may choose to start with even fewer cards.)

Make a comparison	Raise questions (and sometimes answer them)	Give an example/ anecdote	Address the reader directly (You)	Quote an authority
Provide a surprising fact or statistic	Choose words/ phrases that lead the reader to think one way or another	Use text features and/or provide a visual	Define key terms and use technical vocabulary	Incorporate humor

Next, we recommend either projecting an enlarged version of the text you'll be studying, or giving a copy to each group. You'll want students to be able to follow along and study the words and sentences closely. You might begin by quickly reviewing the goals you noticed during the previous minilesson. Then, perhaps you'll say, "As I read, think along with me about whether the author used any of these techniques to help him achieve his goals as a writer."

As always, model the thinking process that goes into this work. For instance, I might begin by saying, "Even before I start reading, I'm thinking about how we noticed that the author hooked us as readers right away. What techniques, I wonder, might he have used? Let's go back to the 'Deadly Droughts' section of the *Hurricane & Tornado* book (page 46) and see if we can specifically name the techniques he used." Model looking frequently between the text and the technique cards. In most cases you will find that several cards will work. We recommend leaving the easier ones for the students to identify.

Deadly Droughts

Any region lacking in water because of lower-than-normal rainfall is in a drought. As rivers, lakes, and soil dry up, crops fail and animals starve, leading to famine among humans. Advances in medicine, transportation, and communication in the 20th century allowed aid agencies to lessen the effects of water scarcity, but droughts are still a problem in much of Africa. Droughts are sometimes caused by human activities, such as over farming.

Skin and Bones
(picture of dead, dried-out animal)

Animal carcasses are a common sight during severe droughts. This unfortunate animal dried out before it had a chance to decay.

For instance, as you read a bit of the text you might pick up the "Provide a surprising fact or statistic" card and point to the image of the mummified animal corpse. Then you can say, "Giving us this fact about animal carcasses and how they dry out is certainly startling and one way that this author 'hooked' me as a reader."

After you model noticing a couple of techniques, turn the reins over to the students. "Now it's your turn," you might say. "With your research teams, continue to read through the *Hurricane & Tornado* excerpt and see if there are any other techniques you see the author using. Remember to give specific examples for the techniques you name." As students talk in their research teams, move the technique cards you hear them calling out into a separate area of the white board or chart paper.

Finally, remind the students of the day's lesson and send them off, technique and goal cards in hand, ready to try this work independently. "Before you go off to read, make sure that each of you has your own copy of the goal and technique cards," you might remind students. "I've got baggies of them up here for those of you that didn't get one during the lesson. Then, off you go to read!"

CONFERRING AND SMALL-GROUP WORK

As mentioned above, similar to the writing checklists in the Units of Study in Argument, Information, and Narrative Writing, you won't want to use the goal and technique cards as teaching tools. Instead, you will want to use specific cards only after teaching students the concepts or craft moves behind them. As students learn more about the nuanced ways in which informational writers write, you'll add to the deck. This is a great thing to do during small groups and conferences today, as you'll know which students can handle a few more cards and then be ready to lead a quick small-group lesson on how to use them.

Alternately, for those who struggle, consider pulling a small group of students together for whom you predict added support will be needed. Pick a text that relates to either their research topic or the topic you are studying as a class, and give each student a copy of the text so that they can annotate it and refer back to specific lines, pictures, and parts. "As I read, I want you to be thinking about the influence this text is having on you," you might say. "What do you think the author is trying to make you think or feel about this topic?" Read it through once, using your voice and think-alouds as tools to highlight places where students might stop and think. "Hmm, . . . that sounds so horrible, doesn't it? Disastrous forest fires . . . malnutrition . . ." Then keep reading. Give partners time to discuss how the author is making them think or feel about the topic after the first reading, and coach them to point to specific lines in the text that evoked those feelings.

After you've read the text through once, you can read it a second time, this time asking students to read with their partners to analyze *how* the author affected them. Talking about each technique card first and then laying them directly onto the text as they notice places where they are applicable can also be helpful to students.

Mid-Workshop Teaching

For your mid-workshop teaching, consider deepening the work students are doing by reminding them that readers don't just ask questions about the goals and techniques writers have—they answer them! You might tell them the story of a former student named Sylvie who was reading books about tornadoes. Sylvie was reading about the way tornadoes are measured in Seymour Simon's book, *Tornadoes*, and she noticed that instead of using captions, he included information about the photograph in the body of his text. Sylvie started to ask, "Why would an author do this? Why not use a caption?" Tell students that you have seen them asking many similar questions and that this is *exactly* what analytical readers do. Then, go on to explain that readers don't stop there. Instead, they investigate, perhaps comparing and contrasting the way Seymour Simon presents information about tornadoes with the way another author does. If you are using *Everything Weather* in this unit, page 25 has a great picture and caption that can be compared to Simon's. Consider ending by reinforcing the idea that readers and researchers go in search of answers to questions, and perhaps offer students a few prompts to do so, such as, "Could it be . . ." or "One possibility is . . ." They can think, talk, or write about these questions and hypotheses as they compare and contrast across texts. Give partners a few minutes to revisit a text in their bin, asking questions about the goals and techniques authors are using and then answering them, before asking students to continue on in their reading.

SHARE

For the share, we suggest that you channel students to elaborate on what they noticed as they read their texts through the lens of their goal and technique cards. To get kids started, you might offer them a few talk prompts such as, "This author uses . . . in order to . . ." and "One example . . . another example . . ." and "This is important because . . ." Consider projecting these prompts or posting them on chart paper so students have access to them.

Coach in as research teams talk using the prompts. For instance, a researcher in the tornadoes group might say something like, "Kathy Furgang uses humor and funny language to make kids interested in the book. One example of this is when she writes, 'Clouds can be naughty or nice.' Another example of this is when she writes that some clouds make people sing 'Oh what a beautiful morning!' This is important because funny language can help readers connect to a topic."

Homework

Readers, we're coming to the end of our nonfiction reading unit. You've learned so much about your extreme weather topics, and now we'll be getting ready to celebrate all you've learned and what experts you've become! So tonight, you'll need to take two steps to get yourself ready for our celebration. You might take a tour through your researcher's notebook, reviewing all of your notes and asking yourself, "What are the biggest things I've learned? How has my thinking about this topic changed?"

You will also want to read anything on your topic that you don't want to miss. Prioritize your texts, and read on, fast and furious, to learn every last bit of information about your topic. In a few days, you'll be sharing what you've learned with others, so try to learn as much as you can tonight!

Sincerely,
Emily and Mike

Session 21

Imagining Possibilities, Celebrating Activism

ear Teachers,

This unit culminates with two days for students to bring their research to a close. One idea we'd like kids to take with them after these investigations and the entire unit has culminated is that passionate nonfiction reading and research can inspire people to change the world. This unit is a chance for your classroom community to celebrate the information they've learned, the ideas they've grown, as well as the ways in which they can apply their research to the problems of the world.

All teachers aim for students to transfer the learning they did with us to other times and other days, long after they have left our classrooms. You will give your children the opportunity to begin this transfer, to begin to apply their learning with independence, so that they may apply it to future learning and life experiences. In this manner, for these two days, we make a rare recommendation that you forgo your traditional minilessons. This removal will allow students to reimmerse themselves in the work of researchers, and it will also allow you to assess the skills that you taught across the unit.

Students' final projects could take on a variety of forms. Some students might choose to create a diagram or a model of a hurricane, inside and out. Another research team might choose to create flyers calling others to action, "10 Things People Need to Do to Prevent Drought and the Overuse of Water!" Still other teams might create a presentation on Google Slides or PowerPoint, or write a persuasive letter, editorial, or speech. Some teams might create a YouTube public-service announcement, urging others to determine whether their homes are located in floods zones as well as the necessary steps to take to avoid floods and flood damage. If possible, bring in examples of the kinds of projects each team selects, to serve as mentors. The possibilities for celebration are countless, but it will be important to remind students that they will be presenting in a mere two days, and so they should choose a manageable vehicle for celebration. Be sure to hone in on teams who have not selected a vision for their final celebration, supporting them right away. This will help the teams' focus and investment in the project remain high.

You might begin by saying, "When we become experts on a topic, it is common to find yourself wanting to share your thoughts and opinions about your topic with the world. In your studies of weather and natural disasters, many of you have uncovered places where your voices would matter, ways in which you wish things were different or where there should be change, and as writers, it's important to remember that you have the resources to fight for that change to happen!"

Then, you might continue, saying, "As this unit comes to a close, we'll invite guests from across our learning community to learn from your work. Before our guests arrive, you'll want to plan with your team what you want to present and how you want to present your information. What is most important for your guests to understand about this type of extreme weather? You might highlight the causes and effects, or maybe there are things your audience can do to be prepared for this kind of natural disaster. Decide what information you most want your audience to learn, or what big ideas you'd like them to leave with."

On these two days, then, you will support students by taking on a variety of roles: cheerleader, coach, tour director, and mentor. You'll move from team to team, channeling students to be successful. You'll also want to help kids find the right resources. You may suggest that teams revisit specific texts, articles, and videos, and read them even more closely. Coach readers to push themselves to consider ideas and information they might not have initially considered. As a part of these few days, you might also arrange trips to the school or public library, or reorganize several bins in your own library so that the right texts are accessible to kids.

Additionally, teams may need help in following through with their celebration plans or with adjusting those plans as predictable problems arise. Some teams might be overly ambitious and will need to modify their plans so they work within reach of what they can actually accomplish in just two days. On the other hand, some groups may under-plan, and they will need your extra help and motivation to add the next steps needed to create a successful celebration.

Tsunami Trigger

Have you ever thought what can cause a tsunami? An earthquake? A volcano to erupt? The answer is yes! Both an earthquake and a volcano eruption. According to the book Volcanic Eruptions, Earthquakes and Tsunamis by Sean McCollum. It says the tectonic plate plunges beneath the continental plate. In other words, the lower plate plunges beneath the upper plate and the edges get stuck. Next, the edges snap free in form of an earthquake. This happens under water.

I found on a website that it starts as what is known called a wave train. All the mini waves get pressure and get bigger and bigger. As the tsunami gets closer to shore the wave comresses and aplatute gets higher. A

Another cause of a tsunami is a volcano. Volcano eruptions set powerful waves. Eruption lawaches can make a wave extremly tall. Imagine a 12 story building made of water coming at you!

What all this cause is, it makes a disaster! 2004 a tsunami struck Khao Lak, Thailand. A car was lifted into a river which drained the river after the tsunami hit. Imagine a river with a car in it instead of water!

FIG. 21–1 This sample shows some of the final presentation options chosen by a student in the pilot classrooms. Some students created their own texts, while others collaborated to make a group project.

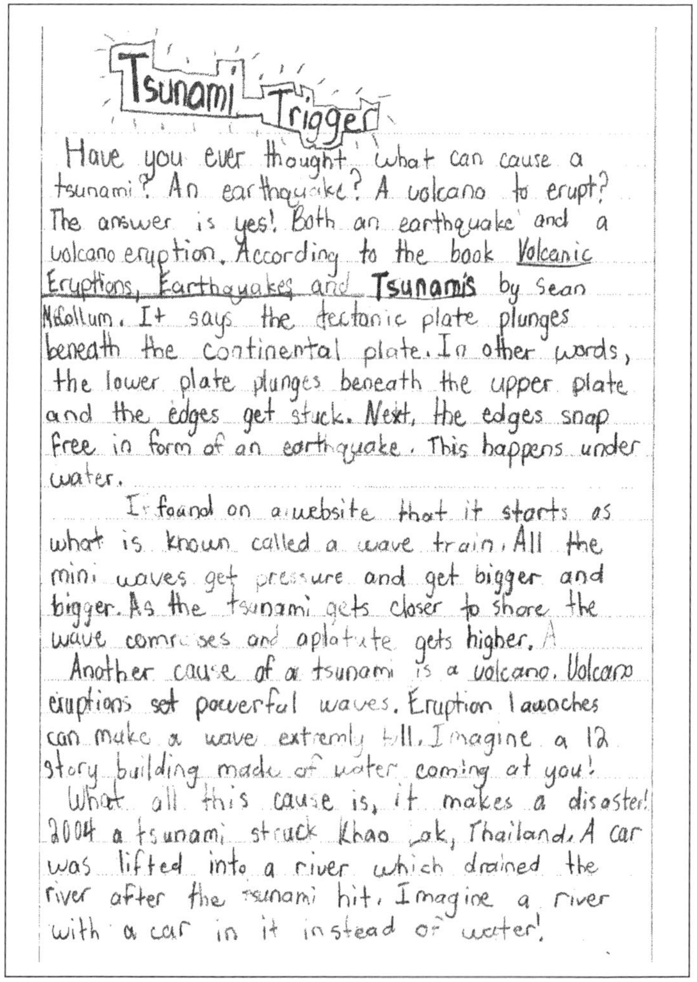

There will be an inevitable buzz of enthusiasm in your class on these two days as research teams work together to prepare their projects. Remember that the end goal is not to produce a beautiful project. Instead, it is for students to apply information they learned through nonfiction reading to teach others and to generate real-world solutions to real-life problems. As teams work together, you might provide pointers, such as, "Always keep in mind the purpose of your project. Illustrations and text features you add should teach about the problem or explain your solution. Don't spend any extra time on the stuff that's not connected to your message!" Your undertaking will be to channel kids to take on ambitious work and to celebrate their ideas. Remember, learning happens in the process, not the product.

If teams struggle to find additional information that adds to their celebration project, perhaps you could recommend a list of ways they could generate ideas to extend their research. Many students may

focus on reading new material for additional information. For these kids, you'll want to remind them of the knowledge they have already accumulated in the unit. You might coach these students by saying, "Your most valuable resources for additional information is your reader's notebook. You can reread your notes, just as you're rereading these books. You can reread your notebook with a purpose in mind—a question in mind—drawing additional information from your notes that fits the purpose of your celebration topic."

Also, it will be important for you to support kids in ways they are collecting and organizing information for presentation. You might offer tips such as, "Keep your solutions to a manageable number—ten or fewer—so your audience will feel they are doable." Or, you might say, "As a team, ask yourselves, 'What is the most important thing for your audience to know about this topic?' and then look at and assess your celebration project to make sure that the most important idea rises to the top."

Additionally, you'll want to channel students to draw upon all the skills they have learned earlier in this unit as well as in previous units. For instance, you might encourage students to draw upon their knowledge of persuasive, boxes-and-bullets essay writing. You may draw attention to some of the charts from the *Boxes and Bullets: Personal and Persuasive Essays* unit from the Units of Study in Opinion, Information, and Narrative Writing to remind students of ways to effectively structure and elaborate upon opinions. A unit's end is a great time for kids to reflect on the work they have been doing. You might also decide to ask students to return to the "Critical Reading" strand of the Informational Reading Learning Progression, as well as other strands of the learning progressions to support self-assessment.

Although you may not conduct traditional minilessons on these two days, you'll certainly conduct mid-workshop teachings and shares, which still give you an opportunity to tuck in teaching tips as well as give a predictable sense of structure to these days. During these times you'll want to spotlight the work particular research teams are doing, that other teams can replicate. We suggest you commend not just ideas different teams generate, but also the *process* they use. For instance, you might call attention to how a team is sticking to or revising its plans, or how a team is using questions to navigate its thinking, or how a team is dividing up its work to be most effective. Then, too, you might highlight how a team used a mentor text or how a group narrowed its research to the most important ideas they wanted to convey to their audience.

To prepare for the final celebration, invite kids to take ownership of their learning and to note how their nonfiction reading has made them experts and advocates for their topics, ready to teach others and urge them to act.

A celebration project always has an audience, and so you'll want to arrange for your class to be an audience for each other's projects. You might even invite other classrooms to celebrate, as well as students' families. On the day of final presentations, teams could set up their work in or around the classroom, perhaps on the outskirts or in the hallways where visitors can move from team to team. Again, your class will buzz with excitement as one team carefully explains to its audience about tornado-safe buildings, flood-watch preparation, or debates on drought prevention. Kids will experience the intellectual engagement of culling information they've learned to purposeful use as they share their ideas with the world.

After the main celebrations end, after the guests leave, save a few minutes to gather children in the meeting area to share and to reflect. Allow them to spend several moments to compliment each other with memorable accounts of their presentations. Ask them to think about what it felt like to teach others, to rally others to action, and to be an expert. Remind students of the power of their work. You might say, "See what has happened? We've all become part of a bigger conversation about how to help people prepare for and prevent catastrophe in a world of extreme weather and natural disasters."

An alternate option for a celebration of this unit allows you the opportunity to tuck instruction that will support work forefronted by high-stakes assessments into your teaching of the curriculum now. One common challenge for students on these assessments is the academic, test-based language commonly used to construct test questions. Helping students become more at home with this language can help prevent their confusion when it appears on the test.

For this version of the celebration, you might ask students to gather several of their favorite texts from their studies in preparation for meeting with their partners. You'll want to give students a few minutes to skim their resources, identifying the texts they learned the most from and remember well. Once students have a selection of texts, you'll want to call them together.

"Readers," you might say, "you've learned so much about your extreme weather topics that you've become true experts. You've asked thoughtful questions and grown sophisticated, complicated ideas. As you know, experts are able to talk about their topic and teach others what they've learned. They do this by synthesizing all the information they've gathered, referring to different examples and evidence to support their thinking. Today, you and your partner are going to do just that, interviewing each other to celebrate your expertise!"

You might ask students to select a text they think they can discuss well, and as students choose, you can distribute question cards. You might use the list of questions below, or you might choose to develop some of your own open-ended questions that incorporate academic language your students would benefit from. Students can use these cards in partnership conversations about their texts. You could direct students to read through the stack of questions before rereading their text. As they read their text, kids can keep the questions in front of them and look for relevant questions. They can pause and discuss the questions using text-based evidence as they go.

Informational Text Questions

- Who would value this information?
- Why did the author introduce the article this way?
- What does the word _____ mean?
- How does the author support the idea that____?
- What is the writer's attitude toward the subject?
- What is the main idea of this article?
- How is the article organized?
- Which statement from the passage best supports the idea that _____?

Or, you may choose to structure this activity as more of a game-like interview. After partners have reread their texts, they can take turns flipping over cards one question at a time and answering the question,

Informational Text Questions	
Who would value this information?	Why did the author introduce the article this way?
What does the word _____ mean?	How does the author support the idea that____?
What is the writer's attitude toward the subject?	What is the main idea of this article?
How is the article organized?	Which statement from the passage best supports the idea that _____?

talking for as long as they can by citing the text and unpacking their evidence. You might time "rounds" of interview questions, challenging students to try answering their question until the buzzer sounds, switching to a new text every few rounds.

To support kids' abilities to cite and analyze text evidence as they discuss their topics, you can give students a list of transitional phrases to help them navigate from their general discussion to a specific text reference to an analysis of the text. Before your students begin their interview rounds, you might choose to model answering a question using these prompts and a passage from *Extreme Weather* or another familiar text, moving from a claim, to a text re+ference, to analysis.

Transitioning to Specific Text References

- For example, according to the text (the character) . . .
- So and so claims . . .
- So and so writes . . .
- One thing to note is that, toward the end of the text, readers learn that . . .

Analyzing Text Evidence

- This illustrates that . . .
- This demonstrates that . . .
- Readers realize that . . .
- The important thing to notice about this is that . . .
- It is important to notice that . . . (didn't), but instead . . .
- What this means is . . .
- In other words . . .

No matter which version of the celebration you choose, on this last day of the unit, you and your class will celebrate not just the endings, but also the beginnings. Celebrate the end of a unit in nonfiction reading, yes, but also celebrate the beginning of letting kids take new knowledge with them wherever they go, to grow new ideas and advocate for beliefs. This beginning allows students to live differently because of all they've learned and all they can teach one another. You might end by saying, "When we finish reading nonfiction texts we love and texts we care about, we become different people. We become the kind of people who work to prevent drought, or help people prepare for earthquakes, or advocate for better tsunami detection systems. We aren't the kind of people who read and then leave information behind. We are the kind of people who carry our nonfiction reading with us, letting those topics live with us, and using that knowledge to find our way in the world."

Congratulations!
Emily and Mike

Transitioning to Specific Text References

For example, according to the text...	So and so claims...
So and so writes...	One thing to note is that, towards the end of the text, readers learn that...

Analyzing Text Evidence

This illustrates that...	This demonstrates that...
Readers realize that...	The important thing to notice about this is that...
What this means is...	In other words...